The Rush for Black Diamonds, Volume One

The Rush for Black Diamonds, Volume One

From John Locke to Thomas Jefferson—The Transatlantic Slave Trade to Chattel Slavery in the UK and the US

GEORGE WALTERS-SLEYON
Foreword by John Witte Jr.

CASCADE *Books* · Eugene, Oregon

THE RUSH FOR BLACK DIAMONDS, VOLUME ONE
From John Locke to Thomas Jefferson—The Transatlantic Slave Trade to Chattel Slavery in the UK and the US

Copyright © 2024 George Walters-Sleyon. All rights reserved. Except for brief quotations in critical publications or reviews, no part of this book may be reproduced in any manner without prior written permission from the publisher. Write: Permissions, Wipf and Stock Publishers, 199 W. 8th Ave., Suite 3, Eugene, OR 97401.

Cascade Books
An Imprint of Wipf and Stock Publishers
199 W. 8th Ave., Suite 3
Eugene, OR 97401

www.wipfandstock.com

PAPERBACK ISBN: 979-8-3852-0136-5
HARDCOVER ISBN: 979-8-3852-0137-2
EBOOK ISBN: 979-8-3852-0138-9

Cataloguing-in-Publication data:

Names: Walters-Sleyon, George, author. | Witte, John, Jr., 1959–, foreword.

Title: The rush for black diamonds, volume one : from John Locke to Thomas Jefferson—the transatlantic slave trade to chattel slavery in the UK and the US / George Walters-Sleyon ; foreword by John Witte Jr.

Description: Eugene, OR : Cascade Books, 2024 | Includes bibliographical references and index.

Identifiers: ISBN 979-8-3852-0136-5 (paperback) | ISBN 979-8-3852-0137-2 (hardcover) | ISBN 979-8-3852-0138-9 (ebook)

Subjects: LCSH: Racism—Atlantic Ocean Region—History. | Slavery—Atlantic Ocean Region—History. | Racism—Atlantic Ocean Region—Philosophy. | Black race. | Enlightenment. | Imperialism.

Classification: HT985 .W356 2024 (paperback) | HT985 .W356 (ebook)

11/14/24

The Rush for Black Diamonds, Volume One is dedicated to Black Africans captured from Africa as capital investments in the transatlantic slave trade. It is dedicated to Black Africans whose grave sites became the Middle Passage in the Atlantic Ocean perpetrated by the international human trade of the Dutch, the Portuguese, the French, the Spaniards, the Germans, the British, the Scots, the Belgians, the Italians, and the Americans. *The Rush for Black Diamonds, Volume One* is devoted to the memories of Black Africans who died on their slave plantation fields, not as human beings but as mere commodities and chattel property. It is devoted to the indelible thoughts of Black African babies who they bred to be sold in the domestic slave trades. These babies never knew their mothers and fathers but were conceived to be used, abused, and discarded as economic units on the slave fields of Western nations while their great philosophers provided the intellectual justifications for Black inferiority and dehumanization.

I MUST FIND MY OWN JUDGE

I must find my own judge,
A judge who respects my dignity.
A judge who rescues me from this bondage of indignity,
I must find my own judge.[1]

---

1. Walters-Sleyon, *Nuggets from the Night*, 44.

Contents

Foreword by John Witte Jr.   ix
Acknowledgments   xiii
Introduction   1

1. A Necessary Background: The Enlightenment Pioneers   6

THE TRANSATLANTIC SLAVE TRADE
1400–1860s

2. W. E. B. Du Bois: The Rush for "Black Diamonds"   27
3. The Making of John Locke   51
4. Locke: The Slave Trader and the British Slave Trade   61
5. Lockean Politics: Once a Slave, Always a Slave   78
6. Lockean Religion: Baptism and Deism   98
7. Lockean Philosophy: Empiricism   120

CHATTEL SLAVERY
1779–1865

8. Lockean Slavery to Jeffersonian Slavery   135
9. Thomas Jefferson: The Slave Master   154
10. Emancipation: Toward the End of Chattel Slavery in the UK and the US   176
11. Walter Rauschenbusch: Sin   186
12. Is Locke a Racist?   194

Bibliography   205
Index   227

Foreword

CHATTEL SLAVERY WAS AMERICA'S *"original sin,"* Justice Thurgood Marshall once said. It was *original* in that chattel slavery was unique to the Americas and other United Kingdom colonies in Africa and the West Indies. Slavery was an ancient and perennial institution in the West and well beyond—born of conquest, surrender, or treaty, or imposed for debts, crimes, or torts. But the status of the slave in earlier legal systems was usually neither permanent nor color-coded, and masters were more closely restricted by law. By contrast, the *chattel* slavery system that slowly emerged in colonial America and culminated in the brutal slave laws and practices of the new American republic was far more sinister. That chattel system reduced each enslaved person to an item of personal property—a piece of "living chattel" like an animal, to be sold, bought, leased, rented, used, abused, beaten, raped, and discarded at the will and whim of the master. American chattel slavery was also color-coded and racist, inflicted primarily on Black people. It was also an inherited condition. A child born to an enslaved mother was, by definition, a slave, even if she had been raped by her white master. And chattel slavery was presumptively permanent. Only emancipation by the master (or in rare instances by a court) would break the bond of slavery. Even a once enslaved person, who escaped to a free state, remained a slave, the US Supreme Court infamously held in *Dred Scott v. Sandford* (1857).

Chattel slavery was also a kind of original *sin*, Justice Marshall insisted. Christian theologians describe Adam and Eve's disobedience to God in the Garden of Eden as the "original sin" of humanity. That first human sin, theologians tell us, destroyed the perfection of creation. It perverted all our human natures. It inclined us all to commit actual sins. And it left all of humanity in need of redemption. The chattel slave system was roughly analogous in effect to the original sin of Adam and Eve, Justice Marshall insisted. To be sure, America was never a perfect Garden of Eden. But the American colonies and young states became increasingly "perverted" in their contorted efforts to routinize chattel slavery even while building an expansive system of rights and liberties for all. The US Constitution likewise perversely extended the chattel slave trade, expanded the fugitive slave laws, and enhanced the power of slave states and masters, even while ratifying an elaborate Bill of Rights. Not all Americans condoned or practiced slavery, and a steady stream of critics and abolitionists challenged this odious institution from the beginning. But all of America benefited from the massive economy built on the backs of the ten-million-plus chattel slaves condemned to work for nothing, and all American states participated in the robust international commerce, fueled in part by the lucrative transatlantic slave trade. Not all Americans committed the "actual sins" of kidnapping, battery, rape, murder, and other abuses of Blacks that were protected by the chattel slave laws, and not all those sins and crimes went unpunished. But America was and remains ravaged by the racism, hatred, and distrust born of the chattel slave system. And American institutions, notably its states and churches, were deeply stained and divided by the vicious battles over slavery and the "badges of servitude" that have persisted to this day. Yes, the American Civil War, the Thirteen through Fifteenth Amendments, the Civil Rights Acts of 1866 and 1964, and countless statutes, cases, and policies have provided measures of liberation and "redemption" for all. But the calls for "truth and reconciliation," let alone for fees and reparations, has only grown louder in recent years, as America continues to struggle with *de facto* if not *de jure* "Jim Crow" regimes in many areas of public and private life, not least its vast prisons filled with Black inmates held in a veritable "penal servitude" from which the establishment amply profits.

In this sweeping two-volume work on *Black Diamonds*, the Reverend Dr. George Walters-Sleyon strives to come to terms with this "original sin" of chattel slavery and the transatlantic slave trade. He works hard to understand its political, legal, economic, and philosophical origins, motivations, and justifications; to identify and study some of its perpetrators, apologists, and beneficiaries; and to document its perversions and permanent stains on Anglo-American culture and institutions.

In the first volume, George (as I know him from his fellowship in our Law and Religion Center) zeroes in on John Locke's early casuistic contributions to the development of chattel slavery and Thomas Jefferson's more blatant exploitation. Locke has long been held up as an ardent defender of natural rights, an early architect of democratic government, and a stern critic of any notion of inherited status whether of royalty or slavery. Indeed, Locke's teachings provided important fuel for the democratic revolutions and constitution-building in America and in many other parts of the vast British Commonwealth, including in twentieth-century Anglophone Africa. Yet, as George shows in this book, Locke was a slave trader. He early on invested in the Royal African Company that he knew profited from the transatlantic slave trade. And the Carolina Constitution of 1669 that Locke helped to draft made blunt provision for slavery: "Every freeman of Carolina shall have absolute power and authority over his negro slaves."[2] Locke was one early and influential example—there were many others—of the pervasive casuistry that helped support the early development of the American and British chattel slavery system.

A century later and an ocean away, pervasive casuistry about chattel slavery gave way to more perverse self-contradictions in the life and thought of many slaveholders in the young American republic. Thomas Jefferson was a glaring case in point, George shows in later chapters of the first volume. Jefferson was the enlightened liberal founder of America, who pressed Lockean and other political teachings into the famous Declaration of Independence: "We hold these truths to be self-evident, that all men are created equal, that they are endowed by their Creator with certain unalienable Rights, that among these are Life, Liberty and the pursuit of Happiness." He was Virginia's governor and then America's president and was famous for his liberalizing reforms of many legal, political, and social topics. Yet Jefferson owned some 600 enslaved persons in his life, including the long-enslaved Sally Hemings, who he kept as his secret concubine and the mother of his illegitimate and presumptively enslaved children.

At the heart of this casuistry and hypocrisy, George argues, was a perverse and pervasive racist greed and lust for power and exploitation of those shiny black diamonds that those enslaved Black bodies represented. And that same racist greed and lust have continued in America, George shows in the second volume, notwithstanding the Reconstruction Amendments and the Civil Rights Acts. So many Blacks over the past century and a half have been forced into exploitative "share cropping" or forced to work multiple menial jobs needed to make thin ends meet. So many Blacks have been consigned to poor and under-serviced

2. Locke, "Fundamental Constitutions of Carolina, 1669," para. 101.

neighborhoods and cities. So many Blacks have been blocked from advancement. So many Blacks have been threatened and brutalized by the police. So many Blacks have been exploited for their athletic, musical, or entertainment gifts—yes, a few make it big time, but so many others are used for others' profits. So many Black men have been dumped into prisons, which has become its own perverse, lucrative industry in America today. The original sin of slavery and servitude continues to infect America, George concludes. We need to find better ways to live together and love each other across racial, economic, and political lines; there are hopeful signs, examples, and pathways that are opening.

The Reverend Dr. George Walters-Sleyon brings learning and experience to these two volumes. He is a scholar, professor, minister, musician, poet, and, most importantly, devoted family man. George was born in Liberia and completed his undergraduate education in Ghana, one of the early African capitals in the transatlantic slave trade. He earned his BA at Central University College in Accra, two master's degrees in theology, social ethics, and philosophy from Boston University, and a PhD in practical theology and ethics with extra training in criminology and comparative criminal justice from the University of Edinburgh. He has known economic hardship both in his youth and now as he struggles to teach and raise his family in Boston, a city known for soaring liberal rhetoric and pervasive structural racism. George has felt the sting of racism; already as a newly arrived American emigrant from Liberia, he was falsely arrested and thrown in prison in 2008 for not having the exact right documentation of his status. He has seen the "new Jim Crow" regime at work in American and United Kingdom (England and Wales, and Scotland) prisons in his research, and he has studied, supported, and written at length about the work of prison chaplains who have sought to ameliorate the lives of the incarcerated. And George has shown us in his ministry, messages, and music how to use Scripture, liturgy, art, literature, and just plain faithful and loving living to chart a better way to love God, self, and all neighbors.

JOHN WITTE, JR.
Center for the Study of Law and Religion
Emory University

Acknowledgments

I AM GREATLY INDEBTED to The Center for the Study of Law and Religion at Emory University School of Law for its support of my work. My sincere thanks to Professor John Witte, Whittney Barth, Amy Wheeler, Peter McDonald, and colleagues of the McDonald Distinguish Fellows. A special thank you to my two sons, George Jr. and William for their constant encouragement and reminders.

Introduction

THIS BOOK IS THE FIRST of two volumes. *The Rush for Black Diamonds, Volume One* and *The Rush for Black Diamonds, Volume Two* cover four eras of the West's legal, political, military, philosophical, racial, and economic actions against Black humanity and Africa as mutually exclusive and inclusive: the *transatlantic slave trade*, the *institution of chattel slavery*, colonialism, and the emergence of *penal slavery* in the United States and the United Kingdom (England, Wales, and Scotland).[1] *Volume One* and *Volume Two* of *The Rush for Black Diamonds* further demonstrate the inhumanity of the slave trade, the reduction of Black humanity to "thinghood," and the "criminalization" of Black humanity post-slavery together with the cruelties and impunity with which Europeans and White Americans dehumanize Black Africans. Both volumes contend that the slave trade, chattel slavery, penal slavery, and colonialism were and are collective efforts with the laws, the courts, the judges, the military, law enforcement, and governments of the superpowers of the slave trade. Portugal, Netherlands, Belgium, Spain, the United Kingdom, France, and the United States were comprehensively involved in the emergence, sustainability, and perpetuation of the human trade, chattel slavery and their future racial implications, leaving Black Africans with no law or court to appeal to.

Both volumes also contend that the transatlantic slave trade, chattel slavery, colonialism, and penal slavery would not have been successful without the injection of the Enlightenment fathers' philosophical justifications for race-based theories, racism, and the assertion of White supremacy against non-Europeans and especially the humanity Black Africans as justification for their enslavement, colonial control, and reduction to chattel property. As a demonstration of the association of the

1. The United Kingdom in *The Rush for Black Diamonds: Volumes One* and *Two* refers to England, Wales, and Scotland.

INTRODUCTION

Enlightenment era with the success of the human trade and its subsequent residues of overt and covert racial treatments of Black people, *The Rush for Black Diamonds, Volume One* and *Volume Two* explore the writings of John Locke, Thomas Jefferson, David Hume, G. W. F. Hegel, and Immanuel Kant, with reference to other philosophers including Voltaire and Joseph Arthur de Gobineau. Finally, Volume One and Volume Two further assert that the economic, technical, and philosophical achievements as well as the success of the Industrial Revolution, from the 1760s in Britain to the 1830s across the rest of Europe and the United States, were predicated on the success of the transatlantic slave trade, chattel enslavement of Black people, and colonialism. For the United States, the concept and continuity of white supremacy existed well after the Emancipation Proclamation of 1863 as penal slavery: the American Black Codes era, the Jim Crow era, the era of the Convict Lease System and mass Black incarceration.

The Rush for Black Diamonds, Volume One explores the immediate historical emergence of the transatlantic slave trade by the Dutch, Spain, Portugal, Britain (England, Wales, and Scotland), and subsequently the United States. This volume provides data on the innumerable Black Africans that Europeans and White Americans first hauled and dragged out of Africa and later bred for slave markets in order to sustain their existing and future slave plantations. Included in this volume are demonstrations of the involvement of the British parliaments, its laws, the British monarchy, the American colonies prior to the Declaration of Independence and afterwards, the United States Congress, its legal system and law enforcement institutions to legally, religiously, and socio-politically perpetuate the claims that Black people are humanly and intellectually inferior to Whites and therefore should be indeterminately perceived and treated as economic units, second-class human beings, and discriminated against on the basis of alleged racial inferiority in Europe and the United States.

With emphasis on the Enlightenment era's association with the success of the slave trade, chattel slavery, colonialism, and penal slavery, *The Rush for Black Diamonds, Volume One* begins with W. E. B. Du Bois's analysis of the slave trade. It then demonstrates the involvement of two prominent Enlightenment philosophers as intellectual architects of the political, legal, economic, and philosophical justifications for the human trade in the United Kingdom and the United States—John Locke (1632-1704), a British philosopher and "Father of Liberalism"; and Thomas Jefferson (1743-1826), the third president of the United States, governor of Virginia, author of the Declaration of Independence, and a prominent Founding Father of the United States. By exploring what I refer to as Lockean slavery and Jeffersonian slavery, this volume reminds readers that Locke and Jefferson were also slave traders and slave masters. The present Western worldview and racial treatment of people of African descent cannot be disassociated from the economic, political, philosophical, and sociocultural claims and practices of Locke, Jefferson, and the Enlightenment pioneers of West.

It is important to note that, unlike in the United States, most of the chattel slavery activities of the superpowers of the slave trade—the United Kingdom, France, Netherlands, Belgium, Portugal, and Spain—took place in their slave territories and colonies. This strategy on the part of the slave-trading superpowers of the West established an immediate continuity from the era of chattel slavery to the eras of colonialism and neocolonialism. *Black Diamond*[2] is a metaphor used to describe Western nations' rush for Black people, from across the Atlantic Ocean to Africa, to be used as economic units. The transatlantic slave trade was Western nations' most disruptive act with substantial implications for centuries in human history. There were no laws or courts of law to which the Africans could appeal.

The transatlantic slave trade was a trade in human beings beginning in the 1400s. Major European nations, including Spain, France, Belgium, Sweden, Portugal, Scotland, Denmark, Germany, Britain, and subsequently what would become the United States, became superpowers in the human trade. The fundamental motivations for the transatlantic slave trade included the quest for economic gains and economic dominance, political control and political dominance, and finally, racial control demonstrated in White supremacist-led laws, practices, and penal codes against the humanity of Black Africans. These claims are poignantly reflected in the writings of John Locke, Thomas Jefferson, Immanuel Kant, David Hume, G. W. F. Hegel, and Joseph Arthur de Gobineau.

The transatlantic slave trade continues to interest us today. The reason for this interest is also the historically unimaginable tolerance of abuse against the humanity of Africans and the impunity with which Western nations engaged and profited from these acts of human suffering. Furthermore, interest in the history of the transatlantic slave trade and chattel slavery have increased because of their legacies and

---

2. Du Bois, *Suppression of the African Slave-Trade*, 176.

influences on the development of the practice of penal slavery and the post-1970s racial consciousness regarding the humanity of Black people in the United Kingdom and the United States. Similarly, Africans and other intellectuals are beginning to ask the questions: What happened? How did it happen? Is there justice in this? How can this be prevented?

Contrary to the claims by some that Africans were selling other Africans to Europeans willy-nilly, the data and records suggest that Europeans and Americans out-maneuvered African leaders with threats and military weapons, inciting wars, pillaging African villages and towns, disrupting communities and institutions, invading the African hamlets, and, like gold diggers, hunting for Africans, artifacts, and treasures to transport across the Atlantic Ocean. James Campbell notes, "Great Britain alone, in a single decade at the peak of the traffic, exported more than one and a half million small arms to West Africa. In such circumstances, Africans who declined to trade with Europeans could quickly find themselves among the traded."[3] Africans were hunted and captured like animals. Their homes, villages, and towns were invaded and destroyed. Their treasures and artifacts were looted. Africans' sociocultural, political, and economic institutions were crippled and distorted, with generational gaps in leadership and institutional continuity from one generation to another.

The transatlantic slave trade was a rush for *black diamonds* that Britain developed after monopolizing the trade and pushing out the Dutch and the Spanish. It was an economic revolution in human trafficking. The traffickers hurled Africans into slave ships, and the British government and the American flag protected these ships. The capturing and trafficking of Africans were legal under the participating nations' laws. The human trade in Africans made Britain, Spain, France, Portugal, Belgium, Scotland, Denmark, Sweden, and the United States economically, socioculturally, and politically dominant.

Like California with the Gold Rush of 1848, Africa became the target of relentless invasion and looting from European nations from the 1400s to the early 1800s. Africans, including those in the coastal areas of Africa especially close to Europe and the Americas, became the target of a slave rush by Britain, Spain, Denmark, Scotland, Belgium, Portugal, Sweden, France, and the United States. They came to pillage and loot

---

3. Campbell, *Middle Passages*, 9.

INTRODUCTION

Africa's institutions, wealth, historical treasures, and artifacts.[4] They came to capture Africans as enslaved people to be monetized, utilized on plantations, and eventually discarded. Africans were the *black diamonds* of the West's rush for gold; wealth creation; and economic, political, military, and racial domination for subsequent generations of Whites. According to Campbell, "While slavery certainly existed in Africa prior to the Europeans' arrival (as it did in virtually every other civilization known to history), the opening of the transatlantic trade radically transformed the institution's scale and character, sparking a vast new demand for slaves and precipitating centuries of war and political upheaval. European traders actively fomented conflict, most notably by offering guns and powder in exchange for slaves."[5]

A structural distinction exists between the transatlantic slave trade and the institution of chattel slavery in this book. While the two are symbiotic and existed concurrently, the slave trade and the institution of chattel slavery were distinct practices. The international slave trade formally ended in the 1850s; the informal slave trade continued for decades.[6] There are thus three slave trades discussed in this book: (1) the international slave trade, which entails the European and the United States governments' legal allowance for their people to travel to Africa to invade, capture, and transport Africans as slaves to the United States and Europe and her territories; (2) the informal slave trade that was conducted by nongovernmental European slave traders, private individuals, and pirates; and (3) the domestic slave trade that entailed the breeding for sale and trading of Black people as slaves before and after the banning of the international slave trade in the 1850s in the colonies and slave plantations of the United Kingdom and in the United States.

While the slave trade and chattel slavery existed concurrently, the slave trade formally mutated into the institution of chattel slavery. The informal slave trade and the domestic slave trade in the United States, and in other British colonies in the West Indies, continued informally into the early parts of the twentieth century.

---

4. Darity, "Numbers Game."
5. Campbell, *Middle Passages*, 9.
6. Du Bois, *Suppression of the African Slave-Trade*, 176.

I

A Necessary Background: The Enlightenment Pioneers

John Locke is a preeminent seventeenth-century British politician, philosopher, and pioneer of the Enlightenment project of reason. He was an academic at Oxford University, philosophically a classical empiricist, religiously a deist, politically an anti-authoritarian, and the "Father of liberal politics . . . [who believed strongly in] the right to private property, popular sovereignty, toleration, and the right to resist an unjust government."[1] Locke is considered an original proponent of the separation between church and state in the United States. He is famous for his defense of human rights, which was influential in America's revolutionary war with Britain for independence. According to Henry Syse:

> John Locke's political thought has had "an enormous influence on the European mind," and—it should be added—on the Americans. The revolutionary movements that swept over America and France in the 18th century owed much of their philosophical basis and rhetoric to *le sage Locke*, as Voltaire famously called him. It can fairly be said that Locke laid the foundation for much of what we commonly refer to as liberal politics. . . . Indeed, Locke has been called "properly the greatest, and certainly the most influential English philosopher."[2]

---

1. Syse, *Natural Law*, 188.
2. Syse, *Natural Law*, 188.

A NECESSARY BACKGROUND: THE ENLIGHTENMENT PIONEERS

However, Locke was also a slave trader.[3] This research contends that Locke was also a theorist of chattel slavery and the subsequent development of race-based constituted penal policies in the United States. Importantly, Locke introduces us to the initial intersections of the law, religion, profit, and race as political and philosophical justifications for the transatlantic slave trade and chattel slavery.

Lockean slavery is also racial slavery. It is different from Roman slavery. The connection of slavery to race and its perpetuation into the twenty-first century is particular to the sixteenth-century Western world. According to Paul Finkelman, "Most strikingly, nowhere in the world before the sixteenth century was enslavement ever confined to a single race or ethnic group. . . . In the United States, only Africans and their descendants could be enslaved; in the ancient world, enslavement could happen to anyone."[4] The Romans enslaved anyone and everyone, including the Jews, the Gauls, the Syrians, the Celts, the Germanic tribes, and Asians. It was not about race but military conquests.

Lockean slavery reflects an irony in Locke's political and philosophical claims. On the one hand, Locke was a pioneer of the Enlightenment project and an advocate of individual rights and egalitarianism. On the other hand, Locke was a theologian, philosopher, and political theorist armed with theological and philosophical claims to validate his divine and natural right to own Africans as property and chattel slaves. Lockean slavery is an ideological, theoretical, and practical concept with socioeconomic, political, and penal implications. It provides an intellectual and conceptual defense for the development of chattel slavery in Britain and its colonies, especially in the United States.

The Rush for Black Diamonds, Volume One contends that Locke's involvement with and defenses of slavery, his rejection of Christian baptism for slaves, and his religiously centered protection of property and punishment in the *Second Treatise of Government* served as important

---

3. Bernasconi and Mann, "Contradiction of Racism."

4. Finkelman, *Defending Slavery*, 9. "This was impossible—unfathomable—in the United States, where slavery was defined by race and race in turn defined the status of blacks, even if they were not enslaved. White people in the South were always free. Only blacks could be slaves, whites, no matter how great their misfortune, could never end up enslaved. While courts struggled at the margins to determine who might be black and therefore subject to enslavement, Southern whites never doubted for a moment that, as South Carolina's highest court put it, 'by law, every negro is presumed to be a slave'. Furthermore, even blacks who were not slaves were always subordinate to whites" (Finkelman, *Defending Slavery*, 10). [*State v. Harden*, 29 S.C.L.(2 Speers) 15In, 155n (1832).

ideological platforms for the historic race-based treatment of Blacks after emancipation in 1863. Locke used Christian theology and biblical claims to justify slavery and racism. In that light, Locke's ideas cannot be divorced from the residues of slavery and the subsequent political and theological defenses of White-supremacist ideologies against Black humanity. Locke's economic, social, and political interests influenced the philosophical, sociocultural, and political worldviews of citizens of a new nation, the United States, mainly through Thomas Jefferson, a reader of Locke who brought many Lockean ideas into mainstream American political consciousness.

In Thomas Jefferson, Lockean philosophy and political theory found a disciple. I refer to Jefferson's brand of slavery as Jeffersonian slavery, and it demonstrates how chattel slavery and its intellectual, religious, sociocultural, and economic influences have been preserved through the American Constitution and various American institutions, including the Thirteenth Amendment, the courts, law enforcement, religion, public policies, and the American penal system. With Locke and Jefferson, slavery in the British empire and the United States transformed into an industry supported by their intellectual prowess.

Locke's influence on Jefferson is well documented, as is Jefferson's paraphrased use of Locke's political, religious, economic, and philosophical claims. Like Locke, Jefferson was a slave trader and a slave master. Like Locke, Jefferson was a deist. Jefferson's philosophical and political arguments for the separation of church and state in the new republic of the United States were inherently Lockean. Unlike Locke, Jefferson was the writer of the Declaration of Independence in 1775 after the Revolutionary War, and the Northwest Ordinance of 1784,[5] which became the initial draft of the Thirteenth Amendment of the United States Constitution in 1865. Jefferson was also the designer of the penal codes of Virginia, and Virginia was the first and most prominent British colony in North America.[6]

Locke's writing highly influenced Thomas Jefferson's views on intellectual, political, religious, social, and racial matters. Jefferson became

---

5. Library of Congress, "Northwest Ordinance."

6. *Finkelman*, "Slavery in the United States," 107. "Virginia was the first British mainland colony to establish slavery, and the rules developed there eventually spread to the other mainland colonies. Virginia would become the largest British colony and the most important of the thirteen that would eventually come to form the United States. From the seventeenth century until the United States Civil War, Virginia continued to maintain the largest slave population on the North American continent."

the most prominent disciple of Locke while the governor of Virginia, as a congressman, and eventually as president of the United States of America. Like his mentor, Jefferson was an avid slave trader and slave master in Virginia as a member of the House of Burgesses,[7] as governor, and in Philadelphia as the third president of the United States. Finkelman argues that "Jefferson—who owned more than 150 slaves when he wrote the Declaration of Independence—did not in fact believe that blacks were entitled to the same rights as other Americans."[8] Like Locke, Jefferson and many of the founding fathers of the United States were defenders of White-supremacist ideas and practices, explicitly and implicitly.

Two important perceptions and legal claims regarding the humanity of Africans are worth introducing from the beginning of this book: (1) the laws of Virginia and (2) the claims of the Enlightenment pioneers concerning Africans.

THE SLAVE LAWS OF VIRGINIA

It is important to note here that Virginia was the largest of the British colonies in America. Furthermore, Thomas Jefferson was a Virginian political and social elite. This understanding is crucial to interpreting the intersections between Locke, Jefferson, the slave trade, and the institution of chattel slavery in the United States. In Virginia, Blacks were first considered legal property, chattel, or commodities to be sold and exchanged. It would require the Civil War for Virginians to recognize Blacks as human beings. Finkelman explains:

> In 1659–60, a Virginia law recognized slavery for the first time, although without defining it. The law provided "That if the said Dutch or other foreigners shall import any negro slaves, the said Dutch or others shall, for the tobacco really produced by the sale of the said negro, pay only the impost of two shillings per hogshead, the like being paid by our owne nation." By this time slaves were seen as commodities being imported into the colony. This was the first clear statement that Africans in new

---

7. Finkelman, "Slavery in the United States," 108. "In the 1640s—before slavery had emerged as an institution in Virginia—the colonial legislature, the House of Burgesses, tackled complex questions of servitude and status. The House of Burgesses was elected by the landowners and dominated by the emerging planter class."

8. Finkelman, *Slavery and the Founders* ix, x.

A NECESSARY BACKGROUND: THE ENLIGHTENMENT PIONEERS

British colonies were considered "things" or property, rather than persons.[9]

Based on this 1659–60 Virginian law, demarcations were made between Africans as slaves and servants of European origin. The new law discouraged interracial friendships and relationships. Its goal was to strengthen the second-class status of Blacks in Virginia.[10] In 1662, another law was passed in the House of Burgesses that held unaccountable men who had affairs with slave women and had children with them. We shall explore the practicality of this law in chapter 8, considering Thomas Jefferson's relationship with Sally Hemings. The law stated that, "WHEREAS some doubts have arisen whether children got by Englishmen upon a negro women should be slave or free [sic], Be it therefore enacted . . . that all children borne in this country shall be held bond or free only accounting to the condition of the mother."[11]

This law gave slave masters the right to have affairs with their female slaves. The children of the affairs would not be the responsibility of the slave master or the White man but of the enslaved woman. Furthermore, if the mother was a slave, her children would be enslaved like her. Also, the slave master could carry on having affairs with many enslaved women to mainly increase his slave population. The only legal attachment between the father and the children was that of a slave master and his slaves. The children were slaves, and they carried the name of the mother, not the father. Under this law, slave women did not control their bodies or the children they gave birth to. No matter how embarrassing the implications of this law were, it was the law.

In 1670, another law was passed establishing that children of enslaved people were from birth enslaved people. An African parent justified their enslavement not their biracial heritage if it was under consideration.[12] Thus, the conditions for defining an enslaved person included non-European origin, a slave status, or Black mother, non-Christian status, and African heritage. Imagine living as a Black man or woman in an era where you could be slapped, raped, shot at, seized,

---

9. Finkelman, "Slavery in the United States," 109.

10. Finkelman, "Slavery in the United States," 109.

11. Finkelman, "Slavery in the United States," 112. (Act XII, December 1662, 2 Hening 170.)

12. Finkelman, "Slavery in the United States," 113.

transported somewhere else, sold on the auction block, or legally robbed of your property and children.

William Paterson, a delegate at the 1787 convention on the Constitution of the United States regarding slavery and the representation of slaves, succinctly captures the state of Black humanity. He writes, "Negro slaves in no light but as property. They are no free agents, have no personal liberty, no faculty of acquiring property, but on the contrary are themselves property, and like other property entirely at the will of the Master."[13] Thus, Virginia and Congress in 1787 became political centers for the legal dehumanization of Black people. While Virginia provided the political and legal justification to define Africans as commodities, the Enlightenment project provided the philosophical and rational justifications.

THE ENLIGHTENMENT PIONEERS AND BLACK HUMANITY

In his book *Lectures on the Philosophy of World History,* based on lectures at the University of Berlin in 1822, 1828, and 1830, Georg Wilhelm Friedrich Hegel (1770–1831) argues that Europeans and especially Germans are intellectually and racially superior to all non-Europeans and especially to all Black Africans—people of what he calls "Africa proper." Hegel contends that Africa consists of three unconnected continents that are "essentially distinct" from each other with profound differences in "spiritual character" and distinct "physical peculiarities."[14] He writes, "One might almost say that Africa consists of three continents which are entirely separate from one another, and between which there is no contact whatsoever."[15] Based on his reading of available texts, Hegel divides Africa into three parts: (1) *Africa proper* as Black Africa, (2) North Africa as European, and (3) Egypt on its own as Asia. He explains: "The first of these is *Africa proper*, the land to the south of the Sahara Desert; it consists of almost entirely unexplored highlands with narrow coastal strips along its shores. The second is the land to the north of the desert, a coastal region that might be described as European Africa. And the third is the region of the Nile, the only valley land of Africa, which is closely

---

13. Finkelman, *Slavery and the Founders,* 16.
14. Hegel, *Lectures on the Philosophy,* 173.
15. Hegel, *Lectures on the Philosophy,* 173.

connected with Asia."[16] Hegel's division of Africa is essential because his perception of the continent and its people would become a part of the standard perception and treatment of those people in these divisions in Europe and the United States.

Hegel contends that *Africa proper* lacks what he calls "historical interest of its own." The inhabitants live in "barbarism and savagery." It is the "land of childhood."[17] Furthermore, Hegel contends that Black Africans are "dominated by passion." He writes:

> The negro is an example of animal man in all his savagery and lawlessness and if we wish to understand him at all, we must put aside all our European attitudes. We must not think of a spiritual God or of moral laws; to comprehend him correctly, we must abstract from all reverence and morality, and from everything which we call feeling. All this is foreign to man in his immediate existence, and nothing consonant with humanity is to be found in his character. For this very reason, we must properly feel ourselves into his nature, no more than into that of a dog.[18]

In 1822, 1828, and 1830, Hegel instructed Europe and his readers to define Black Africans as less human than Whites. Black Africans, he argued, are barbaric savages and animals. For the Europeans to interact with Black Africans, they must be inhumane while expressing zero human sympathies. Europeans must discard the "civilizing" feelings of European nature. According to Hegel, morality, ethics, and godliness are not appropriate to express in Whites' interaction with and treatment of Black Africans.

Fundamentally, Hegel argues that the Black Africans of *Africa proper* must be treated like animals. The virtues of the Enlightenment must not be appropriated to the Black Africans. Hegel gives the most direct instruction to his White audience regarding slavery. He writes: "The only significant relationship between the negroes and the Europeans has been—and still is—that of slavery.... Slavery has awakened more humanity among the negroes."[19] Hegel was basically advocating cruelty against Black Africans. His argument for the maltreatment of Africans by Europeans did not go unnoticed. We shall see the display of brutalities

16. Hegel, *Lectures on the Philosophy*, 173.
17. Hegel, *Lectures on the Philosophy*, 174.
18. Hegel, *Lectures on the Philosophy*, 177.
19. Hegel, *Lectures on the Philosophy*, 183.

A NECESSARY BACKGROUND: THE ENLIGHTENMENT PIONEERS

against the humanity of Africans in subsequent chapters and in *Volume Two* of *The Rush for Black Diamonds*.

The Hegelian definition of Black Africans is critical as a framework. It introduces the reader to the prevailing perceptions and treatments of Black Africans of *Africa proper* from the sixteenth century onward, which manifested in such events as the establishment of the industrial slave trade, the institution of chattel slavery, the transition to penal slavery after emancipation, and the post-1970 phenomenon of penal industrialization in the United Kingdom and mainly in the United States.[20]

While Hegel the German saw Africans as dogs, David Hume (1711–76), the Enlightenment philosopher from Scotland, had his own choice words for Africans' humanity and intellectual capacity. In his essay *Of the Populousness of Ancient Nations*, Hume wrote the following:

> This however is certain, that the characters of nations are very promiscuous in the temperate climates, and that almost all the general observations, which have been formed of the more southern or more northern people in these climates are found to be uncertain and fallacious. . . . I am apt to suspect the negroes and in general all other species of men (for there are four or five different kinds) to be naturally inferior to whites. There never was a civilized nation of any other complexion than white, nor even any individual eminent either in action or speculation. No ingenious manufactures amongst them, no arts, no sciences. On the other hand, the most rude and barbarous of the whites, such as the ancient Germans, the present Tartars, have still something eminent about them, in their valour, form of government, or some other particular. Such a uniform and constant difference could not happen, in so many countries and ages if nature had not made an original distinction between these breeds of men. *Not to mention our colonies*, there are Negroe slaves dispersed all over Europe, of whom none ever discovered any symptoms of ingenuity; though low people without education will start up amongst us and distinguish themselves in every profession. In Jamaica, indeed, they talk of one Negroe as a man of parts and learning; but it is likely he is admired for slender accomplishments, like a parrot who speaks a few words plainly.[21]

This book argues that the sentiments of Hegel and Hume (as well as those of John Locke and Thomas Jefferson) regarding the people of what

---

20. See Walters-Sleyon, *Rush for Black Diamonds, Volume Two*.
21. Eze, *Race and the Enlightenment*, 33.

A NECESSARY BACKGROUND: THE ENLIGHTENMENT PIONEERS

Hegel called *Africa proper* were not fringe racial stereotypes against the humanity and intelligence of Black people. Neither were Hegel and Hume simply repeating the sentiments of "their time"; instead, they defined the sentiments and treatments regarding Black people associated with their time. Hegel, Hume, Locke, and Jefferson provided the fundamental philosophical and sociopolitical justifications for the industrial slave trade and the development of chattel slavery, institutions that still determine how Europe and the United States treat people of *Africa proper*—Black people.

This book considers the depth of Locke's involvement in the transatlantic slave trade. It demonstrates how he provided philosophical, political, and theological defenses for the indefinite and indeterminate existence of the institution of slavery. I refer to this analysis as Lockean slavery. Lockean slavery defines the British role in the transatlantic slave trade. Similarly, the United States' involvement in the transatlantic slave trade and the institution of chattel slavery are expressed through the economic participation, political theory, philosophical arguments, and White supremacist claims of Thomas Jefferson, which I refer to as Jeffersonian slavery. Jeffersonian slavery, like Lockean slavery, provides the theoretical and practical justifications of the transatlantic slave trade and its mutation into the institution of chattel slavery in the United States.

While this book focuses on the United Kingdom and the United States as the leading pioneers and developers of the industrial slave trade and chattel slavery, Scotland's participation in the industrial slave trade and chattel slavery is often subsumed within the involvement of Great Britain. *The Rush for Black Diamonds, Volume Two* addresses the particular role of Scotland in the transatlantic slave trade and chattel slavery. This book further argues that Locke's emphasis on experience, empiricism, natural religion, and his rejection of innateness cannot be extracted from his social, philosophical, and theological justifications for racism. Understanding Locke's ideas and influences provide an essential background to the arguments associated with the transition from the slave industry to a capitalist penal industry in the United States and the United Kingdom.

In the United States, chattel slavery mutated into several forms of racialized bondage after the Civil War and the Emancipation Proclamation of 1863. Like the Industrial Revolution, the transatlantic slave trade and the institution of chattel slavery were revolutionary economic enterprises sustained by wealth accumulation, racism, religion, laws, penal and public policies, and finally philosophical, political, and presidential platforms. John Locke the Englishman and Thomas Jefferson the American provided the religious and philosophical validations for the industrialization of the transatlantic slave trade and the institution of chattel slavery.

Robert Bernasconi and Maaza Mann argue that any attempt to "reconcile" Locke's participation in the transatlantic slave trade with his work as a philosopher of liberal freedom is fraught with contradictions. Firstly, Locke was not ignorant of the argument that colonization of North America without slave labor was untenable. Bernasconi and Mann suggest that Locke's claims in *The Fundamental Constitutions* show how enslaved people should be treated. Secondly, Locke's involvement and defense of the slave trade "was judged to be indispensable to the profitability of the new American colonies."[22] The third contradiction by Locke is his argument about "just war."[23] According to Wayne Glausser, "Every modern scholar who takes him seriously has had to confront an embarrassing fact: John Locke, the preeminent theorist of natural liberties and an influential resource for abolitionist thinkers of the eighteenth and nineteenth centuries, actually participated in the slave trade."[24]

To conclude, Locke, Jefferson, the laws of Virginia, and the rhetoric of Hegel and Hume cannot be separated from the modern sociopolitical, economic, and anti-Black racial ethos and practices of the United States and the United Kingdom. Locke, Jefferson, and their Enlightenment colleagues continue to influence the racial animus against Black humanity. Furthermore, the death and cruelty that Black people have endured at the hands of the United Kingdom and the United States in association with the various mutations of the industrial slave trade, the institution of chattel slavery and penal slavery, are theoretically justified by the ideas of Locke and Jefferson.

Slavery cannot be understood without considering the social, theological, and philosophical contributions of the Enlightenment pioneers. *The Rush for Black Diamonds, Volume One* refers to the experiences of Lockean slavery and Jeffersonian slavery and their consistent implications and adaptations in the twenty-first century. As theological and ethical *situations*, they must be interpreted accordingly in *The Rush for Black Diamonds, Volume Two*.

22. Bernasconi and Mann, "Contradictions of Racism," 90.
23. Bernasconi and Mann, "Contradictions of Racism," 92.
24. Glausser, "Three Approaches," 199.

A NECESSARY BACKGROUND: THE ENLIGHTENMENT PIONEERS

WEALTH FROM THE HUMAN TRADE

Enslaved Africans were a significant economic resource enabling the development and sustainability of major cities in Britain and the United States. Slavery generated capital in Britain for the financial and infrastructural development of cities like Liverpool, London, Bristol, Glasgow, and Manchester.

> The peace of 1713 followed by one year the ending of restrictions on the African trade. With safer shipping, and an increased demand for field-hands in the West Indies, Bristol began mounting a challenge for the Barbados slave trade. In 1715, the port's merchants handled 2,200 of the 5,500 slaves delivered to the island's planters; during the same period, Bristol merchants expanded their sales to the more prosperous sugar cultivators of Jamaica, claiming one-third of this trade by the end of the decade. The postwar period also marked the first significant involvement of Liverpool in the slave trade, especially with Barbados, where over 500 Africans were shipped annually between 1715 and 1718.[25]

The transatlantic slave trade intersected with the development of capitalism and the industrial revolution.[26] The benefits of this intersection continue to intersect with the economic and political dominance of major Western nations in the world today.[27] Similarly, the financial and what would also emerge as the colonial dominance of non-Western nations—especially Africa and her people that the United States,[28] England and Wales, Scotland (the United Kingdom),[29] France, Portugal, Belgium, the Netherlands, Germany, and Denmark developed from the human trade—account for their social-racial, cultural, and civilizational dominance. The English cities of Liverpool, Bristol,[30] London,[31] York, and Manchester are key examples.[32] The port in Liverpool was the epicenter

---

25. Clemens, "Rise of Liverpool," 218.
26. Inikori, "Slavery and the Development."
27. Daudin, "Profitability of Slave."
28. Bailey, "Slave(ry) Trade."
29. The National Trust for Scotland, "Scotland and the Slave Trade."
30. Morgan, "Bristol and the Atlantic Trade."
31. Draper, "City of London."
32. Inikori, "Slavery and the Development."

A NECESSARY BACKGROUND: THE ENLIGHTENMENT PIONEERS

of the slave trade prior to and after the union of the Kingdom of England and Wales and the Kingdom of Scotland in 1701.[33]

According to Paul G. E. Clemens, "When war began in 1739, Liverpool secured its position, for the fighting hindered Bristol's merchants, who cut back their voyages to Africa, the West Indies, and the Chesapeake. The ground they lost during the 1740s was never regained: by mid-century, Liverpool had become the greatest slave port in the world."[34] Clemens contends that Liverpool transformed itself from an "insignificant seaport" starting from the era of English Restoration to "one of England's leading ports" in the "last decades of the seventeenth century," as a member of "the Anglo-American market."[35] The emergence of Liverpool was historic but would later be identified largely with the slave trade and the goods produced and associated with chattel slavery in the territories of the Kingdom of England and the Kingdom of Scotland in the Americas and the Caribbean/West Indies. Clemens notes, "The port's commercial expansion began with its exploitation of American and West Indian trade, and its merchant fleets subsequently carried salt, naval stores, wines, iron, and eventually slaves . . . before the Peace of Utrecht in 1713."[36] The port of Liverpool was efficient in "supplying colonial producers," "marketing the crop," "exploiting news sources," to meet the supply and demands of the Anglo-American market.[37] The prominence of the port of Liverpool and its profitability emerged to challenge the ports of Bristol, Plymouth, London, Bideford, Whitehaven, Glasgow, Chesapeake, ports of Dublin and ports of Drogheda, ports of Maryland, ports of Virginia, and several other ports "for control of much of colonial trade," including the transatlantic slave trade and chattel slavery.[38] Clemens reports, "By 1750 Liverpool stood second only to London in the volume and value of its Anglo-American trade. Sugar and tobacco imports had roughly tripled between 1713 and mid-century, while the port had secured an increasingly larger proportion of English business with Virginia, Barbados, Jamaica, the Leewards, and finally South Carolina."[39]

33. Inikori, "Market Structure," 749–50.
34. Clemens, "Rise of Liverpool," 219.
35. Clemens, "Rise of Liverpool," 211.
36. Clemens, "Rise of Liverpool," 211.
37. Clemens, "Rise of Liverpool," 211.
38. Clemens, "Rise of Liverpool," 212–13.
39. Clemens, "Rise of Liverpool," 216.

As Joseph Inikori has documented, from 1783–93, in the span of ten years, over 300,000 Black Africans were dragged out of various parts of Africa through the Middle Passage by slave traders in Liverpool.[40] Furthermore, at the helm of this slave trading in Africans and economic sponsorship were 359 slave trading firms in the British city of Liverpool.

Several approaches have been used to calculate the enormous wealth acquired from the various forms of commodifying the humanity of Africans.

> Liverpool merchants dealt as readily in sugar as in tobacco. Liverpool firms responded to the economic upswing of the 1730's by expanding their slave trade with Barbados, delivering over 50 per cent of the island's imports after 1735, and then, in the late 1730s, capturing more of the Chesapeake, Jamaica, and Leeward Island slave markets. Paralleling this post-1720 rise of Liverpool's slave trade was a new emphasis on the export of cordage and linens to Africa as well as increased commerce with the Baltic, where wrought iron for Gambia was obtained. Liverpool had over Bristol the advantage of more dynamic urban growth and geographical location.[41]

The first approach is based on a process of generalization. Robert P. Thomas and Richard Nelson Bean are associated with this approach in their 1974 analysis of the profitability of the slave trade. They are particularly apprehensive about any claim of "profitability" associated with the human trade particularly when it comes to the assertions of "Black militants for reparations."[42] Referred to as a "fable," Thomas and Bean contend that "Black slaves, whether shipped directly from Africa, or born in the New World into slavery, served their masters against their wills in return for the subsistence allowed them. Surely there was a substantial difference between the value of what they produced, and the value of the consumption goods allotted to them to allow survival. This essay attempts to trace what happened to the 'fabled' profits of the slave trade."[43] Also, Thomas and Bean argues that the claim for profitability from the slave trade cannot be verifiable since there were several actors involved in the human trade. In explaining their approach, they note:

40. Inikori, "Market Structure," 749.
41. Clemens, "Rise of Liverpool," 219.
42. Thomas and Bean, "Fishers of Men," 885.
43. Thomas and Bean, "Fishers of Men," 886.

A NECESSARY BACKGROUND: THE ENLIGHTENMENT PIONEERS

> We will investigate the market structure of each stage of the slave trade and apply the economic model appropriate to that market structure. Economic theory relates the performance of a market to its structure; a single seller or monopoly, for example, potentially earns economic profits, whereas in a competitive market composed of many sellers the marginal firm will make no economic profits. This procedure allows us to draw conclusions in the absence of direct evidence on the profitability of the trade and substantially adds to our understanding of the economic consequences of the transatlantic slave trade.[44]

Inikori refers to Thomas and Bean's approach as "generalizing about the profitability of the trade on the basis of an *a priori* application of the theory of competition relating profits to market structure."[45] Fundamental to Thomas and Bean's argument is the assertion that "profitability of the trade was relatively low."[46] They further contend that the actual "slave traders" were Africans themselves, thus exonerating Europeans of the accusation. "The importer acquired the slave from a shipper who had brought a cargo across the Atlantic. The shipper purchased the slave from a slave exporter in Africa. The exporter, directly or through intermediaries, acquired the slaves from the fishers of men—the ultimate enslavers. The fishers of men were almost always African, and the exporters usually were African."[47] Instead, Thomas and Bean note that Europeans increased their slave population by breeding Black people as slaves for their plantations. "The planters in British-America could obtain additional slaves either from traders selling blacks directly from Africa or from persons who had reared slaves in the New World."[48]

The second approach, according to Inikori, is "based on the merchants' accounts of individual ventures taken singly or in group."[49] Inikori is associated with this approach. He writes, "The market structure argument is probably the most influential of all recent contributions. Its assumptions and conclusion have far-reaching implications for any calculations based on existing private accounts of the traders. No

---

44. Thomas and Bean, "Fishers of Men," 886.

45. Inikori, "Market Structure," 747. This first approach is attributed to Thomas and Bean, "Fishers of Men," 885–914, particularly, 885–909.

46. Darity, "Numbers Game," 693.

47. Thomas and Bean, "Fishers of Men," 887.

48. Thomas and Bean, "Fishers of Men," 891.

49. Inikori, "Market Structure," 747.

further advance can be made without examining the assumptions and conclusions."[50] According to Darity, "A third approach is to employ 'various sets of data relating to shipping, slave prices, and the like, to estimate total costs and revenues from which overall annual profits are derived.' This last approach was taken by Roger Anstey in two studies that appeared for a time to provide the definitive estimates of the profitability of the British slave trade in the late eighteenth century."[51]

In this entire research, I demonstrate what I call a *cumulative approach to the collateral profitability of the slave trade*. This approach demonstrates the profitability of the slave trade by Western nations and particularly the United Kingdom and the United States. It is inclusive of the commercialization and racialization as both economic and White-supremacist control of Black humanity; the looting, destruction, and usurpation of Black Africans' wealth and artifacts; the breeding of Black people for the market and to sustain the labor forces of the plantations; and the destruction of the sociopolitical and cultural institutions of Africans with impunity. The *cumulative approach to the collateral profitability of the slave trade* also includes the consistent demonstration of the sociopolitical, economic, and racial mutations of the transatlantic slave trade into the institution of chattel slavery, into penal slavery and the post-1970s mutations of the penal industry of mass incarceration.

The National Archives of England notes that "the slave trade was carried out from many British ports, but the three most important ports were London (1660–1720s), Bristol (1720s–1740s), and Liverpool (1740s–1807), which became extremely wealthy. Under the 1799 Slave Trade Act, the slave trade was restricted to these three ports."[52] These cities were built on money from the human trade. Africans were the literal *black diamonds* that provided the foundation for Europe's present financial dominance. According to David Haslam:

> Bristol was more or less built on the commerce in slaves and sugar. Its activity peaked in the 1730s, with up to fifty sailings a year, taking cheap manufactured goods to West Africa, then carrying as many as 17,000 slaves annually from there to the West Indies. An average profit from a voyage was £7,000 to £8,000, a princely sum in those days. Liverpool was founded

50. Inikori, "Market Structure," 747.
51. Darity, "Numbers Game," 695.
52. The National Archives, "Evil Trade," 4. ("Slavery and the British Transatlantic Slave Trade.")

on the trades in slaves and cotton, some of its proceeds being absorbed into the fledgeling Manchester cotton industry. There are differing estimates as to the takings. One estimate put Liverpool's proceeds between 1783 and 1793 at £12 million.[53]

The enslavement of Africans financed the building and sustainability of major economic institutions and infrastructures across Europe and the United States. According to James Pope-Hennessy: "The net profit to the town of Liverpool on an aggregate of 303,737 slaves sold was almost three million pounds.... This was the gold harvest which accounts for all—for the fetid, feverish weeks on the African coast, for the vile and dangerous Atlantic crossing for the sordid scramble in the Guinea-yard, for the callous division of Negro families."[54]

The cities of Bristol, Liverpool, London, and Glasgow in Scotland acquired their wealth and prestige from the sale and use of African humanity. "Liverpool and Bristol were both estimated to have made net profits of more than £12 million from the slave trade. The slave traders, plantation owners, absentee landowners, speculators, and others who were profiting directly from slavery used their wealth to buy political influence."[55] This goes for several other European and American cities. Despite the immorality of the human trade, Europeans exhibited little to no remorse or guilt in exploiting the humanity of Africans. They felt that their military might, backed up by the Enlightenment's claims of White supremacy and civilization, justified their treatment of Africans as property. Similarly, the death of millions of Africans in the slave trade did not strike them as "sinful," notwithstanding their religious distortion, abuse, and racialization of the religion of Jesus Christ.

DEATH FROM THE HUMAN TRADE

Volume One and *Volume Two* of *The Rush for Black Diamonds* also explore four kinds of death tolls of Black people that cannot be avoided: (1) deaths through the transatlantic slave trade and chattel slavery (1600s to 1865); (2) deaths through the Black Codes (also known as Jim Crow laws) in the South/the Convict Lease System in the United States (1865 to 1945); (3) deaths through mob lynching in the United States (1865 to

---

53. Haslam, *Race for the Millennium*, 42.
54. Pope-Hennessy, *Sins of the Fathers*, 146.
55. Kaye, *1807–2007*, 5.

1945); and (4) deaths through mass incarceration in the US and the UK penal systems (1970s to present).

Africans died in exceedingly large numbers in the human trade. They died while capturing them in their villages, towns, and in transit, including the Middle Passage on the rough sea from Africa to the West. Frank Tannenbaum contends that ten to twenty million Africans died during the Middle Passage.[56] He explains, "One-third of the Negroes taken from their homes died on the way to the coast and at embarkation stations, and another one-third died crossing the ocean and in the seasoning so that only one-third finally survived to become the laborers and colonizers of the New World."[57] The Europeans and colonists saw and knew it. Unfortunately, the conscience of their European captors, including Locke and his fellow proprietors, were un-pricked and unsympathetic to the plights of the Africans. They had concluded that the humanity of Africans was inferior to that of Europeans and had thus hardened their hearts and conscience against the Africans. In subsequent chapters, we shall see the demonstration of this mindset toward Blacks on full display. For now, the industry of the slave trade established the initial context by which Europeans (and later Americans) were to define and treat the humanity of people of African descent.

According to Columbus Salley and Ronald Behm: "Slavery was an international phenomenon which developed . . . as one aspect of the expansion of Western European culture into the New World. . . . The Atlantic slave trade was 'officially declared open' in 1441 when 'ten Africans from the northern Guinea Coast were shipped to Portugal as a gift to Prince Henry the Navigator."[58] Despite the high African death toll of the slave trade, Locke and Jefferson were enlightened defenders of the human trade.

---

56. Tannenbaum, *Slave & Citizen*, 35.
57. Tannenbaum. *Slave & Citizen*, 28.
58. Salley and Behm, *Your God Is Too White*, 11.

LICENSED BY THE ENLIGHTENMENT

The Enlightenment Pioneers are the Fathers of Western intellectual racism!
Europeans, the race of supreme intelligence they argued.
White complexion, the superior race,
But Black complexion, the inferior race

Pseudoscientific theories they advanced,
The signs of inferiority they have discovered,
To justify the material distinctions,
Darker skin, they declared inferior.

For David Hume, Black people are intellectually inferior to Whites.
Emmanuel Kant boasted that blackness is a sign of stupidity.
For Georg Hegel, the Germans are the superior race.
But Thomas Jefferson considered Sally Hemings below his
whiteness, yet his mistress with his six children.

Black inferiority, they declared, was anatomical.
Bigger lips and flattened nose,
Bigger buttocks and kinky hair,
With immense disdain for the African complexion,
The Enlightenment pioneers established their names.

The size of the head a sign of brain power.
The African's head a sign of inferior brain.
The European's head a sign of superior brain.
But indeed, the Black skin, they argued an absolute
Degeneration.

The Enlightenment Pioneers provided intellectual justifications.
This racial genocide Darwin also aided.
Monogenesis to polygenesis, White Supremacy they advanced.
With Social Darwinism White Supremacists, they are.[59]

GEORGE WALTERS-SLEYON

---

59. Walters-Sleyon, *Nuggets from the Night*, 107.

THE TRANSATLANTIC SLAVE TRADE

1400–1860s

2

W. E. B. Du Bois: The Rush for "Black Diamonds"

It was not altogether a mistaken judgment that led the constitutional fathers to consider the slave-trade as the backbone of slavery.[1]

THIS CHAPTER DETAILS THE ECONOMIC rush for Africans across the Atlantic Ocean through what is now famously known as the dreadful Middle Passage. From the 1400s, European slave traders, with the backing of their governments, sailed from Europe to Africa to capture Africans as slaves.

In his 1896 dissertation *The Suppression of the African Slave Trade to the United States of America 1638–1870*, W. E. B. Du Bois provides an articulate account of the development of the trafficking and sales of Africans in what he terms the "African Slave-Trade." He describes a human trafficking that was institutionalized, legal, racialized, and strictly profit-oriented. Du Bois's goal was to research the industry of the slave trade in order to determine how it began, how it mutated into the institution of chattel slavery, and how it was "suppressed."[2] To accomplish this, Du Bois meticulously examined the laws, history, treaties, congressional acts, and other historical documents. His aim was to provide an accurate

---

1. Du Bois, *Suppression of the African Slave-Trade*, v, 168.
2. Du Bois, *Suppression of the African Slave-Trade*, 1.

account of the economic, political, and sociological development of the slave trade as "scientific" research.³

In this chapter, the reader is also introduced to the distinctiveness of the transatlantic slave trade. The industry of the transatlantic slave trade preceded the formal institution of chattel slavery. While the two are both considered linked as economic industries, they must be analyzed separately for clarity.

Europeans, Americans, and the British traversed the Atlantic Ocean in fully armed vessels in a scramble to capture Africans from their farms, hamlets, villages, towns, and cities. They sailed from Portugal, Spain, the Netherlands, Bristol, Liverpool, London, Newport, Rhode Island, New York, Great Britain, and other parts of Europe and America in ships armed with the latest ammunitions to invade Africa for Africans as slaves.

However, any exploration of the transatlantic slave trade must begin with the involvement of the Portuguese. Before the British became the most important superpower of the slave trade, there was the Portuguese. The Portuguese started the rush for Black Diamonds from Europe into Africa in the 1400s. Most of their African slaves were taken to Brazil.

THE PORTUGUESE AND THE SLAVE TRADE

The nation of Portugal and her people perfected the capturing and trading of Africans as slaves into Europe and the Americas—North and South America. "Portuguese vessels carried an estimated 5.8 million Africans into slavery."⁴ The capital of Portugal, Lisbon, was considered the slave capital and its ports, the slave ports of Europe. The Portuguese had the "Asiento," "A contractual agreement with the Spanish colonies to provide them with enslaved people for their plantations. Lisbon was the major trade port involved in the African slave trade. From there, ships were sent to West Africa and took enslaved Africans as slaves across the Atlantic Ocean to the Portuguese-owned colonies of Brazil for plantation or mining work."⁵ Prior to the transatlantic transport of enslaved Africans, by around 1444, Portuguese slave traders brought Africans as slaves into Europe. "The Atlantic slave trade started in 1444, when 235 people snatched from the newly discovered coast of West Africa were put up for

---

3 .. Du Bois, *Suppression of the African Slave-Trade*.
4. Ames, "Portugal Confronts," para. 5.
5. Randive, "Case Study," para. 5.

sale in Lagos, now a laidback Portuguese beach resort on Europe's southwestern tip."[6] The Atlantic slave trade gave birth to the transatlantic slave trade. It was the Portuguese and the Dutch and Spain that perfected the Atlantic slave. The French, the English (and eventually the Scots), and the United States perfected the transatlantic slave trade. As a product of the Atlantic slave trade, the transatlantic slave trade mutated into full-blown chattel slavery and colonialism. It is believed that the transatlantic slave trade started when the Portuguese took their initial and recorded load of Africans as slaves into South America. The most imposing structure of the Portuguese trade in African humanity is Elmina Castle in Cape Coast, Ghana. According to Mayur Randive, "The Portuguese used enslaved Africans in their sugar plantation, built in Madeira, a Portuguese island off the western coast of Africa. Later in 1481, the first slave fort, 'Elmina Castle,' was built off the coast of modern Ghana which served as the headquarters for Portuguese slave traders."[7] While this book does not explore in depth the role of the Portuguese as originators of the slave trade, the astronomical number of Africans, 5.8 million (excluding those who died during the dreadful Middle Passage), that Portugal took out of Africa cannot be seen as isolated developments. Portugal and the Portuguese slave traders also provided the blueprint for the human trade that the Dutch, the Spanish, the French, the British, the Belgians, the Germans, the Scots, and the Americans would subsequently adopt and perfect. The Portuguese took most of their slaves to their slave colony—Brazil. The data indicates that 150,000 Africans as slaves were shipped to Brazil between 1721 and 1730. Furthermore, another 200,000 enslaved Africans were shipped to Brazil between 1801 and 1810. Certainly, the slave trade continued between 1730 and 1801 with increasing speed, and with Portugal as one of the most important traffickers in Africans.[8] According to Clive Willis: "The transatlantic trade became the key to the development of the plantations and mines of the New World. . . . The leading perpetrators were Portugal and the United Kingdom."[9] The Portuguese ended their involvement in human trading in 1835. However, the British had already perfected the slave trade and the exportation of their slaves to the West Indies and the region that would become the United States.

6. Ames, "Portugal Confronts," para. 10.
7. Randive, "Case Study," para. 4.
8. "Portugal."
9. Willis, "David Livingstone," 31–49.

THE DUTCH AND THE SLAVE TRADE

The Dutch and the Spanish became the superpowers of slave traders in Europe after the Portuguese but before the British. The Dutch started selling Africans as slaves to Great Britain and were part of the early pioneers of the trade of slaves into America. By 1619, private Dutch slave ships and trading companies had developed "the lucrative African slave-trade."[10]

Du Bois describes the trading companies and ships responsible for the transportation of Africans into the West: "Ships sailed from Holland to Africa, got slaves in exchange for their goods, carried the slaves to the West Indies or Brazil, and returned home laden with sugar. Through the enterprise of one of these trading companies the settlement of New Amsterdam was begun, in 1614."[11] The Dutch West India Company was established in 1621 as a merger of several private slave-trading companies responsible for the importation of slaves into America, but, in four years, it transported 15,430 Africans to Brazil.[12]

It is important to take note of the names of the following slave ships:

- The Dutch: *The Dutch West India Company*—1621.[13]
- Great Britain: *The Company of Royal Adventurers*—1662.[14]
- Great Britain: *The Royal African Company*.[15]
- Great Britain: *Company of Merchants Trading to Africa*.[16]

The packing of Africans on the ships was akin to three or more people squeezed in a casket. According to The National Trust for Scotland:

> A slave ship could take up to two months to sail to the Caribbean islands from West Africa. There might be over 400 people on one ship. Most traders packed in as many people as they could—for maximum profit. (Some opted for fewer slaves in the hope that more would survive.) The men were chained together (with shackles and chains made in Britain), lying or crouching

---

10. Du Bois, *Suppression of the African Slave-Trade*, 2.
11. Du Bois, *Suppression of the African Slave-Trade*, 17.
12. Du Bois, *Suppression of the African Slave-Trade*, 17.
13. Du Bois, *Suppression of the African Slave-Trade*, 17.
14. Du Bois, *Suppression of the African Slave-Trade*, 315.
15. Du Bois, *Suppression of the African Slave-Trade*, 2.
16. Du Bois, *Suppression of the African Slave-Trade*, 4.

next to each other with barely room to move. At times, they could hardly breathe. In one report, the space allowed for each person was 125 x 45 cms (4 x 1.5 ft). Women and children were kept in separate areas of the ship or sometimes on deck (which made them more vulnerable).[17]

However, the Dutch control of the slave trade was not without competition from other European nations, especially Great Britain. Beginning in 1562, Great Britain got involved in the slave trade under Queen Elizabeth I.

This second chapter also provides an introductory background to Lockean slavery and Jeffersonian slavery. It argues that the institution of chattel slavery, the slave-trade industry, the transatlantic slave trade, and the triangular slave trade existed as established practices in the British Empire, other European countries, and the United States. The rush for *black diamonds*[18]—or the extensive capturing, selling, and trafficking of human beings across the Atlantic Ocean in association with the British and the British colonies—legally began in 1638[19] and was legally "suppressed" on March 2, 1870. The suppression of the slave trade took a resolution submitted to the United States Senate by Senator Henry Wilson. However, illegal British and American slave trafficking continued well after 1870 in the West Indies. The kind of slavery discussed in this book—Lockean slavery—is one that Europeans and Americans "fomented" in Africa through threats, wars, and military takeover.[20]

THE BRITISH AND THE SLAVE TRADE THEREAFTER

The British Parliament and the Asiento Slave Trade Treaty

The British Parliament was directly involved in the capturing, transporting, trafficking, and selling of Africans as slaves. Du Bois is meticulous in mentioning the role of the British Parliament in facilitating and fostering the human trade. In the 1500s, Sir John Hawkins became the first

---

17. The National Trust for Scotland, "Scotland and the Slave Trade," 9.
18. Du Bois, *Suppression of the African Slave-Trade*, 176.
19. Du Bois, *Suppression of the African Slave-Trade*, 312. Senate Misc. Doc., 41 Cong. 2 Sess. No. 66.
20. Du Bois, *Suppression of the African Slave-Trade*, 312. Senate Misc. Doc., 41 Cong. 2 Sess. No. 66.

prominent English slave trader and the pioneer of what would become the English slave trading triangle. He violently captured 300 Africans from Sierra Leone prior to the 1560s; these acts earned him a special coat of arm with the image of an enslaved African inscribed on it from Queen Elizabeth I. Hawkins was a member of a group called the "Sea Dogs" of Queen Elizabeth I, which included Sir Francis Drake and Sir Martin Frobisher. They were so called because Hawkins, Drake, and Frobisher were violent and vicious slave capturers, slave traders, and pirates who were also good at destabilizing Spain's naval dominance. Hawkins is also famous for establishing the foundation for the British slave trading interests. He would eventually become a member of Parliament. In 1564 Hawkins received a legitimate commission and investment from Queen Elizabeth I, thus conferring political recognition on the Sea Dogs' slave-trading activities.[21] Du Bois notes: "Sir John Hawkins's celebrated voyage took place in 1562, but probably not until 1631 did a regular chartered company undertake to carry on the trade. This company was unsuccessful and was eventually succeeded by the 'Company of Royal Adventurers Trading to Africa,' chartered by Charles II in 1662 and including the Queen Dowager and the Duke of York."[22]

The English wanted to own "commercial supremacy" of the slave trade. This quest on the part of the English led to two slave-centered wars with the Dutch who controlled the slave trade at the time. As a result, *The Navigation Ordinance of 1651* was enacted with the Dutch.[23] According to Du Bois, Great Britain developed the transatlantic slave trade into a total industry: "It was left to the English, with their strong policy in its favor, to develop this trade."[24]

Wars and other factors affected the trading activities of the English slave company, The Company of Royal Adventurers. In 1672, the owners sold the company to the Royal African Company for £34,000. According to Du Bois, the Royal African Company "carried on a growing trade for a quarter of a century."[25] While admitting that "the exact proportion of the slave-trade to America can be but approximately determined,"[26] Du Bois reports that the Royal African Company shipped 60,783 Africans on

21. "Queen Elizabeth I's Sea Dogs."
22. Du Bois, *Suppression of the African Slave-Trade*, 1.
23. Du Bois, *Suppression of the African Slave-Trade*, 17.
24. Du Bois, *Suppression of the African Slave-Trade*, 17.
25. Du Bois, *Suppression of the African Slave-Trade*, 5.
26. Du Bois, *Suppression of the African Slave-Trade*, 5.

249 ships between 1680 and 1688. Overall, 14,387 Africans died in the Middle Passage during the voyages, with 46,396 delivered to America. In 1701, 104 ships sailed to Africa for slaves.[27] There were many private registered and unregistered trading companies plying the Atlantic Ocean to capture Africans. It was a rush for *black diamonds*.

Following the establishment of the trading apparatus, the British Parliamentary got involved in the slave-trading industry in 1698. According to Finkelman, "The British government gave special protection to the Royal African Company (RAC), which brought more slaves to the American colonies than any other single entity."[28] Furthermore, "private traders, on payment of a duty of 10% on English goods exported to Africa, were allowed to participate in the trade."[29]

Between 1698 and 1707, a total of 25,000 Africans are thought to have been brought to America annually. If so, for nine years, between 1698 and 1707, a total of 225,000 Africans were captured and shipped as slaves to be sold in the human trade.[30] Again, the data does not consider the number of Africans that unregistered and private ships and companies brought to America.

The industry of the slave trade had become the bedrock of the colonies' political and economic survival. Du Bois notes, "That the slave-trade was the very life of the colonies had, by 1700, become an almost unquestioned axiom in British practical economics. The colonists themselves declared slaves the strength and sinews of this Western world, and the lack of them 'the grand obstruction' here, as the settlements 'cannot subsist without supplies of them.'"[31] The British Parliament supported the slave trade as the central economic generator in the British empire.[32] The Europeans' trade in Africans was perceived as an "economic necessity." Particularly, Du Bois writes, "The colonial governors were generally instructed to 'give all due encouragement and invitation to merchants and

---

27. Du Bois, *Suppression of the African Slave-Trade*, 5.
28. Finkelman, *Slavery and the Founders*, 134.
29. Du Bois, *Suppression of the African Slave-Trade*, 2.
30. Du Bois, *Suppression of the African Slave-Trade*, 5.
31. Du Bois, *Suppression of the African Slave-Trade*, 4.
32. The National Archives, "Slavery and the British," para. 5: "Portugal and Britain were the two most 'successful' slave-trading countries accounting for about 70% of all Africans transported to the Americas. Britain was the most dominant between 1640 and 1807 when the British slave trade was abolished."

others . . . and in particular to the royal African company of England."[33] As a result, merchants were clamoring for Africans to turn them into chattel property.

As a result of Parliamentary involvement in the slave trade, Britain displaced Spain as the most successful slave-trading country and assumed a monopoly of the trade in 1713. Du Bois notes that the signing of a treaty—*the Asiento*—between the two countries provided the grounds for this transfer of the human trade monopoly from Spain to Britain. The *Asiento* granted Britain a monopoly of the slave trade in Africans with the advance payment of 200,000 crowns to Spain and a "duty of 33½ crowns for each slave imported." Aside from the advance payment and the duty on each slave, the royal head of each nation was to receive their benefit of the profit. Du Bois notes, "The kings of Spain and England were each to receive one-fourth of the profits of the trade, and the Royal African Company were authorized to import as many slaves as they wished above the specified number in the first twenty-five years, and to sell them, except in three ports, at any price they could get."[34] The signing of *the Asiento* commenced another immediate rush into the continent of Africa, especially West Africa, to acquire Africans as slaves to sell. Captured Africans were taken to the West Indies, Brazil, North America, and other parts of Europe to be sold as chattel property. The experience of being lost in a strange land in chains and being subjected to the most inhumane treatment was real, cruel, ungodly, and with impunity for the perpetrators.

Du Bois admits that the exact number of people taken cannot be ascertained. Many Africans died during the voyages from Africa to Europe, the United States, the West Indies, and South America. Sickness and diseases were rampant. The National Trust for Scotland notes that "in 1788, one ship was reported to have carried 600 slaves—though built for a maximum of 451 people. Slave ships were notorious for diseases such as dysentery and smallpox. Some slaves committed suicide by jumping overboard (nets were put over the decks to prevent it) or by refusing to eat. . . . Another estimation is that 20% of the people died before reaching their destination. Some people put the figure as much higher."[35]

In twenty years, from 1713 to 1733, the English imported 15,000 Africans as slaves annually into America. One-third to one-half of the

---

33. Du Bois, *Suppression of the African Slave-Trade*, 4.
34. Du Bois, *Suppression of the African Slave-Trade*, 3.
35. The National Trust for Scotland, "Scotland and the Slave Trade."

15,000 went to the Spanish colonies. To facilitate the trading, the British Parliament gave an annual grant of 90,000 pounds to the Royal Company from 1729 to 1750.[36] The support of the British Parliament for the slave trade continued well into the nineteenth century in various ways. By 1750 the British controlled and dominated the human trade politically, militarily, and economically. At this point, there was no need for the *Asiento* treaty.

The *Asiento* treaty ended on October 5, 1750.[37] According to Du Bois, "by the Statute 23 George II., chapter 31, the old company was dissolved and a new 'Company of Merchants trading to Africa' erected in its stead."[38] The "old company" in question was the Royal Company. We shall elaborate further in chapters 3 and 4 on Locke's involvement with the Royal Company and its successor: the Company of Merchants Trading to Africa.

It is important to note the number of Africans the Royal Company sold between 1713 and 1733 annually. Based on the quota stipulated in the *Asiento* treaty, with 15,000 Africans to be annually imported into America between 1713 and 1733, a total number of 300,000 Africans were sold. This number does not include the data on imported Africans as slaves that the private and illegal slave ships and companies were bringing into the British colonies including the United States, the West Indies, and Brazil.

Legal importation rose to 30,000 annually between 1733 and 1766. The English imported 20,000 Africans annually into America with the bulk of them going to South Carolina. Du Bois notes, "Before the Revolution, the total exportation to America is variously estimated as between 40,000 and 100,000 each year. [George] Bancroft places the total slave population of the continental colonies at 59,000 in 1714, 78,000 in 1727, and 293,000 in 1754. The census of 1790 showed 697,897 slaves in the United States."[39] Based on Bancroft's research, between 1733 and 1766, 66,000 Africans were legally imported as slaves into the United States. Furthermore, it should be restated that both legal and illegal importations were going on. Africans were imported at alarming rates into the West Indies, South Carolina, Georgia, and other parts of America. Slave codes were enacted to keep the imported Africans from resisting or

---

36. Du Bois, *Suppression of the African Slave-Trade*, 3.
37. Du Bois, *Suppression of the African Slave-Trade*, 3.
38. Du Bois, *Suppression of the African Slave-Trade*, 4.
39. Du Bois, *Suppression of the African Slave-Trade*, 5.

fleeing. These slave codes, like the Black Codes after the American Civil War, were brutal, harsh, and exceedingly inhumane.

THE UNITED STATES AND THE SLAVE TRADE THEREAFTER

The internal slave trade in the United States flourished both before 1770 and long after. Slave trading in the United States was fully industrialized before and after the Revolutionary War (April 19, 1775—September 3, 1783); however, the prices of slaves increased after the war. Unregistered and private companies, slave smugglers, and illegal slave traders resorted to extreme means to acquire Africans as slaves and realized enormous profits.[40] Furthermore, according to Du Bois, "In 1783 the British West Indies received 16,208 Negroes from Africa, and by 1787 the importation had increased to 21,023. In this latter year it was estimated that the British were taking annually from Africa 38,000 slaves; the French, 20,000; the Portuguese, 10,000; the Dutch and Danes, 6,000; a total of 74,000. Manchester alone sent £180,000 annually in goods to Africa in exchange for Negroes."[41] These numbers denote a very concerted and intentional effort to haul Africans as slaves out of Africa. It cast doubts on the claim that African leaders were conspiring willy-nilly with Europeans and Americans. The conclusion here is that Europeans and Americans came to Africa highly weaponized with the latest military gears to pillage, invade, and seize Africans and their wealth at all costs. European slave traders and Americans were not asking Africans for their consent. Instead, they were invading and pillaging African villages, towns, and cities, and capturing Africans to be sold on their auction blocks, used as chattel property, abused, and discarded with impunity.

---

40. Du Bois, *Suppression of the African Slave-Trade*, 8, 14. "In 1760 England, the chief slave-trading nation, was sending on an average to Africa 163 ships annually, with a tonnage of 18,000 tons, carrying exports to the value of £163,818. Only about twenty of these ships regularly returned to England. Most of them carried slaves to the West Indies and returned laden with sugar and other products."

41. Du Bois, *The Suppression of the African Slave-Trade*, 41.

NEW ENGLAND: "MANSTEALING LAW" AND "JUST WAR"

The slave trade flourished in New England. According to Du Bois, "Vessels from Massachusetts, Rhode Island, Connecticut, and, to a less extent, from New Hampshire, were early and largely engaged in the carrying slave-trade. 'We know,' said Thomas Pemberton in 1795, 'that a large trade to Guinea was carried on for many years by the citizens of Massachusetts Colony, who were the proprietors of the vessels and their cargoes, out and home.'"[42] From the Guinean nation of West Africa, New Englanders engaged in the capturing and selling of Africans in America and the West Indies. Du Bois provides a meticulous account of this enterprise.[43]

However, a peculiar mandate existed in Massachusetts regarding the slave trade called the "Mansteeling Mandate." The nature of this mandate is interesting because it provides a clue into one of Locke's arguments for engaging in the slave trade and his defense of the institution of chattel slavery. Du Bois narrates a particular incident that provides insight into the execution of this mandate in Massachusetts:

> The early biblical codes of Massachusetts confined slavery to "lawfull Captives taken in just warres, & such strangers as willingly selle themselves or are sold to us." The stern Puritanism of early days endeavored to carry this out literally, and consequently when a certain Captain Smith, about 1640, attacked an African village and brought some of the unoffending natives home, he was promptly arrested. Eventually, the General Court ordered the Negroes sent home at the colony's expense, "conceiving themselues bound by (the) first opportunity to bear witnes against (the) haynos & crying sinn of mansteeling, as also to Prescribe such timely redresse for what is past, & such a law for (the) future as may sufficiently deterr all oth's belonging to us to have to do in such vile & most odious courses, justly abhorred of all good & just men."[44]

---

42. Du Bois, *Suppression of the African Slave-Trade*, 28.

43. Du Bois, *Suppression of the African Slave-Trade*, 8. "This trade formed a perfect circle. Owners of slavers carried slaves to South Carolina, and brought home naval stores for their ship-building; or to the West Indies, and brought home molasses; or to other colonies, and brought home hogsheads. The molasses was made into the highly prized New England rum and shipped in these hogsheads to Africa for more slaves."

44. Du Bois, *Suppression of the African Slave-Trade*, 30. Read: * Cf. *The Body of Liberties*, § 91, in Whitmore, *Bibliographical Sketch*. And, *Mass. Col. Rec*, II. 168, 176; III. 46, 49, 84.

Referred to as "mansteading," the profit-oriented enterprise of the slave trade was categorically considered a problem to the conscience of some religious Puritans. Among the many reasonings for the immediate transportation of Africans as slaves to Massachusetts were two important justifications. First was the claim that the Africans being traded were captured in a "just war." Secondly, Africans who traded willingly also unwillingly put themselves in the position to be captured or sold by their European trading partners. The Puritans of New England sternly emphasized these two conditions. However, as we shall see, the "just war" argument turned out to be an essential justification for the defense of the slave trade in Britain—the home of the Puritans who came to New England. It is also a major component of Locke's justification of the industrial slave trade. What the "just war" argument demonstrates is that biblical arguments were used to enslave Africans.

In New England, Rhode Island became the biggest slave-trading location and clearing house for slaves in America. Rhode Island was a slave ship–building state. "From the year 1700 on, the citizens of this State engaged more and more in the carrying trade, until Rhode Island became the greatest slave-trader in America. Although she [Rhode Island] did not import many slaves for her own use, she became the clearing-house for the trade of other colonies."[45] It is reported that by 1708, 103 vessels were built in Newport to carry slaves from Africa to the West Indies and to the southern states thereafter. By 1770, 150 slave vessels were built in Rhode Island. According to Du Bois, Samuel Hopkins was disturbed by the level of slave trading in Rhode Island:

> "Rhode Island," said he, "has been more deeply interested in the slave-trade and has enslaved more Africans than any other colony in New England." Later, in 1787, he wrote: "The inhabitants of Rhode Island, especially those of Newport, have had by far the greater share in this traffic, of all these United States. This trade in human species has been the first wheel of commerce in Newport, on which every other movement in business has chiefly depended. That town has been built up, and flourished in times past, at the expense of the blood, the liberty, and happiness of the poor Africans; and the inhabitants have lived on this, and by it have gotten most of their wealth and riches."[46]

---

45. Du Bois, *Suppression of the African Slave-Trade*, 35.
46. Du Bois, *Suppression of the African Slave-Trade*, 35.

This statement demonstrates the industrial and profit-oriented nature of the slave trade. Newport's wealth and prestige were acquired at the expense of the suffering of Black people. The beautiful homes and buildings are the inheritance from the human trafficking and selling of Africans.

In Connecticut, the case of a "moral mandate" to end the slave trade was superseded by the attractive financial benefits of the human trade. Social and moral arguments to end the slave trade were not enough. It took the Civil War to end the slave trade. Du Bois writes: "A feeble moral opposition was early aroused, but it was swept away by the immense economic advantages of the slave traffic to a thrifty seafaring community of traders. This trade no moral suasion, not even the strong 'Liberty' cry of the Revolution, was able wholly to suppress, until the closing of the West Indian and Southern markets cut off the demand for slaves."[47] What was at stake also in the conscience of the slave traders was the competition between the expedience of moral and ethical injunctions and their gross economic interests.

Furthermore, in the absence of a national consensus regarding the end of the slave trade, it was difficult to execute acts binding the slave trade in the British colonies, especially in America. As Du Bois writes, "the laws of the colonies before 1774 had no national unity, the peculiar circumstances of each colony determining its legislation."[48] Du Bois provides six reasons for the decline of the slave trade during the American Revolutionary War:

1. The decline in the economic interest of slavery in the Mid-Middle and Eastern colonies, which led many to believe that the slave trade and slavery would likewise easily decline in the South.

2. The emphasis on "Freedom" and the "Right of man" as the central pillars of the Revolutionary War "made the dullest realize that, at the very least, the slave trade and a struggle for 'liberty' were not consistent."

3. The fear of insurrections from the slaves and the inciting of insurrections by the British among the slaves.

4. From 1774–75, the American "slave markets" were overstocked with slaves.

5. A drop in the price of slaves.

---

47. Du Bois, *Suppression of the African Slave-Trade*, 38.
48. Du Bois, *Suppression of the African Slave-Trade*, 40.

6. "It was long a favorite belief of the supporters of the Revolution that, as English exploitation of colonial resources had caused the quarrel, the best weapon to bring England to terms was the economic expedient of stopping all commercial intercourse with her. Since then, the slave-trade had ever formed an important part of her colonial traffic, it was one of the first branches of commerce which occurred to the colonists as especially suited to their ends."[49]

Again, moral and ethical arguments were not influential in the ending of the slave trade. It was only once these arguments were supplemented by political and legal reasoning that the trade ceased.[50] According to Du Bois: "The movement was not a great moral protest against an iniquitous traffic; although it had undoubtedly a strong moral backing, it was primarily a temporary war measure."[51]

THE END OF THE INTERNATIONAL SLAVE TRADE

May 17, 1775, marks the first international agreement among the superpowers to end the human trade.

> Congress resolved unanimously "That all exportations to *Quebec, Nova-Scotia*, the Island of *St. John's, Newfoundland, Georgia*, except the Parish of *St. John's*, and to *East* and *West Florida*, immediately cease." These measures brought the refractory colony to terms, and the Provincial Congress, July 4, 1775, finally adopted the "Association," and resolved, among other things, "That we will neither import or purchase any Slave imported from Africa, or elsewhere, after this day."[52]

---

49. Du Bois, *Suppression of the African Slave-Trade*, 41–42.
50. Du Bois, *Suppression of the African Slave-Trade*, 42.
51. Du Bois, *Suppression of the African Slave-Trade*, 42, 50. "Nevertheless, the revival of the trade was naturally a matter of some difficulty, as the West India circuit had been cut off, leaving no resort except to contraband traffic and the direct African trade. The English slave-trade after the peace 'returned to its former state,' and was by 1784 sending 20,000 slaves annually to the West Indies. Just how large the trade to the continent was at this time there are few means of ascertaining; it is certain that there was a general reopening of the trade in the Carolinas and Georgia, and that the New England traders participated in it. This traffic undoubtedly reached considerable proportions; and through the direct African trade and the illicit West India trade many thousands of Negroes came into the United States during the years 1783–87."
52. Du Bois, *Suppression of the African Slave-Trade*, 46

However, the slave trade continued well after this date, even with the passing of several congressional acts and prohibitions at the state and federal levels. In the United States and the United Kingdom, the demand for Africans as slaves remained unabated as their citizens brazenly invaded and pillaged Africa with impunity. By now, there were over fifteen million Africans distributed across the Americas: some were captured, some were stolen, and some were bred. Du Bois provides the following data: "At the beginning of the nineteenth century England held 800,000 slaves in her colonies; France, 250,000; Denmark, 27,000; Spain and Portugal, 600,000; Holland, 50,000; Sweden, 600; there were also about 2,000,000 slaves in Brazil, and about 900,000 in the United States."[53]

Between 1789 and 1803, slave traders across America revamped the human trade. According to House Member S. L. Michell of New York in an 1804 speech on the floor:

> It was much to be regretted that the severe and pointed statute against the slave trade had been so little regarded. In defiance of its forbiddance and its penalties, it was well known that citizens and vessels of the United States were still engaged in that traffic. . . . In various parts of the nation, outfits were made for slave-voyages, without secrecy, shame, or apprehension. . . . Countenanced by their fellow-citizens at home, who were as ready to buy as they themselves were to collect and to bring to market, they approached our Southern harbors and inlets, and clandestinely disembarked the sooty offspring of the Eastern, upon the ill-fated soil of the Western hemisphere. In this way, it had been computed that, during the last twelve months, twenty thousand enslaved negroes had been transported from Guinea, and, by smuggling, added to the plantation stock of Georgia and South Carolina. So little respect seems to have been paid to the existing prohibitory statute, that it may almost be considered as disregarded by common consent.[54]

As evident from this speech, the slave trade continued to flourish both across the Atlantic and within US borders, despite the numerous laws attempting to suppress or end it. Many communities in the United States did not think slavery was "evil" or a "crime." Furthermore, many

---

53. Du Bois, *Suppression of the African Slave-Trade*, 131.

54. S. L. Mitchell, quoted in Du Bois, *Suppression of the African Slave-Trade*, 85. See also the speech of Bedinger, quoted in Du Bois, *Suppression of the African Slave-Trade*, 997–98.

considered the act of "manstealing" and the breaking up of Black families as a very "minor offense" rather than a crime.[55]

In 1807, the US Congress passed a pivotal anti-slave trade law, the Act of 1807. However, there were two similar acts enacted around the same time with similar titles: *the Slave Trade Act 1807* in England and the Act Prohibiting Importation of Slaves of 1807 in the US. In this chapter, the Act of 1807 will be referred to as The Act Prohibiting Importation of Slaves of 1807, which came into effect on January 1, 1808.

The Act of 1807 was not an ultimate panacea, as this was not the last time Congress enacted laws prohibiting the importation of Africans as slaves.[56] The Act of 1807 responded to three essential concerns: "the disposal of illegally imported Africans"; "the punishment of those concerned in the importation"; and "the proper limitation of the interstate traffic by water."[57] Along with the Act of 1807, there existed what is known as the "slave-trade clause" of Article 1, Section 9, Clause 1 in the original United States Constitution. However, it does not mention the word "slave" or "slavery." The slave-trade clause was designed to indirectly support the slave trade and its mutation into full-blown chattel slavery. It reads: "The Migration or Importation of such Persons as any of the States now existing shall think proper to admit, shall not be prohibited by the Congress prior to the Year one thousand eight hundred and eight, but a Tax or duty may be imposed on such Importation, not exceeding ten dollars for each Person." A succinct function of the slave-trade clause was to prevent Congress from interfering and stopping the slave trade. It was designed to obfuscate the founders' intention to maintain human trafficking in America.[58]

Violation of the Laws of Humanity

Even after the passing of the Act of 1807, Americans continued the industrial trading and trafficking of Africans to such an extent that the Act became something of a "dead letter." The African Society of London concluded that by 1816, American slave traders took over 16,000 Africans out of Africa annually. Du Bois writes, "So notorious did the

---

55. Du Bois, *Suppression of the African Slave-Trade*, 96.
56. Du Bois, *Suppression of the African Slave-Trade*, 108.
57. Du Bois, *Suppression of the African Slave-Trade*, 95.
58. Finkelman, *Slavery and the Founders*, 146.

participation of Americans in the traffic become, that President Madison informed Congress in his message, December 5, 1810, that 'it appears that American citizens are instrumental in carrying on a traffic in enslaved Africans, equally in violation of the laws of humanity, and in defiance of those of their own country.'"[59]

The laws of humanity have never been written on stones, tablets, or books. Instead, they exist within the conscience of each person. According to President Madison, the industrial slave trade had violated all laws of humanity: empathy, rights, justice, fairness, respect for human dignity, equality, and sympathy. Instead, what was practiced was an abject display of apathy, cruelty, and insensitivity, as Hegel the German philosopher had instructed.

The courts, judges, and sheriffs, like the public, had become complicit in the trafficking of Africans. In Alabama and Mississippi, the courts were directed to sell off Africans who were recently brought in. "The Alabama-Mississippi Territory Act of 1815, directed such Negroes to be 'sold by the proper officer of the court, to the highest bidder, at public auction, for ready money.' One-half of the proceeds went to the informer or to the collector of customs, the other half to the public treasury."[60] This direct involvement of the court, judges, and sheriffs in the selling of Africans was a normal occurrence. We shall also see that law officials were directly involved in leasing Blacks as "convicts" to private companies during the era of Jim Crow and the Black Codes after emancipation. Black humanity did not deserve the justice of the court, judges, or sheriffs. Instead, the justice system became an instrument and facilitator of overt racial injustice with impunity.

On February 17, 1815, the United Kingdom and the United States ratified the *Treaty of Ghent* to end the slave trade, with the conclusion in Article 10 stating that "whereas the traffic in slaves is irreconcilable with the principles of humanity and justice, the two countries agreed to use their best endeavors in abolishing the trade."[61] Yet despite the signing of the Treaty of Ghent in 1815, four years later it was reported that 14,000 Africans were legally brought into the United States as slaves, not counting those that were brought in illegally by slave smugglers and unregistered slave ships. Similarly, 13,000 Africans were brought into Middleton of South Carolina, and 15,000 into Wright of Virginia in 1819, illicitly

59. Du Bois, *Suppression of the African Slave-Trade*, 110.
60. Du Bois, *Suppression of the African Slave-Trade*, 109.
61. Du Bois, *Suppression of the African Slave-Trade*, 135.

as reported.[62] By 1820, 40,000 Africans were transported annually into the United States, territories of the United Kingdom, and other European countries.[63] Du Bois notes that at the Congress of Verona in 1822, Austria, France, Great Britain, and Prussia concluded that the slave trade was still very active. "They said that in seven months of the year 1821 no less than 21,000 slaves were abducted, and three hundred and fifty-two vessels entered African ports north of the equator."[64] With the turn of 1837, the importation of Africans as slaves into America increased to 200,000 annually.

IMMUNITY UNDER THE AMERICAN FLAG

In the industrial slave trade, the American flag became an irresistible symbol of immunity for slave traders of all kinds, including private and unregistered slave traders, pirates, and slave smugglers on the Atlantic Ocean. Slave ships with the American flag were given carte blanche treatment with no harassment and little or no inspection. Any ship with the American flag was unsearchable and unstoppable. According to Du Bois, before 1830, most slave ships were registered under the flags of France, Spain, and Portugal, but, from 1830 to 1840, ships began shifting their registrations under the flag of the United States. The American flag provided the most coverage for legal and illegal slave ships and slave traders. It was the ultimate immunity from countries who enforced the treaties to end the slave trade. Under the American flag, slave ships were not hiding, instead they were blatantly engaging in the capturing and trafficking of Africans through the Middle Passage into Britain, the West Indies, the United States, and Brazil. "Sometimes all disguise was thrown aside" as slave ships like the *Paz*, the *Rebecca*, the *Rosa* (formally the privateer *Commodore Perry*), the *Dorset* of Baltimore, and the *Saucy Jack* would

---

62. Du Bois, *Suppression of the African Slave-Trade*, 124–26. "Between May 1818, and November 1821, nearly six hundred Africans were recaptured and eleven American slavers taken. Such measures gradually changed the character of the trade and opened the international phase of the question. American slavers cleared for foreign ports, there took a foreign flag and papers, and then sailed boldly past American cruisers, although their real character was often well known."

63. Du Bois, *Suppression of the African Slave-Trade*, 143.

64. Du Bois, *Suppression of the African Slave-Trade*, 138.

dock on the coasts of West African countries to invade, capture, and transport Africans.[65]

In 1839, the level of protection the American flag provided to slave shipowners became increasingly obvious. Du Bois writes:

> One well-known American slaver was boarded fifteen times and twice taken into port, but always escaped by means of her papers. Even American officers report that the English are doing all they can, but that the American flag protects the trade. . . . It was proven that the participation of United States citizens in the trade was large and systematic. One of the most notorious slave merchants of Brazil said: "I am worried by the Americans, who insist upon my hiring their vessels for slave-trade." Minister Proffit stated, in 1844, that the "slave-trade is almost entirely carried on under our flag, in American-built vessels."[66]

In 1839, "Pope Gregory XVI stigmatized the slave-trade 'as utterly unworthy of the Christian name,' and at the same time, although proscribed by the laws of every civilized State, the trade was flourishing with pristine vigour."[67] Unfortunately, the trade showed no sign of slowing. In 1847, close to 100,000 Africans were brought into the Western hemisphere annually. It was reported that a single province in Brazil brought in 173,000 Africans as slaves between 1846 and 1849.[68]

Between 1850 and 1860 the slave trade did not dissipate, despite the many Congressional Acts passed in the United States and the treaties signed between the US and the countries of Europe. Throughout it, the American flag served as the most potent form of protection for slave traders. Du Bois notes that in 1860, "The increase of the slave-traffic was so great in the decade 1850–1860" that Lord John Russell, the former prime minster of the United Kingdom, called for a meeting to discuss the American flag, its protection of slave traders and human traffickers as well as the "abolition of the slave trade."[69] Along with the United States, France, Spain, Portugal, and Brazil were invited to send their ministers to London.

---

65. Du Bois, *Suppression of the African Slave-Trade*, 110.
66. Du Bois, *Suppression of the African Slave-Trade*, 163.
67. Du Bois, *Suppression of the African Slave-Trade*, 143.
68. Du Bois, *Suppression of the African Slave-Trade*, 143.
69. Du Bois, *Suppression of the African Slave-Trade*, 149.

It is ascertained, by repeated instances, that the practice is for vessels to sail under the American flag. If the flag is rightly assumed, and the papers correct, no British cruizer can touch them. If no slaves are on board, even though the equipment, the fittings, the water-casks, and other circumstances prove that the ship is on a Slave Trade venture, no American cruizer can touch them." Continued representations of this kind were made to paralyzed United States government; indeed, the slave-trade of the world seemed now to float securely under her flag.[70]

To save the United States, the United Kingdom offered to intervene, even though it was under their control that the slave trade began in North America. The United Kingdom offered to redirect all captured Africans on slave vessels coming into America into the West Indies—a colony of Great Britain. Unfortunately, President Buchanan refused the offer. Du Bois notes that "President Buchanan 'could not contemplate any such arrangement' and obstinately refused to increase the suppressing squadron."[71] One reason for President Buchanan's refusal perhaps was that the majority of the countries in the West Indies were colonies of the United Kingdom. The redirecting of slave vessels there would certainly increase the slave population and slave holdings of the UK. It would further divert the trade and profit to the UK and increase the prices of slaves in the United States. Similarly, the UK would have a dominant economic control of the slave trade. As the United Kingdom, the British and the Scots were still involved in the slave trade even after 1833.

In 1850, the price of slaves had risen astronomically. Owners of slave plantations across the United State were almost brought to bankruptcy.

> *Activity of the Slave-Trade, 1820–1850.* The enhanced price of slaves throughout the American slave market, brought about by the new industrial development and the laws against the slave-trade, was the irresistible temptation that drew American capital and enterprise into that traffic. In the United States, in spite of the large interstate traffic, the average price of slaves rose from about $325 in 1840, to $360 in 1850, and to $500 in 1860. Brazil and Cuba offered similar inducements to smugglers, and the American flag was ready to protect such pirates. As a result, the American slave-trade finally came to be carried on principally by

---

70. Du Bois, *Suppression of the African Slave-Trade*, 149.
71. Du Bois, *Suppression of the African Slave-Trade*, 150.

United States capital, in United States ships, officered by United States citizens, and under the United States flag.[72]

The continuation and inducement of the slave trade were seen as the immediate means of economic revitalization. Du Bois notes that "in 1854 a grand jury in the Williamsburg district declared, 'as our unanimous opinion, that the Federal law abolishing the African Slave Trade is a public grievance. We hold this trade has been and would be, if re-established, a blessing to the American people, and a benefit to the African himself.'"[73] In 1855, the Southern Commercial Convention began to discuss the formal inducement of the slave trade. They met in New Orleans with the introduction of a resolution to repeal the existing slave laws. The Convention met again on May 10, 1858, in Alabama and presented the following resolutions:[74]

1. *Resolved*, That slavery is right, and that being right, there can be no wrong in the natural means to its formation.

2. *Resolved*, That it is expedient and proper that the foreign slave trade should be re-opened, and that this Convention will lend its influence to any legitimate measure to that end.

3. *Resolved*, That a committee, consisting of one from each slave State, be appointed to consider of the means, consistent with the duty and obligations of these States, for re-opening the foreign slave-trade, and that they report their plan to the next meeting of this Convention.[75]

After the Southern Commercial Convention of 1859, the African slave trade was revitalized with the repeal and total rejection of all previous treaties banning the trade.[76] With the revitalization of the slave trade in the South, the trade in human beings increased dramatically between 1850 and 1860 across the United States.[77] The American flag became a symbol of ultimate immunity and protection for both local and foreign slave traders. "In the foreign slave-trade our own officers continue to report 'how shamefully our flag has been used;' and British officers write

72. Du Bois, *Suppression of the African Slave-Trade*, 163.
73. Du Bois, *Suppression of the African Slave-Trade*, 169.
74. Du Bois, *Suppression of the African Slave-Trade*, 170–71.
75. Du Bois, *Suppression of the African Slave-Trade*, 171.
76. Du Bois, *Suppression of the African Slave-Trade*, 172.
77. Du Bois, *Suppression of the African Slave-Trade*, 178.

'that at least one half of the successful part of the slave trade is carried on under the American flag.'"[78]

The economic importance of the slave trade did not escape Du Bois. He mentions the port of New York as a prominent harbor for slave ships. He further notes the laxity and tolerance with which anti-slave trade laws were imposed. The suppression of the slave trade was seen as unattractive due to the trade's economic benefits. Slave traders became powerful economic magnets in New York and across the country, who wielded immense political clout with their ill-gotten money. Du Bois recalls a periodical in New York referencing the economic nature of the slave trade. He writes:

> Slave dealers added largely to the wealth of our commercial metropolis; they contributed liberally to the treasuries of political organizations, and their bank accounts were largely depleted to carry elections in New Jersey, Pennsylvania, and Connecticut. During eighteen months of the years, 1859–1860 eighty-five slavers are reported to have been fitted out in New York harbor, and these alone transported from 30,000 to 60,000 slaves annually.[79]

It is unanimously agreed upon that several of the slave ships bound for Africa from the US came directly from New York and New Orleans.[80] Like President Buchanan, most politicians in Washington, DC, were ambivalent about stopping the human trade. Du Bois notes that "the officials at Washington often remained in blissful, and perhaps willing, ignorance of the state of the trade. While Americans were smuggling slaves by the thousands into Brazil, and by the hundreds into the United States, Secretary Graham was recommending the abrogation of the 8th Article of the Treaty of Washington."[81]

THE CIVIL WAR

The slave trade and human trafficking continued at both the local and international level up to the beginning of the Civil War and thereafter. However, Du Bois contends that the Civil War was not only about the

---

78. Du Bois *Suppression of the African Slave-Trade*, 178.
79. Du Bois, *Suppression of the African Slave-Trade*, 179.
80. Du Bois, *Suppression of the African Slave-Trade*, 179.
81. Du Bois *Suppression of the African Slave-Trade*, 186.

end of the institution of slavery in the United States; it was also inherently about the end of the slave trade. The slave trade was a distinct institution from that of chattel slavery, though the two were concurrent and codependent. President Lincoln's Emancipation Proclamation was also about the end of the slave trade and the use of the American flag to facilitate the slave trade. According to Du Bois, "On the outbreak of the Civil War, the Lincoln administration, through Secretary Seward, immediately expressed a willingness to do all in its power to suppress the slave-trade. Accordingly, June 7, 1862, a treaty was signed with Great Britain granting a mutual limited Right of Search and establishing mixed courts for the trial of offenders at the Cape of Good Hope, Sierra Leone, and New York."[82] However, in his own words, Lincoln made it quite explicit in his communication with Horace Greeley, dated Friday, August 22, 1862, that his major priority was the saving of the union of the United States: "My paramount object in this struggle is to save the Union, and is not either to save or destroy slavery. If I could save the Union without freeing any slave I would do it, and if I could save it by freeing all the slaves I would do that. What I do about slavery, and the colored race, I do because I believe it helps to save the Union."[83] While Lincoln may have had humanitarian inclinations, his paramount political objective was to secure the stability of the union of the United States.

82. Du Bois, *Suppression of the African Slave-Trade*, 150.
83. Lincoln, Abraham Lincoln papers: Series 2. General Correspondence. 1858–64: Abraham Lincoln to Horace Greeley, Friday, August 22, 1862.

FROM EUROPE TO AFRICA: THEIR MILITARY SUBJUGATION

Three Legs of Subjugation they embarked upon,
From Europe to Africa with military artilleries.
From Africa to the Americas with slaves and the booty of gold,
From the Americas to Europe with raw materials.

The Belgians were involved, ask the Congolese.
The Portuguese were involved, ask the Brazilians.
The British were involved, ask the Commonwealth of Nations.
The Spanish, the Scotts, and the French were fierce slave masters ask the Indians, the Jamaicans, the Algerians.

They came with guns, rum, and sugar.
They came with religion, greed, and racial superiority.
They left with gold, the young and the old their human cargos.
The Continent of Africa, they came to pillage.

The sowing of internal conflicts was their strategic choice,
Divide and conquer among the chiefs the only means,
To threaten the local chiefs with invasion was very strategic,
The African bodies and raw materials their utmost choice.

Africans in nativity have seen the white man!
In the Ghanaian language, "a god" is seen,
Hospitality abounds to appease their gods,
Yet with motive ungodly, their gods are consumed.

Africans on Africans was a sure recipe,
Tribes on tribes the perfect strategy,
While tribalism prevailed in the West and the East,
African tribalism the worst, they claim,
Over 11 million they dragged through the Middle Passage![84]

GEORGE WALTERS-SLEYON

---

84. Walters-Sleyon, *Nuggets from the Night*, 107.

3

The Making of John Locke

JOHN LOCKE WAS BORN ON August 29, 1632, to parents of Puritan background in Wrington, England.[1] His father Nicholas Locke, a lawyer, fought in the English Civil War on the side of the Parliamentary Army.[2] Locke's birth took place during the reign of Charles 1.[3] According to Roger Woolhouse, business ran in Locke's family. Woolhouse writes:

> John Locke's great-grandfather, Sir William Locke, was said to be "the greatest English merchant under Henry the Eight." His activities as a mercer dealing in silk and velvet were continued by his son Nicholas, who moved from Buckland Newton, Dorset, to Pensford, in Somerset, where he built up a flourishing business, collecting in, and shipping on, the woollen cloth woven in cottages throughout the west of England.[4]

Locke remembers his father, the grandson of Sir William Locke, as being a disciplinarian. In his book *Some Thoughts Concerning Education*, he reminisces about his upbringing: "For, methinks they mightily misplace the treatment due to their children, who are indulgent and familiar, when they are little, but severe to them, and keep them at a distance when they are grown up. For liberty and indulgence can do no good to

---

 1. For a more complete biography of John Locke, see Uzgalis, "John Locke"; Locke, *Locke: Political Essays*.
 2. Cranston, *John Locke*, 1.
 3. Faiella, *John Locke*, 18.
 4. Woolhouse, *Locke*, 5.

children; their want of judgement makes them stand in need of restraint and discipline."⁵

Political theorist John Dunn contends that Locke's life can be structured into three important movements: "The first move, to Westminster and then to Christ Church" at Oxford University. Second, Meeting Lord Ashley, who later became the first Earl of Shaftesbury, in 1666. This meeting was "momentous" for it launched Locke's political, medical, and philosophical careers. Lord Ashley became Locke's paramount patron. Finally, "The commitment to philosophical understanding, [which] was, of course, far less obvious to the outsider and more gradual than either the shift to Westminster and Oxford or the entry into Shaftesbury's service."⁶

Locke entered Westminster School in London in 1647 as a Puritan. According to Maurice Cranston, "Westminster did purge Locke of the unquestioning Puritan faith in which he had grown up; and thus, however ironically, Dr. [Richard] Busby, the great conservative pedagogue, must be given the credit for having first set Locke on the road to liberalism."⁷ Through his father's career connection as a secretary/attorney for Alexander Popham, Locke was admitted into a prestigious British educational institution.⁸

> Nicholas Locke, in spite of financial standing was a bit well connected. He served as a secretary and attorney of Alexander Popham, a prominent magistrate in Somerset and Wiltshire. Popham became a member of the House of Commons in Parliament in 1640 and eventually a "colonel in the Parliamentary Army." With his new title he led an army and appointed Nicholas Locke a captain. In 1643, the Royalist defeated Colonel Popham and his army the British Civil War. However, the Civil War was won in 1647 and Colonel Popham was back in Parliament with the prestigious Westminster School under his supervision.⁹

---

5. Locke, *Some Thoughts Concerning Education*, 41.
6. Dunn, *Locke*, 3–8.
7. Cranston, *John Locke*, 19.
8. Cranston, *John Locke*, 17. "Among the institutions which the Long Parliament took under its control was Westminster School. As Member of Parliament for Bath, Colonel Popham was thus in a position to nominate boys for that distinguished foundation. His attorney's elder son was fifteen years of age, not too old to be a candidate. Colonel Popham put up his name and in the autumn of 1647, the boy was admitted to the school. Such was the decisive beginning of a career from which all else flowed."
9. Cranston, *John Locke*, 21.

Admission into the Westminster School was not open to everyone. Not all the children of the upper class had the privilege. His admission into the school was Locke's initial entrance into the world of political, social, and economic connections that would prepare him for his future as a political theorist and philosopher.

OXFORD UNIVERSITY

In 1650 Locke was elected to the prestigious position of a King's Scholar. While it was not financial, this honor catapulted Locke from a "minor election" to a "major election" with a scholarship to Christ Church, Oxford, when he turned twenty in 1652. At Oxford, he read philosophy, law, theology, Greek, Latin, Hebrew, and Arabic with an interest in medicine. "The education of an Oxford undergraduate was still medieval" in Locke's days.[10] Cranston notes, "All undergraduates, and Bachelors of Arts as well, had to go every Sunday evening between six and nine o'clock to 'give an account to some person of known ability and piety of the sermons they had heard,'" and later they had also to pay nightly visits to their tutors "to hear private prayers and to give an account of the time spent that day."[11]

Locke made many influential friends at Oxford, including two men who particularly affected his life due to their theological influences and associations: Thomas Blomer and John Mapletoft. They were theologically Latitudinarians. Furthermore, Mapletoft was the son of a high church clergyman.

During his Oxford academic experience, Locke's mother took ill and died on October 4, 1654, at the age of fifty-seven in Somerset.[12] Additionally, the political and military events in Britain at the time were of grave concern. Her death affected him greatly and briefly slowed his academic motivations.

In his academic pursuits, Locke earned his Master of Arts degree and became a Senior Student of Christ Church on June 28, 1658. In 1660, Locke was promoted to the position of Lecturer in Greek at Christ Church Oxford.[13] Cranston provides insights into the responsibilities of the position:

10. Cranston, *John Locke*, 21.
11. Cranston, *John Locke*, 31.
12. Cranston, *John Locke*, 29, 37.
13. Cranston, *John Locke*, 45, 69.

A tutor's duties were not merely pedagogic; he stood in *loco parentis*; he would commonly have charge of his pupil's money and he would advise him in the conduct of his private life, though he had not, after 1660 to ensure the salvation of his soul. Locke kept a record of his pupils' names, and the fees they paid him, in the same little account book in which, as a schoolboy and undergraduate, he had kept note of his income and expenditure.[14]

Locke's burgeoning career as a philosopher was marred by his father's death on February 13, 1661, at fifty-four. From Westminster to Christ Church at Oxford, Locke's desire to become a prominent clergyman in the Church of England was guaranteed.

LOCKE REJECTS PASTORAL APPOINTMENT

In 1663, the possibility of being a clergyman was becoming quite imminent for Locke, as the position at Christ Church came with increased prestige and financial stability. However, he was developing an interest in medicine.[15] While exploring this interest, Locke met a close friend named Robert Boyle with whom he worked alongside. Cranston writes that "Boyle was an earnest Christian, and he encouraged the fashion among the Oxford *virtuosi* of combining theological with scientific studies. Boyle knew his Bible well and would have made an excellent clergyman. Indeed, urged him to become one and proposed if he did so to make him Provost of Eton."[16] Boyle declined the offer for the position of a layman, and Locke followed his friend.

In December of 1663, Locke was elevated to the position of Senior Censor or Censor of Moral Philosophy at Christ Church for twelve months, at the end of which he "died." This "death" was a metaphor for Locke's refusal to go into the ministry. According to Cranston, this kind of death was academically expected. He writes:

> When his term of office ended, Locke, according to the Christ Church tradition, died, and made his own funeral speech in Latin at the ceremony of burying the outgoing Censor. The speech was made up partly of Baroque conceits on this desirability of death, partly of farewell greetings addressed in turn to the Dean and other dignitaries of the House. Locke compared

---

14. Cranston, *John Locke*, 71.
15. Cranston, *John Locke*, 74.
16. Cranston, *John Locke*, 76.

life on earth to a prison, where there was no peace. Philosophy, he protested, offered no consolation.... Wealth brought nothing but anxiety, nausea and surfeit: *Ferre vitam tot calamitatibus onustam miserum est, miserius certe amare.*[17]

However, while Locke was jokingly "dying" as Censor of Christ Church, his brother was truly dying. Thomas Locke died around Christmas in 1663. Unlike Locke, Thomas was married; he left behind a widow and daughter.

Locke didn't hold in any high esteem those he referred to as religious "enthusiasts," such as the Puritans and the Quakers. Locke was now a "layman" in the Church of England, concerned with deriving knowledge through practical engagements and experiments, which provided a rational, experiential knowledge of the world.

In 1666, upon his return from his diplomatic mission to Europe, Locke was again encouraged to become a clergyman. Like the previous times, he declined the position to pursue his interest in medicine and science.[18] By finally rejecting the position of a clergyman, Locke had rejected a handsome guarantee of financial stability. He had to find something to fill the gap.

LOCKE MEETS LORD ASHLEY

Locke's friendship with Lord Anthony Ashley Cooper is pivotal both to his life and to this book. Brad Hinshelwood notes, "In 1662, Lord Anthony Ashley Cooper joined with seven other leading statesmen to form a company dedicated to colonizing the land between Virginia and the Spanish settlements in Florida, but the earliest attempt to colonize the area failed by the end of 1668."[19]

Locke met Lord Ashley, a man with significant political, financial, and social connections, at Oxford in 1666. According to Woolhouse, Ashley was around forty years old when Locke met him. However, at the

---

17. Cranston, *John Locke*, 78.

18. Eisenach, *Two Worlds of Liberalism*, 3. "The implicit teaching of Locke's natural history becomes of paradigmatic importance in the writings of Adam Smith and David Hume, and it is a commonplace of twentieth-century histories of ideas.... Locke concludes that his own religious duty is to further the progress of philosophy by examining the entire range of political and moral duties on the basis of reason—in short, to construct a demonstrable moral philosophy."

19. Hinshelwood, "Carolinian Context," 567.

same time, Woolhouse contends, Ashley "had been subject for twenty years to almost daily attacks of violent pain in his side. He also suffered from jaundice, with its accompanying ill-effects of weakness and loss of appetite, and in the earlier months of his health had been particularly poor. He found acidic mineral waters to be something of a tonic."[20] Locke became a close confidant of Ashley while serving in the following capacities: friend, physician, secretary, researcher, and an astute political assistant.

There have been various accounts of Lord Ashley. Cranston provides a bewildering account. He writes: "Ashley was never a handsome man. Besides his dwarfish stature, he had a plain face with big ears and monkey's eyes. His critics have made much of his reputed addiction to the pleasures of the brothel. The king is supposed to have called him 'the greatest whoremonger in England.'"[21] Woolhouse disagrees with Cranston's conclusion that Ashley was ugly. For Woolhouse, "Ashley was a man of great charm, affable, cultivated, and confident."[22] Furthermore, Woolhouse notes that "Locke was no less attracted to Ashley, as he told friends in later life, 'but if my Lord was pleased with the company of Mr. Locke, Mr. Locke was yet more so with that of my Lord Ashley: and he has often said, that it perfectly charmed him.' Indeed, so pleased were the two with each other that Locke accepted Ashley's invitation to drink the waters at Astrop with him."[23]

Lord Ashley was a wealthy man. He generated his money from trading between England and the colonies. Prominent among his trading interests was the transatlantic slave trade. By entering Ashley's confidence, Locke entered a world not only of wealth, political, and social prominence, but also one intimately bound up with the prevailing economic industry—the rush for black diamonds in Africa. It is this aspect of Locke's history that this book is mainly concerned with.

After meeting Ashley, Locke used his new connection to appeal for a formal letter from the King and Queen of England who were at the time staying at Oxford. According to Cranston, the letter came directly from the king on November 14, 1666, to the dean. It was signed by the

20. Woolhouse, *Locke*, 70.
21. Cranston, *John Locke*, 107.
22. Woolhouse, Locke, 71
23. Woolhouse, *Locke*, 71.

Secretary of State, Sir William Morrice, also the "best friend" of Ashley.[24] The letter read as such:

> Trusty and well-beloved, we greet you well.
> Whereas we are informed that John Locke, Master of Arts and Students of Christ church in our university of Oxford, is of such standing as by the custom of that college he is obliged to enter into holy orders or otherwise to leave his student's place there; at his humble request that he may still have the further time to prosecute his studies without that obligation, we are graciously pleased to grant him our royal dispensation, and do accordingly hereby require you to suffer him, the said John Locke, to hold and enjoy his Students' place in Christ Church, together with all the rights, profits and emoluments thereunto belonging, without taking holy orders . . . and for so doing this shall be your warrant.[25]

With this letter, Locke's residency at Christ Church was secured.

In September 1666, Locke went to the home of Lord Ashley in response to the medical need of victims who were affected by the plague and the fire. Cranston contends, against the claims of Lady Masham and the grandson of Ashley, in the person of the third Earl of Shaftesbury, that "it was not until the following Easter that Locke was asked to make Exeter House his home."[26]

Locke's Pursuit of Medicine

Due to his interest in medicine, Locke sought a "dispensation" to avoid becoming a clergyman and remain at Christ Church—an unconventional request at the time. On November 3, 1666, a gentleman from Clarendon wrote a letter on Locke's behalf to the vice-chancellor, requesting that he be awarded a Doctor of Medicine, "but not having taken the degree of bachelor's in physics, he has desired that he may be dispensed with to accumulate to that degree, which appears to me a very modest and reasonable request."[27] Cranston intimates that Ashley was involved in the writing of these letters. The above letter caused much hullabaloo among the medical faculty. "It was clear to the faculty that Locke wished

---

24. Cranston, *John Locke*, 97.
25. Cranston, *John Locke*, 97.
26. Cranston, *John Locke*, 95.
27. Cranston, *John Locke*, 96.

to take the advanced lectures or doing other work required for a junior medical degree." In addition, "Locke had more than one motive for seeking a medical degree. He wished, not unnaturally, to have academic recognition for its own sake, but he also wanted the degree to secure a layman's place as a medical don at Christ Church. He was now quite resolved against taking holy orders."[28] The letter was eventually ignored. With the royal dispensation granted to stay at Oxford with or without a teaching position, as well as the unfortunate circumstances under which he could not teach medicine, Locke's desire to continue serving as a college tutor for grammar and philosophy began to wane during the winter of 1666–67.[29]

Locke did not attend formal classes to receive a Doctor of Medicine degree. Instead, he learned the practice of medicine through an apprenticeship and collaboration with his friends, including Robert Boyle and David Thomas, who were established medical practitioners. Unfortunately, his pursuit of medical credentials did not go well.

Moving in with Lord Ashley in London had a lot more to offer Locke concerning scientific research and resources than Oxford.[30] In 1670, Locke tried one more time to achieve the degree of a medical doctor with a nomination from Lord Ashley. It was not successful, and Cranston notes that "he never received the degree of D.M."[31]

In the spring of 1667, Locke packed his belongings and moved to the home of Lord Ashley to become his "personal physician." Living with Lord Ashley came with new interests. According to Cranston,

> It was Ashley who discovered and helped Locke to discover his own true genius. Before he went to Exeter House, Locke was a minor Oxford scholar, an ex-diplomatist of small experience, an amateur scientist, an unpublished writer and unqualified physician. In Ashley's home he blossomed into a philosopher, an economist and a medical virtuoso; and a part of the credit for his doing so must go to the ugly little nobleman who was his patron and host.[32]

---

28. Cranston, *John Locke*, 96.
29. Cranston, *John Locke*, 99.
30. Cranston, *John Locke*, 103.
31. Cranston, *John Locke*, 139.
32. Cranston, *John Locke*, 113.

Cranston's analysis of Locke's involvement in the transatlantic slave trade raises the question as to who was responsible for getting Locke involved. Cranston, it seems, holds Lord Ashley responsible and wants to separate Locke from "the ugliness" of Ashley. He intimates that "Locke did not get much material reward for the work he did for Ashley."[33] Cranston also notes that "Locke was easily infected with Ashley's zeal for commercial imperialism, seeing as clearly as his patron saw the possibilities it offered for personal and national enrichment."[34] Cranston's depiction of the relationship as rather one-sided is challenged by the following reflection from the grandson of Lord Ashley.

> He (Lord Ashley) put him (Locke) upon the study of the religious and civil affairs of the nation with whatsoever related to the business of a Minister of state, in which he was so successful that my grandfather began soon to use him as a friend and consult with him upon occasions of that kind. He was not only with him in his library and closet but in company with the great men of those times, the Duke of Buckingham, Lord Halifax and others, who, being men of wit and learning, were as much taken with him, for together with his serious, respectful and humble character, he had a mixture of pleasantry and becoming boldness of speech. The liberty he could take with these great men was peculiar to such a genius as his.[35]

From 1683 to 1689, Locke traveled throughout Western Europe. Yolton argues that these travels were prompted by Locke's expulsion "from his college, Christ Church, by order of the king himself. 'Fled' may be too strong a word, but Locke did end up, by a route not entirely known, in Holland."[36] The circumstances surrounding Locke's flight to Holland became interesting and shrouded in secrecy even with the arrest of Algernon Sidney, his friend.

---

33. Cranston, *John Locke*, 114.
34. Cranston, *John Locke*, 119.
35. Cranston, *John Locke*, 114.
36. Yolton, *Locke*, 6.

CAN A MAN DECLARE HIMSELF INNOCENT?

With the wings of his thoughts, he thinks of a thing,
With the stirring of his thoughts, he discerns a thing,
With the wings of his thoughts, he flees to a thing,
With the flight of his thoughts, he plans a thing.

When with the plans of his thoughts, he creates a thing,
When with the plans of his thoughts, he crafts a thing,
When with the crafting of his thoughts, he births a thing,
We behold the manifestation in awe or disgust.

The ears only hear what is said,
The eyes only see what is birthed,
The hands only touch what is made,
The heart only feels what it senses.

The eyes judge what it sees,
The ears judge what is heard,
The hands judge what is touched,
The heart judges what it feels,
Can a man declare himself innocent?[37]

GEORGE WALTERS-SLEYON

---

37. Walters-Sleyon, *Nuggets from the Night*, 139.

4

Locke: The Slave Trader and the British Slave Trade

LOCKE'S POLITICAL CAREER EXISTED IN tandem with his participation in the transatlantic slave trade. This book contends that Locke's political theory was fundamentally based on the experiences gathered from his political appointments in the government of Great Britain.[1] I begin this chapter with Locke's political appointments to demonstrate the relationship between Locke's political engagements and the development of his political theory.

LOCKE: WRITER OF THE FUNDAMENTAL CONSTITUTIONS OF CAROLINA

In 1668, Locke was appointed secretary to the Lords Proprietors of Carolina. According to Hinshelwood, the Lords Proprietors were basically managers of Carolina and profiteers of the slave trade.

> Locke had been a member of Ashley's household for over a year, having taken up residence on a semi-permanent basis in the spring of 1667; at this point Ashley made Locke secretary to the lords proprietors. Locke and his new employers immediately turned to crafting a constitution. The first edition of the

---

1. Armitage, "John Locke."

Fundamental Constitutions of Carolina is dated July 21, 1669, and portions of the manuscripts are in Locke's hand.[2]

He supported Lord Ashley and seven other noblemen who possessed the right of proprietorship of Carolina.[3] According to Woolhouse, "Locke acted as secretary of the lords proprietors until 1675, arranging and keeping minutes of their meetings, summarizing, and taking notes of official letters sent between England and Carolina, exchanging letters himself with officials in the colonies. His interest in the colony extended to devoting some thoughts to constructing a decimal system of coinage and measurement for it."[4] Concerning Locke's position as secretary, Cranston notes, "The lords proprietors, who had the power to grant titles of nobility, bestowed on him in April 1671 the rank of landgrave in the aristocracy of Carolina—the title to be his and his heirs' forever. At the same time, they gave him four thousand 'baronia,' or estates of land, in the colony."[5]

The Lords Proprietors were also slave traders.[6] As members of the British Parliament, their responsibilities included managing the British colonies and all forms of colonial trade, including the slave trade. They also personally owned and controlled shipping companies plying the Atlantic Ocean from Britain to Africa to the West Indies and America. In addition, the Lords Proprietors managed the colony of Carolina in America. "Locke was granted the second highest rank, of 'Landgrave'

---

2. Hinshelwood, "Carolinian Context," 567.

3. Glausser, "Three Approaches."

4. Woolhouse, *Locke*, 90–91. "In April, the proprietors began fitting out three ships with 140 prospective settlers and the goods, arms, implements, and other paraphernalia necessary for the settling, planting, and general working of the colony. In July, before the ships left, they approved a formal 'Fundamental Constitutions of Carolina' to govern the colony. This specified various government positions to be filled by the proprietors themselves; it imposed certain divisions of the land (into counties, subdivided into various hereditary baronies and land for 'the people'); set up a number of supreme courts; and determined the constitution of the Parliament, which was automatically to meet every two years."

5. Cranston, *John Locke*, 120.

6. Hinshelwood, "Carolinian Context," 563. "Close examination of the policies of the lords proprietors of Carolina reveals a remarkable similarity between their attitude toward the Indian slave trade and Locke's, hardly surprising given Locke's position as secretary to the proprietors. Unlike Locke's investments in African slavery, which did not call for high-level theorizing about the legitimation of slavery, in Carolina just-war arguments over slavery were part of a regular dialogue between the colonists and the lords proprietors due to the massive trade in Indian slaves and their method of capture—war, either between the colonists and local tribes or intertribal conflict."

and forty-eight thousand acres that came with the title" as well as the provision that "every freeman of Carolina shall have absolute power and authority over his negro slave of what position or religion so ever."[7]

The legal justification for slavery in Britain was based on common and commercial legal concepts. Finkelman notes, "Slavery in the British Empire would be governed by local laws, haphazardly passed by colonial legislatures or developed by colonial courts responding to specific events and cases. This would lead to a complicated legal structure for slavery in the colonies and later in an independent United States of America."[8] In the United Kingdom, politicians of all stripes were involved in the slave trade as ship owners and plantation owners in the West Indies and the Caribbean. According to Mike Kaye:

> All of Liverpool's Lord Mayors between 1787 and 1807 were involved in the slave trade, as were 37 of the 41 members of Liverpool's governing body in 1787. Eleven of Bristol's mayors owned shares in slave ships while Lord Mayors of London were shareholders in the Royal Africa Company when it had a monopoly on the slave trade courtesy of King Charles II. One Lord Mayor of London, William Beckford, was England's first millionaire and the richest absentee plantation owner of his time, using more than 2,000 slaves on his properties in Jamaica. According to Gentleman's Magazine, in 1766 there were over 40 MPs who had interests in plantations in the West Indies.[9]

On March 1, 1669, John Locke wrote the Fundamental Constitutions of Carolina, the state's founding document, which included the stipulation that "every freeman of Carolina, shall have absolute power and authority over his negro slaves, of what opinion or religion soever."[10] Locke and his fellow Lords Proprietors needed a constitution to govern this colony, and the Fundamental Constitutions of the Carolinas was produced in 1669 as a response to this need.[11]

7. Glausser, "Three Approaches," 203.
8. Finkelman, "Slavery in the United States," 107.
9. Kaye, *1807–2007*, 5.
10. Cranston, *John Locke*, 115. "Drawn up by John Locke (1 March 1669). [Historical research suggests that this constitution was drawn up jointly by Locke and his patron, the Earl of Shaftesbury.] From the 1 Statutes at Large of South Carolina 43 (Columbia SC 1836)."
11. Hinshelwood, "Carolinian Context," 563. "Known for a stirring exposition of inviolable natural rights and the claim that 'slavery is so vile and miserable an Estate of Man, and so directly opposite to the generous Temper and Courage of our nation'

As secretary, Locke served as the architect of the Fundamental Constitutions,[12] a significant document stipulating the power and authority a slave owner had over his slaves, including "liberal policies and restrictive social hierarchies."[13] According to Armitage, "no major political theorist before the nineteenth century so actively applied theory to colonial practice as Locke did by virtue of his involvement with writing the Fundamental Constitutions of the Carolina colony."[14] Armitage contends that the Fundamental Constitutions reflect the intersection between Locke's "political theory and his colonial interests." In addition, it "assumed the existence of slavery and affirmed the absolute powers of life and death of slaveholders. They also erected the first hereditary nobility on North American soil."[15] Cranston, however, rejects the claim that Locke was responsible for the Fundamental Constitutions. He notes: "A copy, in Locke's hand, of The Fundamental Constitutions for the Government of Carolina which reposes in the Public Record Officer, has long been familiar to students of Locke. The fact of its being in Locke's hand has led many such scholars to conclude that Locke composed it, whereas that circumstance is in fact evidence only of Locke's secretarial services to the lords proprietors."[16] Cranston makes this argument notwithstanding Sir Peter Colleton's appeal to Locke in a letter written in 1674 referencing "that excellent form of government in the composure of which you had so great a hand."[17]

Sir Peter Colleton had a brother by the name of Sir John Colleton. He was also one of the most prominent Lords Proprietors of Carolina. Sir Peter Colleton was in all earnest referring to the Fundamental

---

(1.1.1), Locke also helped author the Fundamental Constitutions of Carolina, which guaranteed Englishmen absolute power and authority over African slaves in the colony, and created a just-war theory of legitimate slavery in the Second Treatise. The evidence for his involvement with the slave trade constitutes 'an embarrassment of riches, a tale of intimate and informed involvement with all manner of slavery,' and his theoretical views—which utilize a just-war theory that is grossly incongruous with the reality of the slave trade as we know it—have attracted considerable interest from Locke scholars."

12. There are six versions of the Fundamental Constitutions of Carolina: 1669, 1670, January 1682, August 1682, 1698, and 1699. The original version is the 1669 version. All subsequent versions are revisions of the original. Locke is considered the original author of the Fundamental Constitutions of Carolina.

13. Farr, "'So Vile and Miserable an Estate,'" 265.

14. Armitage, "John Locke," 603.

15. Armitage, "John Locke," 607.

16. Cranston, *John Locke*, 119.

17. Cranston, *John Locke*, 120.

Constitutions. Based on minutes recorded in a notebook in 1672, Locke was present at all expected gatherings of the Lords Proprietors of Carolina up to June of 1675.

Woolhouse disagrees with Cranston's position that Locke was not responsible for the Constitutions. He notes that:

> Locke's first editor included the "constitutions" as one of his works: Locke himself, Desmaizeaux said, had "presented it, as a work of his, to one of his friends, who was pleased to communicate it to me." Locke did indeed ... speak in terms which could imply that the "Constitutions" were his. ... But whatever his involvement in the composition of the "Constitutions," Locke seem to have a close attachment to it. Over the years he gave copies to friends, and just months before his death he was still interested enough for it to be a topic of discussion.[18]

Just about the time the Fundamental Constitutions were published in 1669, the state of Virginia was passing laws regarding slavery. The following stipulations from the Fundamental Constitutions state:

> Our sovereign lord the King having, out of his royal grace and bounty, granted unto us the province of Carolina, with all the royalties, properties, jurisdictions, and privileges of a county palatine, as large and ample as the county palatine of Durham, with other great privileges; for the better settlement of the government of the said place, and establishing the interest of the lords proprietors with equality and without confusion; and that the government of this province may be made most agreeable to the monarchy under which we live and of which this province is a part; and that we may avoid erecting a numerous democracy, we, the lords and proprietors of the province aforesaid, have agreed to this following form of government, to be perpetually established amongst us, unto which we do oblige ourselves, our heirs and successors, In the most binding ways that can be devised.
>
> 1. The eldest of the lords proprietors shall be palatine; and, upon the decease of the palatine, the eldest of the seven surviving proprietors shall always succeed him.
>
> 2. There shall be seven other chief offices erected, viz: the admirals, chamberlains, chancellors, constables, chief justices, high stewards, and treasurers; which places shall be enjoyed by none

---

18. Woolhouse, *Locke*, 90.

but the lords proprietors, to be assigned at first by lot, and, upon the vacancy of any one of the seven great offices, by death or otherwise, the eldest proprietor shall have his choice of the said place. . . .

4. Each signiory, barony, and colony shall consist of twelve thousand acres; the eight signiories being the share of the eight proprietors, and the eight baronies of the nobility; both which shares, being each of them one-fifth of the whole, are to be perpetually annexed, the one to the proprietors, the other to the hereditary nobility, leaving the colonies, being three-fifths, amongst the people; so that in setting out and planting the lands, the balance of the government may be preserved. . . .

108. Assemblies, upon what presence soever of religion, not observing and performing the above said rules, shall not be esteemed as churches, but unlawful meetings, and be punished as other riots. . . .

110. Every freeman of Carolina shall have absolute power and authority over his negro slaves, of what opinion or religion soever.

111. No cause, whether civil or criminal, of any freeman, shall be tried in any court of judicature, without a jury of his peers.[19]

Central to the Fundamental Constitutions are the rights of slave masters, including the Lords Proprietors. In addition to the slave owners, Carolina contained many freemen. According to the Fundamental Constitutions, the slave masters and freemen of Carolina had "absolute power and authority over his negro slaves." The slave had no right that the above masters were obliged to recognize, respect, or implement. In Article 111, Locke makes it absolutely clear that the freemen, the Lords Proprietors or the ordinary slave masters could not be brought before the court for any "civil or criminal" offence "without a jury of his peers." As we shall see more evidently in *The Rush for Black Diamonds, Volume 2*, the Constitutions also implied impunity and immunity for any White person who offended a Black person.

Slave masters acted with absolute impunity. In 1669, an Act was passed in Virginia stating that if a master kills a slave by punishment, the death was not considered a crime. The slave was property and part of the

19. Locke, "Fundamental Constitutions of Carolina, 1669."

estate; because of this, the slave master could not face punishment for the death of a slave. The law stipulated that the death of the slave at the hand of the master was a casual occurrence and could not be based on a "prepansed malice" (premeditated).[20] In 1680 and 1691, new laws were enacted mandating the killing of Blacks or mulattos found protesting, hiding from their masters, or "lurking in obscure places." Finkelman notes:

> A decade later the legislature authorized local justices of the peace to order sheriffs to "kill and destroy ... by gunn or any otherwise whatsoever" any "negroes, mulattoes, and other slaves unlawfully absent[ing] themselves from their masters and mistresses service" who "lie hid and lurk in obscure places." These laws effectively reduced slaves to the legal status of wild beasts, to be "destroy[ed]" by public authorities without any trial or hearing. Slaves were property, except when they might "lie hid and lurk" and then they were reduced to the legal status of wild creatures.[21]

The industry of the slave trade and the institution of chattel slavery were eras of blatant White supremacist brutality against Black humanity and personhood. The *black diamond* was a thing of economic utility, sexual abuse, and cruel destruction. Just as they were denied Enlightenment justice and fairness, Blacks were denied common-law justice, fairness, and protection as slaves. Slaves were "wild beasts" and property to be protected against and to "protect" as economic units. Finkelman notes: "With these two statutes Virginia had adopted one of the central aspects of the Roman law of slavery—that it was not a criminal act to kill a slave."[22] One can argue that the Virginian laws of 1680 and 1691 regarding the punishment of slaves became the preamble to the post-1970 increase in rates of police brutality against Black people. Virginia established the

---

20. Finkelman, "Slavery in the United States," 114. "'An act about the casual killing of slaves', Act I, October 1669, 1 Hening 270. This was a variation of the biblical rule 'And if a man smites his servant, or his maid, with a rod, and he die under his hand; he shall be surely punished. Notwithstanding, if he continues a day or two, he shall not be punished: for he is his money'. Exodus, 20:21–22 (King James Translation). However, the biblical rule would have punished a master whose punished slave did not linger, and the Virginia law did not. Nor, of course, did Virginia or any other slave jurisdiction follow the biblical rule on maiming a slave. 'And if a man smites the eye of his servant, or the eye of his maid, that it perishes; he shall let him go free for his eye's sake. And if he smites out his manservant's tooth, or his maidservant's tooth; he shall let him go free for his tooth's sake'. Exodus, 20:26–27."
21. Finkelman, "Slavery in the United States," 114.
22. Finkelman, "Slavery in the United States," 114.

legal foundation by which Black people were legally defined as slaves, property, and real estate.

Take for instance the case of *State v. Hoover.* John Hoover punished and tortured his female slave Mira when she was pregnant in her late trimester. The court documents report:

> He beat her with clubs, iron chains, and other deadly weapons, time after time; burnt her; inflicted stripes over and often, with scourges, which literally excoriated her whole body; forced her out to work in inclement seasons, without being duly clad; provided for her insufficient food; exacted labour beyond her strength, and wantonly beat her because she could not comply with his requisitions.[23]

Mira died because of a fatal blow to her head. Hoover was guilty of "extreme punishment." In the 1800s, slave masters in the South had the right to carry out "common-law criminal homicide" even against slaves who did not pose any resistance to their authorities. According to Scott Howe, a simple murder conviction was imposed in the North Carolina Supreme Court in this case because of the "torturous punishment" involved.

According to Howe, "In *Hoover,* for example, the court took pains to clarify that a 'master may lawfully punish his slave; and the degree must, in general, be left to his own judgement and humanity, and cannot be judicially questioned.'"[24] If she had not died, her punishment would still have been legal, and Hoover would have been acting within the limits of the law as a slave master. Mira's torture was considered an example of legal "corporal punishment" under the law. Slave owners had the right to kill their slaves. "The rule was also clear, however, that a master was free to inflict corporal pain on his slave . . . that an accidental killing that resulted from such an episode was not criminal homicide."[25] The right of the master over his slave is clearly stated in Locke's *Fundamental Constitutions of the Carolinas,* in which he argues that the slave master has total power over their slave.[26]

---

23. Howe, "Slavery as Punishment," 1002.
24. Howe, "Slavery as Punishment," 1003.
25. Howe, "Slavery as Punishment," 1003.
26. Eisenach, *Two Worlds of Liberalism,* 103. "The relationship between Locke's 'strange doctrine' of the right to kill in the state of nature and the transformation of men in nature has been stressed. . . . What requires elaboration before looking at Locke's natural history of man's political relationships in the *Two Treatises* is his treatment of the problem of the right to kill in his earlier *Two Tracts of Government.* Elaboration is

Commenting on the North Carolina Supreme Court decision in the case of *State v. Hale*, Finkelman notes that the court instead decided to protect the property right of the slave master by allowing a White man to be punished for harming the slave of another White man. He adds: "At the same time, in the iconic case *State v. Mann* (Document 13), which set out legal rules that the right of the South followed, the North Carolina Supreme Court affirmed the right of masters to treat a slave however they wished, short of murder."[27] The laws were designed to protect the slaveholding interests of the master and not the slave. This sentiment is quite explicit in the statement of North Carolina's Justice Thomas Ruffin, who contends in the case of *State v. Mann*,

> The end is the profit of the master, his security and the public safety; the subject, one doomed in his own person and his posterity, to live without knowledge and without the capacity to make anything his own, and to toil that another may reap the fruits. . . . The power of the master must be absolute to render the submission of the slave perfect.[28]

The court and the legal system positioned themselves to protect the institution of slavery by not allowing:

> The right of the master to be brought into discussion in the courts of justice. The slave, to remain a slave, must be made sensible that there is no appeal from his master; that his power is in no instance usurped; but is conferred by the laws of man at least, if not by the law of God.[29]

The slave was without justice and legal defense. The slave was a mere object and treated like an animal to be abused before the law. The laws of European nations and the United States were intentionally not designed to protect the slaves or Black folks but enacted to subjugate and abuse Black humanity.

In 1673, Locke lost the position of Secretary of Presentation to Shaftesbury in Parliament. However, the same year, Locke "was sworn

---

required because the *Treatises* discuss the natural evolution of political authority from paternal authority and the *Tracts* discuss the origins of the right to kill in paternal authority. The paternal origins of 'executive power' are identified in the Tracts as religious origins as well. Paternal authority and its history connect the *First Treati*se to the *Second Treatise* and his political writings generally to prophetic history and toleration."

27. Finkelman, *Defending Slavery*, 36.
28. *North Carolina v. Mann*.
29. *North Carolina v. Mann*.

in" as the secretary of the Council of Trade and Foreign Plantations; the earl served as the council's president. Locke's positions brought him into personal contact with the regulators of British trade, including the slave trade in the North American colonies.

LOCKE: SECRETARY AND INVESTOR IN THE SLAVE TRADE

In addition to the theoretical and bureaucratic responsibilities of his position, Locke was also personally involved in the slave trade. He was a merchant adventurer—one of the many highly placed investors and slave traders within British trading companies. Locke invested his initial 200 pounds in the industry and continued to invest in the industry throughout his life. Cranston intimates:

> Locke's interest in the colonies was not purely theoretical and bureaucratic. Toward the end of 1672 Shaftesbury had inaugurated a new company of merchant adventurers to trade with the Bahamas, which the King had ceded to the lords proprietors of Carolina two years before. Locke himself became one of these merchant adventures: the others included John Mapletoft, Thomas Stringer and Henry Aldrich. Locke put up 200 Pounds in the first instance, which was more than some of the others did.[30]

In his position as secretary, Locke was meticulous in gathering information about the "colonial trade and plantation life." He served in the Council of Trade and Foreign Plantations until 1674 and received a handsome annuity from Shaftesbury.[31]

In 1676, Locke was elevated to the position of secretary to the Council of Trade and Plantations. According to Wayne Glausser, "One of the Council's directives was to oversee the provision of slaves and to investigate disputes between the chartered slaving company and the American plantations."[32] His role as secretary of the Council of Trade and Foreign Plantations was also based on how well he had executed his responsibilities as secretary of the Lords Proprietors. In this position, Locke had a bigger platform to craft and structure the policies of the British Empire

---

30. Cranston, *John Locke*, 153, 155.
31. Cranston, *John Locke*, 156.
32. Glausser, "Three Approaches," 199–216.

regarding the slave trade, a business that he had a personal stake in. In all of these positions, Locke was not an idle bystander and accidental participant. His intellectual ability and socio-political connections were integral to the perpetuation of slavery. Woolhouse explains that "in October (1676), Locke was sworn in his place, at an annual salary of 500 Pounds, taking on further responsibility the next month as Treasurer (at 100 Pounds a year). Many of his letters in this and the following year are witness to his involvement with both the Council and the lords proprietors of Carolina, and also to his own interest in the Bahamas."[33]

In his many prestigious positions, Locke became one of the most sought-after architects of the slave trade in the British Empire. He had expertise regarding the practice and policies of the slave trade at the local, national, and international level. Locke's knowledge and influence extended to the British colonies in America including the Carolina colony and Virginia—the home of Thomas Jefferson.

In 1696, Locke became commissioner of King William's New Board of Trade. The focus of this board was on crisis management in the colonies of England, including those in North America.[34] The board intervened in colonies with poor governance and attempted to solve problems including piracy and ineffective trade regulations. Glausser notes that "in this position, [Locke] was unquestionably an active policy-maker... the leading Commissioner in nearly everything which was undertaken."[35] Locke's positions as regulator and policy adviser were related to the slave trade, and his elevation to these prominent positions was not coincidental.

On March 30, 1695, Locke wrote to his friend Molyneux to inform him of his decision to accept the position and mentioned the salary that comes with it.

> The business of our money has so near brought us to ruin that, till the Plot broke out, it was everybody's talk, everybody's uneasiness. And because I had played the fool to print about it, there was scarce a post wherein somebody or other did not give me fresh trouble about it. But now Parliament has reduced guineas to two and twenty shillings a piece after the 10th instant, and prohibited the receipt of clipped money after the 4th of May next. The bill has passed both Houses, and, I believe, will speedily receive the Royal Assent. Though I can never

---

33. Woolhouse, *Locke*, 114.
34. Turner, "John Locke," 280.
35. Glausser, "Three Approaches," 199–216.

> bethink any pains or time of mine, in the service of my country, as far as I may be of any use; yet I must own to you this, and the like subjects, are not those which I now relish, or that do with most pleasure employ my thoughts; and therefore shall not be sorry if I escape a very honourable employment, with a thousand pounds a year salary annexed to it, to which the King was pleased to nominate me some time since. May I have but quiet and leisure, and a competency of health to perfect some thoughts my mind is sometimes upon, I should desire no more for myself in this world, if one thing were added to it, viz. you in my neighbourhood.[36]

On December 12, 1695, Locke received a letter of assurance from Lord Monmouth, a gentleman of King William III's Bedchamber.

> I was some days ago extremely pleased when the King was brought to so reasonable a resolution as to determine upon a Council of Trade, where some great men were to assist but where others with salaries of 1000 pounds a year were to be fixed as the constant labourers. Mr. Locke being to be of this number made me have a better opinion of the thing and comforted me for our last disappointment upon your subject; but according to our accustomed wisdom and prudence when all things had been a good while adjusted, the patent ready for the seal, and some very able and honest men provided for your companions, it was impossible to get the King to sign it; but delaying it from day to day, the Parliament this day fell upon it, and are going to form such a commission to be nominated by themselves.... At last the Secretary informs the House at the latter end of the Debate and much consultation that the King had just formed such a commission.... What the event will be, I know not, but for the little I am able, I shall endeavour that Mr. Lock may be the choice of the House as well as the King's.[37]

On January 2, 1696, Parliament debated the issue of the Commission. Locke received a direct letter regarding the proceedings in Parliament from William Popple.

> I must discharge my promise of writing to you, though I know it was be done more particularly by other hands than I possibly can. But when I tell you what I know, if it be comparatively impertinent, you must blame yourself, and not me, for the trouble

---

36. Cranston, *John Locke*, 401.
37. Cranston, *John Locke*, 401.

of reading it.... This morning the Party that have promoted the design of the Committee of Trade in the House, being offended at the postpoining of that business, shuffled off the coinage without doing anything remarkable in it and brought on the subject of the Committee which had before been appointed. The whole day was spent in Debates. And in the end without resolving anything about the powers that this intended Committee should have, but agreeing that the nature of it should be perfectly different from that intended by the King (which was mentioned and opined, not by the Court but themselves) this being only for speculations, as they said, about the improvement of Trade in time of Peace; this for the effectual security of it in time of war. After much more of this nature then I can tell, and without agreement upon the number of Commissioners, at seven o'clock at night, the question was put, whether the Parliament by one single voice; on that side being 175 and on the other side 174.... This about the Committee I have, now late, from one that was present at the Debate. And this is all I can say.[38]

The above communication confirms that Locke was not a bystander or accidental participant in the transatlantic slave trade. He was involved at the highest level of the slave trade as a political appointee of the British Parliament. Locke was responsible for formulating and executing policies related to the human trade and all trade relations for the British Empire. Furthermore, these communications showed that the concept of "Lockean slavery" received its formal origin in the British Parliament. Lockean slavery is Britain as a slave trader, slave master, and a colonial master of Africans in the Americas, the West Indies, and Africa. It was Locke's responsibility to provide the philosophical and political justification of the transatlantic slave trade, the institution of slavery, and chattel slavery with the blessings of the British Parliament. While Du Bois's account reflects the industrialization of the slave trade as Jeffersonian slavery in the United States, Locke is, on the other hand, the embodiment of the British account of the industrialization of the slave trade and its political and philosophical justification before the American Revolutionary War and thereafter.[39]

A central argument in this book is Locke's participation in the transatlantic slave trade and his defense of the institution of slavery. Let's

---

38. Cranston, *John Locke*, 402–3.
39. Cranston, *John Locke*, 404.

look at the companies organized in Britain to facilitate the slave trade.[40] Locke's involvement in the slave trade took a new turn in 1671 after the dissolution of the old Company of Royal Adventurers.[41] In its place, the Royal African Company emerged and, with the full participation of Locke, Ashley, and Colleton, transported close to ninety thousand slaves from Africa to the British colonies.[42] Britain collected taxes on slaves imported through the slave trade, which became the ultimate source of profit, revenue, and labor.[43] According to Finkelman, "the Royal African Company's investors reached the highest echelons of British society, including members of the royal family. Even after the demise of the Royal African Company in 1750, the slave trade continued to be an important part of Britain's mercantile policy."[44]

In 1672 Locke, by now a Landgrave of Carolina, joined Ashley's new company of merchant adventurers with the purpose of trading with the Bahamas. According to Farr, "In his portfolio, then, he smartly complimented stock in the Royal African Company with stock in a company of Merchant Adventurers with much investment in the human trade."[45]

Locke invested six hundred pounds in the Royal African Company (which had a monopoly over the trade in the British Empire) not long after its establishment in 1672.[46] His patron Lord Ashley also invested two thousand pounds. Ashley was a ship owner and a nobleman who owned slaves and lands in Barbados and a significant share in the *Rose*, another slave-trading ship. He became the sub-governor of the new Royal African Company from 1673 until 1677.[47] According to Glausser, "No doubt

40. See chapter 1 for a confirmation of this list as well from Du Bois.
41. Farr, "'So Vile and Miserable an Estate.'"
42. Bernasconi and Mann, "Contradictions of Racism," 89.
43. Finkelman, *Slavery and the Founders*, 134.
44. Finkelman, *Slavery and the Founders*, 134.
45. Farr, "'So Vile and Miserable an Estate,'" 267.
46. Cranston, *John Locke*.
47. Cranston, *John Locke*, 153–55. "The Council was a fact-finding, not an executive body, and its secretary was, for this reason, a more important man than any of the councilors. . . . The work of the Council was conscientiously done, meetings were frequent, complaints and memorials from the colonies were sedulously examined, and information on colonial conditions accepted from all with experience, local or English, of the conduct of colonial relation. The instructions to be given to Governors were carefully prepared, and colonial legislation scrutinised. The Council had also to investigate home trade, to consider the improvement of produce and of manufactured goods, the development of fisheries, harbours and navigable rivers, the increase of exports and the elimination of abuses in trade."

Locke and Ashley looked carefully both at the company's charter—which granted a monopoly for the trade of 'Gold, Silver, Negroes, Slaves,' and any other minor Guinea goods—and at a report of its first year's activities, which mentions gold, elephants' teeth, and a few other items, but places by far the greatest emphasis on slave shipping and slave factories."[48]

Locke was a partner with Ashley in the Bahamas venture along with five Carolina businessmen who served as custodians of the Bahamas islands in 1672.[49] He was also one of eleven "Adventurers to the Bahamas" whose goal was to bring development to the Bahamas through the slave trade. Glausser explains that Locke had initially invested £100 in the Royal African Company and later took over the share of his partner John Mapletoft. "He was present on the 8th of November [1672] at a meeting on board the ship *Bahamas Merchant*, moored in the Thames, and ready for the sailing."[50]

The institution of slavery was important for two main reasons: (1) slaves were economic units, and (2) slavery provided cheap labor and wealth generation. The slave trade and slavery were legal and legitimate means of income, as the Laws of the United Kingdom of Great Britain supported it. Kaye notes that:

> By the end of the 18th century, some 40 per cent of British exports went to Africa or the Americas and the Caribbean. The slave trade also provided thousands of seamen, merchants, carpenters, shipbuilders, gunsmiths and many others with employment. The custom duties on slave grown imports were an important source of government income. In 1773, the value of British imports from the island of Grenada were worth eight times more than those from Canada. As well as driving demand for exports, the money made from slavery boosted the domestic economy as individuals and institutions funded businesses and other projects with profits from the plantations.[51]

In 1673, Locke invested in The Company of Royal Adventures in England and Trading into Africa. The company was given a monopoly on the slave trade on the West Coast of Africa. Robert Bernasconi and Anika Mann explain that "by 1665 one quarter of the company's trade was in

---

48. Glausser, "Three Approaches," 201.
49. Glausser, "Three Approaches," 201.
50. Glausser, "Three Approaches," 202.
51. Kaye, *1807–2007*, 5.

slaves, and in 1667 it claimed to be delivering six thousand slaves to the plantation each year."[52]

Slavery brought Locke financial and social elevation as secretary, controller, and regulator of the British trade and the American colony. According to Cornel West, the "racialization of American slavery was rooted in economic calculations and psycho-cultural anxieties that targeted black bodies. Thus, the profitable sugar, tobacco, and cotton plantations of the New World were housed and husbanded by African labor, with the result that African men, women, and children defined the boundaries of European culture and civilization."[53]

Locke's participation in the slave trade was for economic gain.[54] According to Farr, "he also gained financially from his service under Ashley, investing alongside his patron in the Royal African Company (£400 in 1674 and £200 more in 1675) and in the Bahamas trade (£100 in 1675), which he liquidated at profit (in 1676). Locke remained in Shaftesbury's colonial affairs until late 1682 when Shaftesbury fled to Holland and fell mortally ill."[55] While this research examines Locke and Thomas Jefferson as important intellectual supporters of the slave trade and chattel slavery, it is important to note that the widespread appeal of the human trade was evident in several countries of Western Europe.

52. Bernasconi and Mann, "Contradictions of Racism," 89.
53. West, *Cornel West Reader*, 89.
54. Glausser, "Three Approaches," 202.
55. Farr, "Locke, Natural Law," 497.

FROM AFRICA TO EUROPE: THE MIDDLE PASSAGE

The trade in human beings was their ultimate goal.
Elmina Castle and Sudan, the absolute reflection,
To enrich the West in the human trade,
While the East, its Arabization spread.

They pillaged the culture of their savage host!
The strongest from 10 to 40 were deliberately stolen!
Men and women to perpetuate the community,
They were placed on ships through the Middle Passage!
With slave-sticks on their necks, they hauled their African cargo across the Atlantic!

The bodies of Africans were branded with hot metals,
Their feet and wrists were shackled for bondage,
To keep them in line, Africans were hauled in chains.
Their human dignity was not a question to the civilized Conscience!

It was called the Triangular Trade System,
From Europe to Africa to the Americas.
It was called the Transatlantic Slave Trade.
On the Atlantic Ocean from Africa to the Americas through the dreadful Middle Passage,

Packed in ships from top to bottom,
Like sardines in a can, Africans craved fresh air.
Through pain and hunger, they died in the dungeon,
And to the shirks, the Europeans threw the dead to feast.

To the Indies and Britain, their cargo was taken,
In the streets of Paris and Belgium, a spectacle they were.
But in America, the vilest form of human slavery
John Wesley said he saw firsthand.[56]

GEORGE WALTERS-SLEYON

---

56. Walters-Sleyon, *Nuggets from the Night*, 114.

5

Lockean Politics: Once a Slave, Always a Slave

THE SLAVE IS A SLAVE for life in civil society and nothing can change it. This chapter demonstrates a relationship between Locke's political appointments, his involvement in the slave trade, and the development of his political theories. Locke worked as a secretary for the British colony of Carolina in London from 1663 to 1696.[1] Locke's secretarial positions precede the beginning of the formulation and publication of his major political and philosophical theories.[2] It contends that a holistic understanding of Locke's political theories can only be derived from reading them in relation to his many appointments as secretary of the British slave-trading enterprises and his investments in the trade itself.

Between 1689 and 1692, Locke published the *Two Treatises on Government*. In the same year, he published *A Letter Concerning Toleration*. This book contends that these two publications came after Locke's extensive engagements in the transatlantic slave trade and chattel slavery in the British colonies and America. By 1689, Locke had established

---

1. Armitage, "John Locke."

2. 1689: *A Letter Concerning Toleration*. 1690: *A Second Letter Concerning Toleration*. 1692: *A Third Letter for Toleration*. 1689/90: *Two Treatises of Government* (published throughout the eighteenth century by London bookseller Andrew Millar by commission for Thomas Hollis). 1689/90: *An Essay Concerning Human Understanding*. 1691: *Some Considerations on the Consequences of the Lowering of Interest and the Raising of the Value of Money*. 1693: *Some Thoughts Concerning Education*. 1695: *The Reasonableness of Christianity, as Delivered in the Scriptures*. 1695: *A Vindication of the Reasonableness of Christianity*.

himself politically, socially, and financially through his many high-profile positions and connections. It was time to focus on writing his philosophical and political treatises—many of which defended slavery and private property, in addition to natural rights and other Enlightenment concerns. This chapter explores Locke's political argument that the social and economic status of the (Black) slave will always be one of indeterminate and perpetual bondage. According to Locke, to be a slave is to be a slave indeterminately. He writes in the Fundamental Constitutions, "But yet no slave shall hereby be exempted from that civil dominion his master hath over him, but be in all things in the same state and condition he was in before."[3] Religiously, Locke was a deist and an empiricist. He believed in the supremacy of natural law and reason. For Locke, that which reason and experience cannot validate must be rejected as a relic of religious dogmatism.

LOCKE AND THE PRIVATIZATION OF THE NATURAL RIGHTS

The support for rights, justice, fairness, respect, and equality are pivotal cardinal virtues regarding the treatment of other human beings. The foundations are religious. In Christianity, God is the embodiment of justice. This religious association of God with justice is fundamentally ontological. It ascribes ontology or beingness to justice. The ontological foundation of justice serves as an ideal against the excesses of man-made justice, natural justice, and socially constructed forms of justice. This chapter focuses on Locke's concept of "rights."

According to John Witte, "Religion has long been a critical foundation and dimension of human rights. Religion and human rights still need each other for each to thrive."[4] However, as we shall see, John Locke's conception of rights differed drastically from Witte's. For Locke, natural reason serves as the foundation for the interpretation and construction of rights as political, legal, social, or even religious. Witte contends that:

> Rights defined the claim that one legal subject could legitimately make against another to protect their person, property, business, reputation, and interest, or to compel another to live up to their contracts, promises, and other obligations. Rights

3. Locke, "Fundamental Constitutions of Carolina, 1669," para. 98.
4. Witte, *Blessing of Liberty*, xi.

and liberties also defined limits to the actions, duties, or charges that authorities could legitimately impose upon their individual and corporate subjects. And rights and liberties language set out the procedures and principles that were to be followed in all of these legal interactions, sometimes casting them in terms of justice, equity, liberty, equality, due process, and other ideals.[5]

Witte's definition of rights justly underscores what is normative about rights, and what rights ought to entail. Witte's definition implies an objective and subjective understanding of rights as actions and expressions of fair and legitimate treatments and engagements.

Nagamitsu Miura intimates that Locke based his political philosophy on natural rights. "The natural right of self-preservation (preservation of life, liberty and possession) of all men as well as the equality of all and the mutual respect for natural rights of others. Man was created as God's creature, and since God wills that men live in this world, they have the right of self-preservation."[6] For Locke, everyone has natural rights endowed by God. Natural rights are the "law of nature"[7] and are given for "the peace and preservation of all mankind." Thus, in the state of nature, any encroachment on another's right to self-preservation may lead to punishment and reparation. Nevertheless, with the emergence of the political society, both natural rights and the law of nature are relinquished within the political society. The political society has the ultimate right to punish.[8] However, for Locke, the element of "self-preservation" is fundamental. "Being endowed with his own body, reason, and liberty, man has the right of appropriating materials and possession necessary for his life by the use of these capacities. These rights are natural in the sense of native rights conferred on everyone by God the creator."[9]

---

5. Witte, *Blessing of Liberty*, 4.

6. Miura, *John Locke*, 12.

7. Sahakian and Sahakian, *John Locke*, 32. "The expression 'law of nature' did not originate with Locke, for the term was employed in the seventeenth century by two English divines and philosophers in their attack on the egoism of Hobbes: Nathanael Culverwel (d. 1651) in his *An Elegant and Learned Discourse of the Light of Nature* (1652); and Richard Cumberland (1631–1718) in his *A Philosophical Enquiry into the Laws of Nature: Wherein the Essence, the Principal Heads, the Order, the Publication, and the Obligation of These Laws Are Deduced from the Nature of Things; Wherein Also the Principles of Mr. Hobbes's Philosophy, Both in a State of nature and of Civil Society, are Examined into and Confuted (1672)."*

8. Miura, *John Locke*, 13.

9. Miura, *John Locke*, 13.

Locke insists that the law of nature seeks the welfare of all men. "And that all men may be restrained from invading other's rights and from doing hurt to one another, and the law of nature be observed, which wills the peace and preservation of all mankind, the execution of the law of nature is, in that state, put into every man's hand."[10] He does not define what determines property; neither does he invoke a moral compunction to legislate against that which ethically and ontologically, one cannot "own" as property.

As Locke saw it, natural rights exist as the ground for positive laws, with positive laws becoming established in natural rights.[11] As to the origin of the law of nature, Locke refers to the "mind" and "divine law as the will of God" as the basis for natural rights and the law of nature. According to Locke:

> The divine law, whereby I mean, that Law which God has set to the actions of men, whether promulgated to them by the light of nature, or the voice of revelation. That God has given a rule whereby men should govern themselves, I think there is no body so brutish as to deny. He has a right to do it, we are his creatures: He has goodness and wisdom to direct our actions to that which is best. . . . This is the only true touchstone of moral rectitude: and by comparing them to this law, it is, that men judge of the most considerable moral good or evil of their actions (EHU.II.28.8).[12]

It is implied that Locke's "divine law" also refers to the law of nature. "The light of nature" refers to every individual's reason and "the voice of revelation" refers to the Bible as the revelation of God's word. With the above explanation, Miura contends: "Therefore, Locke now speaks of 'reason, which is that law [law of nature]' (TT.II.6), then quotes a passage from the Bible when explaining a provision of the law of nature (TT.II, 31). One can thus find the law of nature as God's will by one's own reason and the Bible."[13] In another place, Locke refers to the law of nature as the teacher of every individual. He writes: "Reason, which is that law [law of nature], teaches all mankind, who but consult it, that being all equal and independent, no one ought to harm another in his life, health, liberty,

---

10. Locke, *Second Treatise of Civil Government*, sec. 7.
11. Miura, *John Locke*, 17.
12. Miura, *John Locke*, 18.
13. Miura, *John Locke*, 18.

or possession" (TT.II.6).[14] As an empiricist, Locke is invariably emphatic about the centrality of reason; we shall discuss his related rejection of innateness later.

Locke compares his concept of self-preservation to the "immortality" of the soul, which also serves as the ground for "eternal happiness."[15] Individuals' right to self-preservation in the state of nature is also transferred to the government in a political society. The right of self-preservation serves as a fundamental element in Locke's law of nature. A poignant example of this is found in Locke's assertion that religion cannot be legislated.

According to Locke, everyone is responsible for their eternal salvation and no one else, nor the state, can claim this responsibility. The state cannot force religion on anyone, because the choice to become a part of any religion or denomination is the natural right of the individual. The state ought to stay out of the business of eternal salvation and eternal happiness. This argument has become the basis for the separation of church and state in the United States.[16] Jack Turner rejects this conclusion considering Locke's "evangelical commitments" and "defense of toleration of Christian missions." He contends that Locke was not "advocating disestablishment" between church and state but "advocated disestablishment only in the limited sense of prohibiting the use of coercion to enforce established religion."[17] Furthermore, Turner argues that Locke "personally contributed" to the "global reach of Protestantism through an imperial practice of toleration" in England's "evangelical project."[18]

Henrik Syse intimates that Locke's theory of human rights must be interpreted considering the preceding view of rights, natural rights, and law, from those whom Syse regards as his "predecessors." These include Francisco Suarez (1547–1617), Hugo Grotius (1583–1645), and St. Thomas Aquinas.[19] Characteristic of the debate about right and natural

---

14. Miura, *John Locke*, 19.
15. Miura, *John Locke*, 15.
16. Miura, *John Locke*.
17. Turner, "John Locke," 296–97.
18. Turner, "John Locke," 297.
19. Syse, *Natural Law*, 191, 193. They "pointed out that *ius* has at least two meaning: (a) that which is *iustum* (just) and (b) that which signifies a person's relationship to that which he or she, in exclusion of all others, possesses. This is what we earlier in this work have referred to as the difference between (a) 'objective' right and (b) 'subjective' right(s) (the will, leading to voluntarism); or, in other worlds between a 'system' of law or right on the one hand and a personal right on the other. . . . The turn toward

right was the ambiguity associated with the word *ius*. It is right as subjective-voluntaristic and right as objective-philosophical and intellectual.[20] According to Locke, "[The law of nature] teaches all Mankind, who will but consult it. That being all equal and independent, no one ought to harm another in his Life, Health, Liberty, or Possession."[21]

This book considers Locke's concept of rights qua property ownership in relation to his defense of the slave trade and chattel slavery. Syse notes that "Locke's concept of property involves the use of the term 'right' in the subjective sense. One has a 'right' to the property with which one mixes one's labor, according to Locke. But to whom belongs that which no one has appropriated"?[22] Rights are associated with property ownership. This form of ownership is radically subjective. It makes little or no provision for constraints regarding what is considered accountability regarding ownership. Locke does not comment on the intersection between right, property, and ownership. He argues that God has given the right to own everything but stops short of mentioning God's limitation on what can be owned. God is against "owning" human beings. The intersection of Egypt, Pharoah, Moses, the Ten Plagues, and the liberation of the Jews in slavery is a clear example.

For Locke, God owns the universe and has given man the power to possess it. As such, there is no limitation on what one can own from the earth and the universe. God is all-powerful and has given that power to human beings, especially "rational" beings. In contrast to Hobbes, Strauss, Grotius, Aquinas, and Spinoza, Locke radicalizes the concept of rights into an individualized concept of right. Syse contends that Locke has privatized the concept of rights to be very subjective.

> Locke paves the way for the concept of a sphere of "private jurisdiction," a sphere within which no one but the person with the "right" can determine the right or wrong of an action. Locke makes this point by saying that "every Man has a Property in his

---

a subjective use of the term *ius* does not appear in a vacuum; it is preconditioned by an extensive legal, political, theological, and philosophical debate. This becomes an important clue (albeit one of many) to understanding Locke. So many of his writings are responses to concrete political, philosophical, and not least, theological challenges."

20. Syse, *Natural Law*, 194. "The crucial point is that there is a possible link between 'divine' voluntarism—i.e., the idea that natural/divine/eternal law has its basis in God's *will* rather than reason—and an ethical and political voluntarism which stresses the will of the community or of the individual."

21. Locke, *Second Treatise of Civil Government*, 6. Pt. 1.

22. Syse, *Natural Law*, 212, 216.

own person" (that man's rights are "ownership" rights, most basically a *self*-ownership right). From a hierarchically ordered reality expressed through divine and natural laws (the great chain of being), we have arrived at a universe of property-owners, with God as the greatest and mightiest.[23]

Locke's privatization of right was done to protect owning Africans as chattel property. One may argue that Lockean right is synonymous with Lockean individualism and inevitably Western individualism. Individualism and private property are rooted in the justification of chattel slavery and the owning of Black humanity as property.

Locke used biblical claims to establish his argument for private property. On the question of slavery, human rights, and Locke's inconsistency, Woolhouse notes, "On the face of it, the black slaves who formed part of the trade of the Royal African Company were people who had been robbed of their natural rights and 'subject to the arbitrary will of another' quite without their consent. Is there an inconsistency between Locke's having investments in that company and the political theory he was developing here"?[24] Locke's notion of natural rights is theoretically universal but was in practice private and subjectively racial. This practice of circumscribing natural rights is reflected in the works of all the major pioneers of the Enlightenment project. On the one hand, natural rights, concepts of justice, and equalitarianism are defined as universal concepts for all. On the other hand, those same natural rights and concepts of equalitarian justice are denied to the people of African descent. It is an obvious inconsistency in Locke's political theories that cannot be dismissed.

LOCKEAN NATURAL RIGHTS AND SLAVERY

This section provides the immediate background narrative to some of Locke's arguments on the intersection between natural rights and slavery. Locke railed against slavery but with a back hand defended it in his political theory. The question remains: what kind of slavery did Locke

---

23. Syse, *Natural Law*, 217. "Nonetheless, while not being as radical in his concept of the *ius naturale* as Spinoza and Hobbes, Locke does extend and radicalize the rights concept. While the *ius naturale* was originally (in medieval philosophy) an expression of what is right to do, meaning what one can do within the jurisdiction ordained by superior authorities (in the last instance, by God or nature)."

24. Woolhouse, *Locke*, 187.

condemn and what kind of slavery did he advocate? In the *Second Treatise of Government*, Locke argues, "Slavery is so vile and miserable an estate of man and so directly opposite to the generous temper and courage of our nation, that is hardly to be conceived that an Englishman, much less a Gentleman, should plead for it."[25]

Locke, the slave trader, and slave master was writing from experience. He had seen and endorsed the brutality of slavery against the humanity of Africans. There was no way Locke could imagine or condone the enslavement of any Englishman. The immediate political context for Locke's defense of the enslavement of African and chattel slavery is found in Locke's rejection of the claims of another English man, the royalist Sir Richard Filmer.

THE LOCKE AND FILMER DEBATE ON SLAVERY

In his defense of slavery and its institutionalization, Locke was also attacking a proponent of the "divine right of kings" by the name of Sir Robert Filmer.[26]

Sir Filmer was a British intellectual who was taken to task for suggesting some form of absolute power for the king in his book *Patriarcha*. The first person to have written against Sir Filmer was James Tyrrell in his book *Patriarcha Non Monarcha,* published in 1681. Tyrrell argued "that Mankind is naturally endowed and born with Freedom from Subjection, and at liberty to choose what form of government it please; and that the Power which any man hath over others was at first bestowed according to the direction of the multitude."[27]

In contrast to Filmer, Tyrrell contended that the king was not free from the constraints of the law. Cranston argues that Tyrrell and Locke

---

25. Locke, "Second Treatise of Civil Government," pt. 1.

26. Dunn, *Locke*, 39. "There was, therefore, nothing eccentric about Locke's choice of a target. Filmer stood out from other royalist ideologues, dead and living, by the uncompromising character of his theory of political authority, devout enough in tone and premises to reassure any Anglican, but also sufficiently absolute in its claims to match the practical appeals of the distressingly less devout theory of Thomas Hobbes. It is not altogether clear whether the choice of Filmer as an enemy in the early 1680s was a tribute to his popularity amongst supporters of Charles II or whether it was more a reflection of his attractions as an intellectual target. But here too what mattered for the quality and content of the book which Locke wrote was not the original motive which led him to undertake it, but the intellectual effect of organizing his thinking to such a large degree, in the *Second Treatise* as well as in the *First*, around an attack on Filmer."

27. Cranston, *John Locke*, 205.

met but never collaborated. However, Locke's *Two Treatises of Government* vehemently attacked Filmer's argument. For Cranston, Locke's ideas in the *Two Treatises of Government* were inherently Lockean. Cranston notes that "the first of the *Two Treatises* is a detailed refutation of Filmer, and the second sets out an alternative political philosophy to Filmer. This definite connection helps to date Locke's book as one written, like *Patriarcha Non Monarcha*, when the writings of Filmer were at the height of their fashion after the first publication, in 1680, of *Patriarcha*."[28] Filmer's view of the power and "regal authority" of the monarchy was based on paternity, like Adam as the first parent passing his right to have dominion over the earth down to his children. Woolhouse notes that "Filmer addressed the question, 'what is the basis for the authority of a government and for the obedience of subjects to that government?'; are rights and liberties 'derived from the law of natural liberty', for example, or 'from the grace and bounty of princes?'"[29] What are the sources of rights and liberty? Are they based on the concept of man-made liberty, i.e., the authority of the prince? Locke fundamentally rejected Filmer's argument.[30] According to Locke:

> Freedom then is not what *Sir Robert Filmer* tells us, *Observations, a liberty for everyone to do what he lists, to live as he pleases*, and *not to be tied by any laws: but freedom of men under government* is, to have a standing rule to live by, common to every one of that society, and made by the legislative power erected in it; a liberty to follow my own will in all things, where the rule prescribes not; and not to be subject to the inconstant, uncertain, unknown, arbitrary will of another man: as *freedom of nature* is, to be under no other restraint but the law of nature.[31]

Locke contends that Filmer suggested a form of *political absolutism, arbitrary power* for the monarchy, and the theory of the divine right of kings. In Locke's view, mankind's natural state is not entirely subjected to divine concepts or oriented institutions. "Our natural state is one of 'liberty ... free from any superior power on earth, and not ... under the will ... of man but [with] ... only the law of nature for [our] rule.'"[32]

28. Cranston, *John Locke*, 207.
29. Woolhouse, *Locke*, 182.
30. Woolhouse, *Locke*, 183.
31. Locke, *Two Treatises of Government*, 22–23; italics original.
32. Woolhouse, *Locke*, 185. "Locke did not think of people as being 'alone' in the state of nature. God has so constituted human beings that 'necessity, convenience, and

For Locke, reason is how the "law of nature" is discovered. However, like Filmer, Locke appropriated biblical and religious ideas to establish his claim for the discovery of the law of nature. In his *Essays on the Law of Nature*, Locke notes that mankind is the "workmanship of one omnipotent and infinitely wise maker," as God's servant "sent into the world by his order, and about his business," having been "furnished with like faculties, sharing all in one community of nature." Thus, he concludes it is inappropriate to assume "any . . . subordination among us that may authorize us to destroy one another, as if we were made for one another's uses, as the inferior ranks of creatures are for ours." In that light, we are preservers of one another's humanity and dignity. Beyond the state of nature is the formation of the political society and submission of rights to the political authority for the "preservation of property"—which in this case included life, liberty, and estate.[33]

Locke's contention is based on the freedom of will and conscience. It is freedom from the conscience of arbitrary and absolute power toward self-preservation. Locke rejected "the supremacy of the king" for "the supremacy of parliament."[34] He thought it repugnant for a man or woman to own another person, and felt Filmer's argument in favor of the king's authority to hold his subjects as "slaves" negated God's theological and natural right. Notwithstanding his rejection of English enslavement to the monarch, Locke refuses to appropriate the same argument and contention for Black folks. Dunn notes that there are contradictions in Locke's argument against Filmer. He writes:

> This proviso should have been extremely embarrassing for Locke himself in his capacity as stockholder of the slave-trading Royal Africa Company, since it clearly implied that the status of a slave could not legitimately be inherited from one generation to another. All legitimate servitude was intrinsically penal and the crime of the father or mother could not descend to their children.[35]

Locke's hypocrisy is on full display in his contention with Sir Filmer. In contrast to Filmer, Locke advanced the notion that the monarch was

---

inclination . . . drive [them} into society.' There are though different kinds of society: for example, society between man and wife, between parents and children, master and servant, and, finally, political society."

33. Woolhouse, *Locke*, 186.
34. Miura, *John Locke*, 15.
35. Dunn, *Locke*, 51.

fundamentally a "servant."[36] Filmer advocated some form of theoretical slavery for Englishmen as subjects of the monarchy, which Locke vehemently opposed. For Locke, the freedom of an Englishman is non-negotiable. He believed that the Englishman cannot "enslave himself to anyone, nor put himself under the absolute, arbitrary power of another to take away his life when he pleases. Nobody can give more power than he has himself; and he that cannot take away his own life, cannot give another power over it."[37] However, Locke subscribes to the notion that the Englishman has the absolute right of divine authority to terrorize, capture, and perpetually enslave the Africans.

LOCKE'S JUST WAR AND VOLUNTARY ENSLAVEMENT

Locke defines slavery as giving up one's *will* and *consent* to be ruled by another. The one who gives up his will and consents to be ruled has relinquished their capacity for self-determination and become subject to the will of the master. He writes:

> Indeed, having by his fault forfeited his own life, by some act that deserves death; he, to whom he has forfeited it, may (when he has him in his power) delay to take it, and make use of him to his own service, and he does him no injury by it: for, whenever he finds the hardship of his slavery outweigh the value of his life, it is in his power, by resisting the will of his master, to draw on himself the death he desires. This is the perfect condition of slavery, which is nothing else, but the state of war continued, between a lawful conqueror and a captive.[38]

Locke is particular about the conceptual structure of his argument. The slave is to blame for his or her enslavement. The slave has forfeited every right. The slave has willingly become a slave. Therefore, the slave master is a lawful conqueror because the slave has willingly submitted themselves to the master. The slave master as the lawful conqueror, therefore, has absolute authority over the slave. Locke writes:

> This is the perfect condition of *slavery*, which is nothing else, but *the state of war continued, between a lawful conqueror and a*

36. Dunn, *Locke*, 52.
37. Locke, *Two Treatises of Government*, 23–24.
38. Locke, *Two Treatises of Government*, 23–24.

captive: for, if once compact enter between them, and make an agreement for a limited power on the one side, and obedience on the other, *the state of war and slavery* ceases, as long as the compact endures: for, as has been said, no man can, by agreement, pass over to another that which he hath not in himself, a power over his own life.[39]

For Locke, slavery is the voluntary surrender of one's will. He believes that Africans who were enslaved were made slaves because they voluntarily submitted their wills to the slave masters. According to James Farr, Locke condemns slavery as "vile" and "miserable."[40] On the one hand, Locke argues against slavery in any civilized society but on the other hand, he endorses the enslavement of Africans. He was only condemning the enslavement of Englishmen. While Locke condemns slavery in the state of nature and the civil society as antithetical to the preservation of natural rights, he makes provisions for slavery in the civil society established on reason. This kind of slavery, he argues, is tolerated based on his concept of "just war."

Hinshelwood disagrees with Farr's analysis of Locke's theory of slavery. According to Hinshelwood, Farr is arguing that Locke's justification of slavery is a "domestic motivation" against Filmer and should not be taken to justify the enslavement of Africans or Indians in Carolina.[41] For Hinshelwood, Locke's theory of slavery in the *Second Treatise* argues for a legitimate class of slaves based on Locke's experience in Carolina as one of the Lords Proprietors and profiteers. Hinshelwood notes that "Carolina also helps explain why Locke is concerned with defining a class of legitimate slaves in the first place; if he were purely interested in English affairs, as Farr contends, Locke would gain nothing out of a theory that both creates the opportunity for legitimate slavery while failing to justify any of its colonial forms."[42]

---

39. Locke, *Two Treatises of Government*, 23–24; italics original.
40. Farr, "'So Vile and Miserable an Estate,'" 270.
41. Hinshelwood, "Carolinian Context," 581.
42. Hinshelwood, "Carolinian Context," 581.

LOCKE AND THE LEGITIMATE CASTE OF BLACK SLAVES

Locke was interested in establishing a perpetual and legitimate class of slaves comprised mainly of Africans. In the *Second Treatise*, Locke argues that slaves are captives from conquest through "just war."[43] They have voluntarily given up their rights as captives and are therefore rightless. The condition of slavery is associated with "total servitude for an unjust aggressor of just war."[44] Locke sees no incompatibility between "unjust aggressors and just conquerors."[45] He writes:

> But there is another sort of servant to which we give the special name "slave." A slave is someone who, being a captive taken in a just war, is by the right of nature subjected to the absolute command and arbitrary power of his master. A slave has forfeited his life and with it his liberty; he has lost all his goods, and as a slave he is not capable of having any property; so he can't in his condition of slavery be considered as any part of civil society, the chief purpose of which is the preservation of property.[46]

Locke's statements on slavery and his concept of just war are inconsistent with his arguments regarding Enlightenment values. There must have been an underlying reason for Locke, the promoter of human rights, to make such incoherent claims. Glausser notes, "However tortured and incomplete this chain of logic, it is not simply an illusion conjured up by imaginative interpreters. Locke the opponent of slavery cannot entirely suppress Locke the landgrave, eager to make his mark on the *tabula rasa* of American waste land."[47] Unused land was up for grabs in America and Locke wanted to justify owning some of it.[48] In his writing, Locke associates slavery with the concept of war. He writes, "So someone who tries to enslave me thereby puts himself into a state of war with me."[49] Locke used his just war theory to justify slavery, just as the lords proprietors of the colony of Carolina used it to support their treatment of American Indians.

43. Hinshelwood, "Carolinian Context," 580.
44. Farr, "Locke, Natural Law, and New World Slavery," 496.
45. Farr, "'So Vile and Miserable an Estate,'" 271.
46. Locke, *Second Treatise of Government*, sec. 85.
47. Glausser, "Three Approaches," 209.
48. Glausser, "Three Approaches," 210.
49. Locke, *Second Treatise of Government*, sec. 17.

As Hinshelwood shows, the Lords Proprietors worked diligently to frame their enslavement of Native Americans in the terms of just war. "Often traders actually incited intertribal warfare to profit from the sale of captives. By 1675, the colonists had recognized the importance of portraying their slaves as captives taken in just wars. On December 10, 1675, the Grand Council of the colony heard testimony from 'Mr. John Boon the English Interpreter, and Capt. Titus the Indian Interpreter.'"[50] The Proprietors "accomplished two goals: [they] argued loosely that the method of capture was a just one, and . . . skirted the 1671 law banning Indian slavery."[51]

THE LOCKEAN SLAVE IS RIGHTLESS

Locke argues that the slave is perpetually rightless. Slavery is rightlessness. Witte notes that it wasn't the Bible alone that influenced the construction of the concepts of rights in the Western tradition. Classical Roman laws provided ample background. He provides a distinction between "objective rights" and "subjective rights." These distinctions are crucial to understanding Locke's use of the language of right and the status of the slave in the British colonies. Witte explains:

> Both before and after the Christian conversion of Emperor Constantine in the fourth century CE, classical Roman jurists used the Latin term *ius* to identify a "right" in both its objective and subjective senses. *(Ius* also meant law or legal order more generally.) The objective sense of *ius*—to be in proper order, to perform what is right and required, "to give to each his due" (*ius suum cuiuque tribuere*)—dominated the Roman law texts. But these texts also sometimes used *ius* subjectively, in the sense of

---

50. Hinshelwood, "Carolinian Context," 570.

51. Hinshelwood, "Carolinian Context," 570. "This experience led to Locke's participation in a substantial set of revisions to the Fundamental Constitutions in the summer of 1682. On August 17, a new edition of the Fundamental Constitutions was published. One draft of the August edition with emendations survives, and three people suggested revisions: Peter Colleton, Locke, and an unidentified third hand. Locke's revisions are extremely detailed, and all of them made it into the August edition of the Fundamental Constitutions. These revisions betray concern with the course of Indian affairs in Carolina. The proprietors continued to insist that "no person whatsoever shall hold or claim any Land in Carolina, by Purchase, gift, or otherwise, from the natives or any other whatsoever, but merely from and under the lords proprietors," but the constitutional rules about warfare and trials in the colony change significantly, a response to wars with the Indians and the Woodward affair."

a subject or person having a right that could be defended and vindicated. Many of the subjective rights recognized by classical Roman law involved property.[52]

Considering Witte's explanation of objective and subjective rights, one may conclude that objective rights provide the ground and argument for what ought to be done, that is, what is the "proper" and "appropriate" action or decision to take. Objective rights are universal, humanitarian, and inherently equalitarian. On the other hand, subjective rights are particular and immediate. Subjective rights concern property ("the right to be free from interference with or invasion of one's property . . . the right to alienate property") and personal issues ("the rights of fathers and mothers over children," and the "rights of masters over slaves"). Other aspects of subjective rights include "public rights: the right of an official to punish or deal with subjects in a certain way" and "procedural rights in criminal and civil cases."[53] Based on the above, subjective rights did not precede objective rights. Furthermore, subjective rights are particular and have the tendency to be socially constructed, situational, and discriminatory. In this book, I argue that the Lockean concept of right is subjective, individualistic, and private.

Locke argues that slaves are property and made rightless through conquest. He defines slaves as property of their captors and inherently rightless politically and civilly. They have forfeited their natural, civil, and economic rights among free men. The slave is the property of his captor and will perpetually be his captor's property. For Locke to logically justify slavery, Africans and American Indians are considered "aggressors" in a "just war." He writes, "These men, having, as I say, forfeited their lives and with it their liberties, and lost their estates, and being in the state of slavery not capable of any property, cannot in the state be considered as any part of civil society, the chief end whereof is the preservation of property."[54] For Locke, to have another Englishman advocate some form of political slavery for Englishmen under the monarchy as Filmer did was an affront to English dignity.

---

52. Witte, *Blessing of Liberty*, 23.
53. Witte, *Blessing of Liberty*, 23.
54. Locke, *Second Treatise of Civil Government*, sec. 85.

LOCKEAN SLAVERY IS CHATTEL SLAVERY

Slaves had no claim to their own labor power. Locke sees no incompatibility between "unjust aggressors and just conquerors" and so justifies the institution of slavery.[55]

According to Farr, "three facts of Afro-American slavery, facts of which he was abundantly aware, violate Locke's just-war theory of slavery: (1) the methods of capture, (2) the demography of enslavement, and (3) the institution of hereditary bondage. The first two occurred in Africa, the third in America."[56] Evidence abounds to debunk Locke's claim that Africans were enslaved because of his concept of just war.[57] Du Bois's writing on the slave trade provides enormous background to the process of capturing Africans and negates Locke's concept of this process as a "just war." Locke was one of the wealthy investors in the slave ships that were fueling wars and tribal conflicts in Africa. It was a blatant disruption of the lives of Africans in their villages and towns. Based on his experience from trading in Carolina, Locke was interested in the establishment of a perpetual castes system of Black people.[58] Hinshelwood explains, "Viewing Carolina as the animating concern behind the specific content of the theory helps us to understand Locke's interest in agricultural reparations, as well as Locke's concern with creating a carefully limited class of legitimate slaves."[59] Unfortunately, taking into consideration Locke's Enlightenment prowess and his theory of knowledge, he considers these actions "just." Woolhouse contends that "the *Second Treatise* does allow the taking of slaves as 'captives . . . in a just war,' such as a defensive war waged by innocents against an aggressor; for such captives have, by putting themselves into a state of war; forfeited their lives. . . . Though there is no consensus on this whole question, there certainly seems to be 'a glaring contradiction between his theories and Afro-American slavery.'"[60]

For Locke, slaves had no claim to their own labor power. Slavery was a state of economic disempowerment and social oppression. The slave had no rights and property but was the property of a free person

---

55. Farr, "'So Vile and Miserable an Estate,'" 271.
56. Farr, "'So Vile and Miserable an Estate,'" 274.
57. Rawley, *Transatlantic Slave Trade*.
58. Hinshelwood, "Carolinian Context," 581.
59. Hinshelwood, "Carolinian Context," 581.
60. Woolhouse, *Locke*, 187.

in civil society. Locke's argument that the slave is a perpetual property of their master and rightless can be best seen in the illegality of Black marriages at the time. Black families were raised as economic units and chattel bodies that were frequently broken up and sold. According to Du Bois, under slavery, Blacks had no "legal marriage, no legal family, no legal control over children."[61] Civil society enforced the law against the Black family structure and relationships. It has been argued that the root of the contemporary breakdown of the Black family structure can be traced to the American practice of delegitimizing Blacks' relationships and marriages through slavery and mass Black incarceration. Du Bois notes a particular case:

> Fifty dollars reward—Ran away from the subscriber his Negro man Pauladore, commonly called Paul. I understand General R. Y. Hayne has purchased his wife and children from H. L. Pinckney, Esq., and has them now on his plantation at Goose Creek, where, no doubt, the fellow is frequently lurking. "T. Davis."[62]

Locke is well regarded for his arguments concerning private property as an expression of individual natural rights. But while Locke may seem to be inclusive in his argument for the recognition of the rights of every individual and their right to own property, Black people were not included. He regarded Black people as slaves with no right in civil society. For Locke, a slave is a property and cannot own property.

This book contends that Locke's concept of property is best understood alongside his economic activities as a slave trader. According to Judith Richards et al., Locke's use of the term "property" in the *Two Treatises of Government* is "consistently inclusive."[63] Locke provides three major arguments in support of the right to own property. Furthermore, in these arguments, Locke references the Bible and Christian theology as justifications of this right—like his argument against baptizing slaves, as we shall see. Locke constructs his argument for property as a theo-political argument. The references to "God," "the Bible," and "Scripture" provide support for Locke's argument and give slavery a divine validation.

> One: the individual has right to acquire property freely—"How men might have come to have property in several parts of that

---

61. Du Bois, *Darkwater*, 169.
62. Du Bois, *Darkwater*, 169.
63. Richards, Mulligan, and Graham, "'Property' and 'People,'" 29.

> which God gave to Mankind in common, and that without any express compact of all the commoners."[64]

Two: "man must control his own person by owning property. 'Though the Earth and all inferior creatures be common to all men, yet every man has a property in his own person. This nobody has any Right to but himself. The labor of his body, and the work of his hands, we must say, are properly his.'"[65]

Three: an individual is a person who owns property in himself as a person. "Whatsoever he removes out of the State that Nature hath provided, and left in it, he hath mixed his Labor with and joyned (joined) to it something that his own, and thereby makes it his property."[66]

Locke argued that God has granted the right to all to own property. This seemingly egalitarian notion of property is tainted by Eurocentrism and racism. Similarly, the poor, illiterate, unenlightened, and uncivilized cannot be property owners and as such cannot be political leaders. The right to own property is only given to the "rational." For Locke, rationality is not innate. It is an empirical experience. According to Richards et al., Locke contends:

> God gave the world "to the use of the Industrious and Rational." Thus, Locke was able to justify the ownership of property by the contemporary landowners and gentry, since appropriation had marked that class as the most rational. . . . With Locke the difference in rationality was not inherent in men, not implanted in them by God or Nature; on the contrary, it was socially acquired by virtue of different economic positions.[67]

Locke did not believe in the innate intellectual capacity of all. This rejection enables Locke to argue for rights as socially and politically engendered. According to Thomas Peardon, "There is an obvious inconsistency between the concept of inherent individual rights contained in the *Second Treatise* and the rejection of innate ideas which is so prominent in his general philosophy."[68] Richards et al. note: "Slaves were carefully distin-

64. Locke, *Two Treatises of Government*, sec. 25.
65. Locke, *Two Treatises of Government*, sec. 27.
66. Locke, *Two Treatises of Government*, secs. 25–51, 123–26.
67. Richards, Mulligan, and Graham, "'Property' and 'People.'"
68. Locke, *Second Treatise of Government*, xxi.

guished from all other men by the loss of those attributes; this argument was also part of Locke's answer to Filmer's insistence that originally all men but the king had been slaves. Locke said that slaves were those men who had, by their actions."[69]

He asserts the value of one's labor as the fundamental condition for owning property. If labor is the necessary means of owning property, what prevents one's use of labor to hold another human being as property?

In Lockean slavery, the master owns the entire production of the slave labor as his property. The slave's existence is to meet the demands of the master.[70] Lockean slavery is also forfeiture of the right to one's power of labor.[71] The master owned the labor-power and production of the slave.

Locke's defense of slavery perpetuates the claims of a legitimate caste system based on race and economic interest.[72] According to Cornel West:

> The great paradox of Western modernity is that democracy flourished for Europeans, especially men of property, alongside the flowering of the transatlantic slave trade and New World slavery. Global capitalism and nascent nationalism were predicated initially on terrors and horrors visited on enslaved Africans on the way to, or in, the New World. This tragic springboard of modernity, in which good and evil are inextricably interlocked, still plagues us. The repercussions and ramifications of this paradox still confine and circumscribe us—in our fantasies and dreams, our perceptions and practices—in these catastrophic times.[73]

---

69. Richards, Mulligan, and Graham, "'Property' and 'People,'" 37.
70. Bair, *Prison Labor in the United States*, 12.
71. Bair, *Prison Labor in the United States*, 13.
72. Bair, *Prison Labor in the United States*, 12.
73. West, *Cornel West Reader*, 52.

AFRICANS ON THE AUCTION BLOCK IN EUROPE

With the arrival of the ships, the human auction began.
On the slave market, Africans were bought and sold.
The trading was public, with the human goods advertised.
The auction was private, with red ribbons on the doors.

Like things, Europeans sold their African slaves off.
For their plantations, they were auctioned for all to purchase.
Like cows and horses, they reduced Africans to cattle.
For pleasure, Europeans scrambled for a Buck or a Wench.

Pieces of cotton they picked for their superiors' comfort,
For rum and sugar, they were worked to death.
Cities they built like Liverpool, Bristol, London, DC, Paris...
For the slave had no right that the Whiteman must recognize.

African dignity Europeans painfully sought to distort.
Their African dignity Europeans spit upon.
Their human dignity Europeans destroyed for gain.
This human cruelty Europeans could not abandon.

As goods of pray, Africans were their means of wealth.
The economic gains were worth the cruelty.
To trade in humans, their hearts were cold.
The Africans they saw as economic units.[74]

GEORGE WALTERS-SLEYON

---

74. Walters-Sleyon, *Nuggets from the Night,* 181.

6

Lockean Religion: Baptism and Deism

Since charity obliges us to wish well to the souls of all men, and religion ought to alter nothing in any man's civil estate or right, it shall be lawful for slaves, as well as others, to enter themselves, and be of what church or profession any of them shall think best, and, therefore, be as fully members as any freeman.[1]

THIS CHAPTER PROVIDES AN IMPORTANT analysis of what I refer to as *the Lockean religion*. The chapter considers the framework of Locke's concept of religion and his theological arguments concerning slavery and the status of the slave in civil society. It analyzes Locke's religious arguments based on his theological views: latitudinarianism, natural theology, and deism.[2]

    1. Locke, "Fundamental Constitutions of Carolina, 1669," para. 98.
    2. Eisenach, *Two Worlds of Liberalism*, 84. "Locke's attempt to reconcile natural law, psychological empiricism, and religious faith was continuous. His purposes in writing the *Reasonableness* and its vindications confirms this larger task. These works are efforts to convince deists and other 'skeptics' that Scripture does not stand in the way of constructing a coherent world on the basis of reason. Locke, however, has another purpose as well, that of relating both moral knowledge and religious faith to history and to political life" (*Reasonableness*, no. 241, 170–71, and no. 243, 178, in Eisenach, *Two Worlds of Liberalism*).

Locke vehemently rejected religious faith as the ground for any intellectual, sociopolitical, legal, and economic worldview. He believed that reason is the fundamental means by which worldviews are established and sustained. Locke was resistant to the concept of innateness: the idea that every human being is born with an inherent capacity to think, to derive knowledge either by revelation, inspiration, or nonempirical means without reference to physical experiences. For Locke, what we know and how we know it must be based on experience. Innateness, he argued, is based on "opinions," religious dogmatism, and the domain of religious enthusiasts.[3] He contends that knowledge is based on and derived primarily from physical experience. It is the assertion of a materialist and naturalist means of knowing. Locke's refusal to accept the importance of innateness demonstrates his rejection of revelation. In the *Essay Concerning Human Understanding*, he writes, "There can be no evidence, that any traditional Revelation is of divine Original, in the Words we receive it, and in the sense, we understand it, so clear, and so certain, as that of the Principles of Reason."[4] Locke refers to the five senses as the basis of knowledge.[5] What is called revelation is not validated by religious inspiration, intuition, or illumination, but rather by the senses and human rational capacity.[6]

This book contends that Locke's naturalist rejection of the concept of innateness is inextricable from his rejection of the concept that every human has inherent dignity. The logical trajectory of this naturalist and materialist perception of human beings is the wholesale support of some as perpetual slaves and others as perpetually free, as demonstrated in Locke's engagement in the slave trade.

3. Biddle, "Locke's Critique," 412. "On the other hand, he sought to refute those who would extend man's inquiries beyond the capacities of human understanding. Such efforts to know more than the limits of understanding allowed and to claim certain knowledge where only probability could be attained, led in Locke's view only to disputes, wranglings, increased doubts, and in turn to 'perfect Scepticism.' What 'gave the first Rise to this *Essay* concerning the Understanding,' then, was the concern 'to search out the *Bounds* between Opinion and Knowledge,' and to examine the means by which man ought to regulate his assent in matters of probability and thereby govern his actions. With such a purpose in mind he attacked the theory of innate principles, not only because it granted more to human understanding than could rightly be claimed, but also because it seemed to Locke to threaten morality and revealed religion."

4. Locke, *Essay Concerning Human Understanding*, 10. "Principles of reason" here refer to particular knowledge associated with intuition or demonstration.

5. In this context, Locke's epistemology is Aristotelian and materialist.

6. Biddle, "Locke's Critique," 417. "Locke seems to have believed that reason could confirm some of Scripture and could falsify none of it; thus reason's judgment of Scripture's content corroborated its conclusion from external evidence."

The analysis in this chapter, therefore, begins with Locke's opinion on the prevailing practice of baptizing slaves. Locke concludes that while slaves might be baptized, baptism does not absolve them of their social status either religiously or politically as slaves. For Locke, the slave remains a slave in the church and a slave in the civil society and baptism cannot change it.

CHRISTIAN BAPTISM IS NOT FREEDOM FROM SLAVERY

In the early part of the seventeenth century, baptizing slaves in Britain and the colonies was considered a form of Christianization that led to both social and spiritual freedom for slaves. In 1610 Walter Aubrey, a slave from Sudan, became Haringey's first Black person to be baptized followed by Francis in Bristol in 1645.[7] According to Peter Fryer:

> Katherine Auker asked the Middlesex sessions in 1690 to discharge her from her master; a Barbados planter called Robert Rich, who had brought her to England about six years before. When she had herself baptized—a ceremony widely but wrongly supposed to confer freedom on slaves—her master and mistress "tortured and turned her out"; her said master refusing to give her a discharge, she could not be entertained in service elsewhere.[8]

According to Folarin Shyllon, slaves in Britain sought baptism as a form of freedom from their masters. Similarly, some ministers argued that baptism implied freedom in the church and in civil society.[9] Baptism was viewed as a form of "emancipation."

> 1664, March 12. Duke of York's Patent: Slavery Regulated.
> "Lawes establisht by the Authority of his Majesties Letters patents, granted to his Royall Highnes James Duke of Yorke and Albany; Bearing Date the 12th Day of March in the Sixteenth year of the Raigne of our Soveraigne Lord Kinge Charles the Second." First published at Long Island in 1664.
> "Bond slavery": "No Christian shall be kept in Bondslavery villenage or Captivity, Except Such who shall be Judged thereunto by Authority, or such as willingly have sould, or shall sell themselves,"

---

7. Shyllon, *Black People*.
8. Fryer, *Staying Power*, 23.
9. Fryer, *Staying Power*.

etc. Apprenticeship allowed. Charter to William Penn and Laws of the Province of Pennsylvania (1879), pp. 3, 12.[10]

The above patent shows the extent to which Christianization of slaves became a major challenge to slave traders, slave masters, and advocates of African slavery in the church and the larger society.

However, considering the rush to baptism, laws were enacted forbidding slaves from being baptized.[11] In 1667, the state of Virginia passed "An Act declaring that baptisme of slaves doth not exempt them from bondage."[12] The practice of baptizing for freedom was not unheard of. In 1670 and 1682, laws were passed in Virginia, making the designation "Christian" a mark for enslavement or freedom from enslavement. These laws and those that follow serve as part of the legal foundation for the racialization of Christianity. Furthermore, these laws provided the platform for the religious justification of slavery.[13]

David B. Davis notes that it was established in English law in the 1700s when "the Attorney-General and Solicitor-General gave their formal opinions that baptism could not alter the temporal condition of a slave within the British Kingdoms."[14] Furthermore, there was a debate in Virginia as to whether to use the term "Christian" to refer to converted or baptized slaves. The implication was that no Christian could be a slave or enslaved; conversion, and particularly baptism, was perceived as a form of emancipation. According to Finkelman, Virginia had to stop the practice because it did not favor the economic welfare of slave masters. "English settlers in seventeenth-century Virginia initially believed that conversion would emancipate slaves. Thus, many masters apparently refused to allow the Church of England to teach and convert their slaves.... The goal of this act was to 'more carefully endeavor the propagation of Christianity by permitting' slaves 'to be admitted to that sacrament.'"[15] Thus, it was just and legal to enslave none-Christians.[16] Locke's reason for the rejection of baptizing slaves is based on his argument that baptism is a religious practice and slavery is a social and economic enterprise. These

10. Du Bois, *Suppression of the African Slave-Trade*, 202.
11. Woodson, *History of the Negro Church*.
12. General Assembly, "Act Declaring That Baptisme."
13. Finkelman, "Slavery in the United States," 113.
14. Davis, *Problem of Slavery*, 209.
15. Finkelman, *Defending Slavery*, 12.
16. Finkelman, *Defending Slavery*, 110.

are two distinctions in his claims. Similarly, to keep slaves unbaptized meant they could not be accorded Christian sympathies and tolerance. Locke basically decided that baptized or unbaptized, Blacks were slaves and second-class human beings, not even citizens in the civil society.

Locke's rejection of baptism for slaves is couched in religious terms. As secretary and author of the Fundamental Constitutions of Carolina, Locke was aware of the angst associated with slavery in the seventeenth century. Slaves were beginning to perceive baptism and membership in the church as a means of freedom. According to Jennifer Welchman,

> If Locke was defensive about anything, it was about his advocacy of tolerance for slaves' religious beliefs. It was sometimes argued in the seventeenth century that the Old Testament injunction against the enslavement of Jews by Jews was a ban against the enslavement of one's co-religionists that applied to Christians as well. So if a Christian's slave were to become a Christian, the owner would be obliged to set his slave free. Religious tolerance could thus cost a slave-owner dearly.[17]

Slave owners refused to baptize their slaves for fear they could be convicted of the immorality and ungodliness of slavery and the slave trade after they were baptized. They were also afraid that they could be forced to abandon the slave trade and the institution of slavery, and Locke was no exception. The prevailing belief was that Christians could not enslave Christians. For his part, Locke argued that Christian baptism could not change the civil status of any slave: once a slave always a slave.[18] He writes, "Religion ought to alter nothing in any man's civil estate.... But yet no slave shall hereby be exempted from that civil dominion his master hath over him, but in all other things in the same state and condition, he was in before."[19] Locke established a clear distinction between religious freedom and civil freedom. The slave was a slave in civil society. For Locke, the slave is always a slave regardless of whether he or she went to church. In *Paraphrase and Notes on the Epistles of St Paul* Locke writes, "A man should not think himself discharged, by the privilege of his Christian state and the franchise of the Kingdom of Christ which he was entered into, from any ties or obligations he was in as a member of

---

17. Welchman, "Locke on Slavery," 74.
18. Farr, "'So Vile and Miserable an Estate,'" 266.
19. Farr, "'So Vile and Miserable an Estate,'" 266.

the civil society. . . . The thinking themselves freed by Christianity were very apt to run into."[20]

In his book *The Negro's and Indian's Advocate, Suing for Their Admission into the Church,* Morgan Godwyn, an Anglican missionary in Virginia and Barbados, challenged wealthy elites regarding the religious state of slaves and Indians from 1665 to 1680. Farr quotes Morgan to support his claim that Locke was justified for not accepting the argument and practices of those who saw baptizing slaves as initiation into the church and freedom in civil society.[21] He claims that Locke had a "supplemental" copy of Godwyn's book.[22]

Godwyn saw the proselytization of slaves as an important religious obligation in the British colonies. According to John Fout, Godwyn argued that converted slaves and slave masters "were spiritual equals."[23] Regarding proselytization in the colonies, Godwyn wrote that "we are only charged with the Neglect [of proselytizing], I shall not add the opposing of it; that being the Crime of such degenerated English, who with that air, have imbibed the Barbarity and Heathenism of the Countries they live in: And with whom, through the want of Discipline, Christianity doth seem to be wholly lost, and nothing but Infidelity to have come in its place."[24] Fout contends that Godwyn's proselytization of slaves did include the baptism of "two enslaved Africans while in Virginia," a claim that is contested.[25] However, slave baptism engendered resistance from slave masters including the religious and social elites.

In 1657, Richard Ligon visited the Island of Barbados and recorded his experience in *True & Exact History of the Island of Barbados.* While Christianity was foreign to most slaves, Ligon nonetheless concluded that slaves were candidates for Christian evangelism. He recorded a statement from a slave master whose slave Ligon had wanted to convert to Christianity. He writes, "Being once a Christian, he could no more account him a Slave, and so lose the hold they had of them as Slaves, by making them Christians; and by that means should open such a gap, as all the Planters in the land would curse him."[26] The slave master was afraid that by allow-

20. Welchman, "Locke on Slavery," 74.
21. Farr, "'So Vile and Miserable an Estate,'" 266.
22. Farr, "'So Vile and Miserable an Estate,'" 266.
23. Fout, "Explosive Cleric," 55.
24. Godwyn, *Negro's & Indian's Advocate,* iv.
25. Fout, "Explosive Cleric," 55.
26. Gerbner, "Ultimate Sin," 60.

ing his slave to be baptized, he was establishing a precedent that other slave masters would frown upon and hold him in contempt.

It was common knowledge that slave masters in Barbados treated their slaves with extreme cruelty. This can be seen in the Barbados law codes of 1661, in which slave masters in Barbados referred to Africans as "heathenish, brutish and dangerous people."[27] In 1676, slaves in Barbados were barred from accessing "skilled craft professions"; a further pronouncement in 1681 declared Africans "wholly incapable of conversion to Christianity."[28] According to Katharine Gerbner, "For proselytizing Christians in the late seventeenth century, Barbados was not a welcoming place. For those concerned with the souls of Africans and Creole slaves, it was openly hostile."[29] Proselytizing slaves was deemed "pointless" and "destructive" to the financial interests of those in power.

In contrast to the slave owners, the Quakers of Barbados converted slaves and brought them into their worship meetings. In 1676, the Assembly of Barbados passed a Quaker Negro Act called "An Act to Prevent the People called Quakers from bringing Negroes to their Meeting." The Act ignited the persecution of Quakers for their tolerance and conversion of slaves. Gerbner notes that "Quakers were persecuted for allowing their slaves to meet for worship. These arrests marked the first time any Protestant group in the British West Indies had been persecuted for missionary activity."[30]

For his part, Godwyn provided "logical justifications" for including Africans and Indians in the Anglican Church. In one of these writings, Godwyn notes:

> That the Negro's (both Slaves and others) have naturally an equal Right with other Men, to the Exercise and Privileges of Religion; of which 'tis most unjust in any part to deprive them.
> *First*, That *naturally* there is in every Man an equal *Right to Religion*.
> *Secondly*, That *Negro's* are Men, and therefore are invested with the *same Right*.
> *Thirdly*, That being thus qualified and invested, to deprive them of the *Right* is the *highest injustice*.[31]

27. Fout, "Explosive Cleric," 66.
28. Fout, "Explosive Cleric," 66.
29. Gerbner, "Ultimate Sin," 57.
30. Gerbner, "Ultimate Sin," 58.
31. Godwyn, *Negro's & Indian's Advocate*, chap. 1.

LOCKEAN RELIGION: BAPTISM AND DEISM

Anti-slavery advocates like the Quakers registered their disgust for the human trade as anti-biblical and anti-Christian. They saw the institution of slavery as sinful and a gross distortion of the image of God—the *imago Dei* in every human being. According to Gilbert Osofsky, abolitionists condemned slavery as reducing human beings to "thinghood." He writes,

> Enslaving men is reducing them to articles of property—making free agents, chattels—converting *persons* into *things*—sinking immortality into *merchandise*. We repeat it, the reduction of persons to things! Not robbing a man of privileges, but of himself; not loading him with burdens, but making him a beast of burden; not restraining liberty, but his neighbor of a cent, yet commission him to rob his neighbor of himself? . . . Slaveholding is the highest possible violation of the eight[h] commandment.[32]

However, Fout contends that Godwyn had another agenda: the defense of the Church of England and the British Crown. "Godwyn's challenges to Barbadian slaveholders and Virginian vestrymen threatened to take away the high societal positions they had grasped for themselves. Godwyn's intention was to counteract the trends he observed in English colonial societies."[33] Fout explains that Godwyn was concerned about wealthy slave merchants using their wealth to amass sociopolitical and economic control. "To Godwyn, power was properly placed in the hands of the English Crown and its spiritual arm, the Church of England. Together these two entities had ruled England and should continue to rule."[34] According to Fout, Godwyn was also a missionary in Virginia and Barbados who advocated the proselytization of slaves into the Anglican Church in Virginia.

In contrast to some of Fout's claims about Godwyn, in *A Supplement to the Negro's & Indian's Advocate*, Godwyn explicitly refused to endorse baptizing slaves. Farr also notes that Locke "owned" a copy of Godwyn's *A Supplement*.[35] According to Bernasconi and Mann, Locke was in "full agreement with Godwyn's position"; interestingly, Godwyn "was also a former student of Locke."[36]

---

32. Osofsky, *Burden of Race*, 88–89.
33. Fout, "Explosive Cleric," 17.
34. Fout, "Explosive Cleric," 17.
35. Farr, "'So Vile and Miserable an Estate,'" 285.
36. Bernasconi and Mann, "Contradictions of Racism," 94.

Bernasconi and Mann disagree with the claims of Fout. They argue that Godwyn was mainly interested in harmonizing the religious and economic interests of the Church of England, which was concerned about the planters and slave traders who needed slaves. In addition, Bernasconi and Mann indicate that "in an effort to reassure the planters further, he [Godwyn] later wrote a tract that portrayed the slave as more interested in baptism than freedom."[37] According to Turner:

> Notwithstanding his insistence on Negroes' humanity, Godwyn does not characterize their enslavement as unjust. *The Negro's & Indian's Advocate* takes for granted that African slavery will continue indefinitely. Godwyn even recommends in *A Supplement to the Negro's & Indian's Advocate* that colonial assemblies pass laws stipulating that baptism in no way alters slaves' civil status as property; this way, owners have no financial incentive to prevent slaves' baptism.[38]

Turner contends that Locke was an avid supporter of evangelizing Indians and slaves. He argues that Locke's collaboration with James Blair on the Board of Trade Bishop of London's Commissary in Virginia led to the publication of the "Grievances of Virginia."[39] This document focuses on "the reorganization" of Virginia's government and its economy. However, a major portion reflects on the Christian mission and religion. Locke and Blair criticized that "little care is taken to instruct the Indian and Negroes in the Christian faith. . . . The Conversion, and Instruction of Negroes and Indians is a work of such importance and difficulty that it would require a Treatise of itself."[40] Turner emphasizes that Locke and Blair felt that they had a Christian mission to "negroes." The problem is that Locke did not care whether they were baptized or not in civil society. Blacks and Indians were second class and at most slaves including their children. Also, Locke and Blair were focused not on Negroes as free people, but rather on Negroes as slaves. The document emphasizes the importance of baptizing Negro and Indian children in contrast to adult Negroes or Indians. Locke had already rejected the practice of baptizing slaves. The document states:

---

37. Bernasconi and Mann, "Contradictions of Racism," 94.
38. Turner, "John Locke," 273.
39. Turner, "John Locke," 282.
40. Turner, "John Locke," 282.

> That all Negroes be brought to Church on Sundays.... That a law be made, that all Negroes children be baptized—catechized, and bred Christians.... That as many Indian children be educated at the College [of William and Mary] as may be; and these well instructed in the Christian Faith (but with all keeping their own language), and made fit to evangelize others of their nation and language.[41]

Turner also notes that Locke rejects what he calls "mandatory church attendance."[42] This was Locke's way of rejecting King Louis XIV's mandate that all French Protestants attend Catholic mass. In "A Third Letter of Toleration," Locke refers to baptism as a "truly essential Christian rite."[43] However, Locke's seemingly positive description of Christian baptism must be viewed skeptically considering his previous claims about Christian baptism and slaves, just as his support of African slavery must contextualize his rejection of slavery for "English men" or Europeans.

Locke, like Godwyn, did not endorse the baptism of slaves and Indians. The question of Christian baptism for slaves as a means of emancipation was important in seventeenth-century North America. Turner notes that in 1664, the colony of Maryland enacted a law stipulating that the term "African servitude" was a *durante vita*. Similarly, Virginia passed a law in 1667 that Christian baptism was not equivalent to manumission. Turner writes, "The Virginia House of Burgesses framed this latter law as an effort to 'free masters from doubt' about the effects of baptism on their slaves' civil status, and thus to make them more likely to allow evangelization on their plantations."[44]

An apparent contradiction in Locke's defense of slavery and reflection on baptism is shown in his reference to St. Paul's first letter to the Corinthians. According to Locke, baptizing slaves and admitting them to Christianity does not alter their civil status as slaves. Christianity cannot change their legal status as property. To provide a biblical justification for his argument, Locke quotes the apostle St. Paul from 1 Corinthians 7:20–24:

> Christianity gives not anyone any new privilege to change the state ... which he was in before. Wert thou called, being a slave? In whatsoever state a man is called, in the same he is to remain, notwithstanding any privileges of the gospel, which

---

41. Turner, "John Locke," 282.
42. Turner, "John Locke," 284.
43. Locke, *Third Letter for Toleration*, 154–56.
44. Turner, "John Locke," 279.

gives him no dispensation, or exemption, from any obligation he was in before (*The Works of John Locke* [10 vols.' London, 1801] VIII, 116–17).[45]

Locke failed to acknowledge the fact that St. Paul would have condemned the capturing, trafficking, and cruelties meted on Africans in the name of Christianity. First Corinthians 7:20–24 was one of the pivotal passages proslavery advocates used to defend the industrial slave trade and the institution of chattel slavery. Locke was conversant with the practice and in quoting 1 Corinthians 7:20–24, Locke was reaffirming his proslavery and White-supremacist positions as well as his full participation in the industrial slave trade and chattel slavery.

Unfortunately for Locke and the proslavery advocates, Christianity asserts a fundamental concept of equalitarianism found in the sayings, writings, and healing ministries of Jesus Christ and the apostles, including St. Paul. Witte explains, "The New Testament also called for equality. Saint Paul's manifesto to the Galatians famously declared: 'There is neither Jew nor Greek, there is neither slave nor free, there is neither male nor female; for you are all now in Christ Jesus.'[46] This radical Christian message of human equality trumped conventional Greco-Roman hierarchies based on birth, nationality, social status, gender, and more."[47] In contrast to Saint Paul, Locke advanced arguments for the propagation of a system of inherent social inequality found in the enslavement of Africans.

Locke's conclusion on the issue of baptizing slaves as a precursor to freedom provides insights into his notion of religion and religious "tolerance."[48] Locke's concept of tolerance is limited and not equalitarian. He was certainly intolerant of people of African descent. In contrast to Locke, Jesus Christ teaches and exemplifies the concepts of tolerance, justice, right, fairness, respect, and liberty. According to Witte, "The New Testament was even more radical in its call to treat the 'least' members of society with love, respect, and dignity. Jesus took pains to minister to the social outcasts of his day—Samaritans, tax collectors, prostitutes, thieves, traitors, lepers, the lame, the blind, the adulteress, and others."[49]

45. Glausser, "Three Approaches," 204.
46. Gal 3:26–28; see also Col 3:11; Eph 2:14–15.
47. Witte, *Blessing of Liberty*, 23.
48. Locke, *Letter Concerning Toleration*.
49. Witte, *Blessing of Liberty*, 21. "See e.g., Luke 10:25–37; Matthew 9:10; Luke 7:36–50; Matthew 21:31; Mark 15:27; Matthew 8:3; Mark 2:1–12; Mark 8:22–25; John 8:1–15."

LOCKE AND DEISM

Locke was an avowed deist.[50] He rejected and, on numerous occasions, spoke and wrote against orthodox Christianity.[51] It became common knowledge that Locke was a latitudinarian and a member of the latitudinarian club of the Church of England. In 1668, Benjamin Whichcote, a prominent latitudinarian of the Cambridge School, was appointed vicar of St. Lawrence Jewry parish in London. It was this parish Locke selected to attend regularly. Cranston notes that latitudinarians "believed that Christians should unite on the broad common ground of essentials in religion while agreeing to differ over nonessentials; they all believed that reason could be relied upon to determine what was and what was not essential."[52] According to Woolhouse, "Locke concluded that the natural means by which we *do* acquire our knowledge of natural law indeed is 'the light of nature.'"[53]

Latitudinarianism was associated with the emphasis on rational theology in the Church of England. It began as a theological movement at Oxford University in the 1630s under the leadership of Lucius Cary, Viscount Falkland, William Chillingworth, and John Hales. According to Cranston:

> These men were loyal Anglicans, conservatives and Royalists, and Laud, a man liberal in theological opinion however imperious in ecclesiastical government, protected them. Chillingworth and Hales did not recommend toleration for mere prudential reasons, but they did believe that to strip the Christian doctrine

---

50. Reedy, "Socinians," 186. "The exact origins of deism are hard to trace. Herbert of Cherbury's *De religione laici* (1645) may or may not make him the father of deism in England; Herbert's modern commentator doubts that any school can be traced to him. 'The deists,' writes Harold Hutcheson, 'were individual religious malcontents.'"

51. Hefelbower, "'Deism Historically Defined,'" 223. "In an age that was rationalistic and critical, when all progressive thinkers, many of whom were conservative, felt that they must justify religion by proving it from reason and nature, the deists developed those tendencies in a radical way, and fostered a hostile attitude toward traditional supernaturalism. They denied the possibility of any religious truth above reason; they challenged external revelation and criticized its records and the miraculous; they emphasized the perfection of natural religion, which man of his own unaided powers could know, and set it up as supreme over all positive religion, which was imperfect because of 'mysteries,' 'uncertainties,' 'contradictions,' and 'confusion.'"

52. Cranston, *John Lock*, 125–27.

53. Woolhouse, *Locke*, 56.

down to its bare essentials would have the effect of broadening the national Church so that all could join.⁵⁴

Their focus was on the rational analysis of theological claims and the centralization of reason in theological discourse. The movement's goal was the intentional disintegration of church dogmas with adherence to a minimum number of creeds. In other words, latitudinarians were also Socinians—but minimally and with pejorative connotations. According to Syse, "the Socinians were a religious group, founded by Faustus Socinus (d. 1604), with a unitarian and minimalist theology. They were deemed heretical by most factions of the Church.... Locke was quite obviously influenced by the Socinians; yet, he repeatedly defended himself against accusations of actually being a Socinian."⁵⁵ The main doctrinal positions of Socinianism are summarized as:

4. Immortality is a supernatural gift.
5. The meaning of Christ's death is to show that man can partake in life after death.
6. Before Christ's coming, mankind had no reason to believe that there was a law of right and wrong, enforced by other-worldly punishment.⁵⁶

According to Gerard Reedy, the doctrinal claims of Socinianism can be summarized as such.

- That God is one person, not three.
- That Jesus is a messenger, minister, servant, creature, and son of God, but not God almighty and eternal.
- That the Holy Spirit is the power of God, but not God himself.
- That Jesus is a man raised up by the Father
- Rejects the implications of Christ's death and resurrection as evidence of God's redemptive act for humanity and Christ as the sacrifice for sin.⁵⁷

The Socinians rejected the standard Christian doctrines including the Trinity, the divinity of Jesus Christ, and the divinity of the Holy Spirit.

54. Cranston, *John Locke*, 125.
55. Syse, *Natural Law, Religion, and Rights*, 225.
56. Syse, *Natural Law, Religion, and Rights*, 225.
57. Reedy, "Socinians," 285.

Philosophically, latitudinarianism was associated with the Cambridge Platonists—a school of metaphysical philosophy. According to Cranston:

> Socinianism was Latitudinarianism pushed to its logical conclusion; and a particular characteristic of the Latitudinarians was that they did *not* push things to their logical conclusion. They would not have thought of doing anything to immoderate. . . . The Latitudinarians were attached to their Church, which, like Hooker, they regarded as a national institution to which all Englishmen could properly belong, not as a brotherhood of saints or as a society of men of identical persuasions. The Church of England allowed considerable variety of interpretations of her creed, and the Latitudinarians believed in taking every advantage of that liberty.[58]

As Gilbert Burnet, a colleague of Locke and fellow Latitudinarian of the Cambridge School, wrote in 1663, the Latitudinarians did not believe in the supernatural or what they refer to as religious "enthusiasm."[59]

The publication of Locke's *Reasonableness of Christianity* in 1695 generated much controversy due to its theological arguments. John Edwards wasted no time in making public the Socinian bent of the book. According to John Dunn, "Socinianism, [is] a recondite Continental heresy stressing the authority of reason and scripture which rejected the doctrine of the Trinity and which Edwards himself roundly equated with atheism."[60] In 1696, Locke also encountered a "formidable" attack consisting of accusations that he was a Socinian. These attacks came at the hands of the famous Anglican apologist and Bishop of Worcester Edward Stillingfleet. During the "Exclusionary controversy," these attacks were "especially damaging." Dunn intimates that "Socinianism (unlike that of atheism) was an extremely plausible one to level at Locke's religious views."[61]

Stillingfleet chose to accuse Locke based on the content of his argument in the *Essay* instead of the *Reasonableness*. Locke was concerned about these attacks on his works in 1690. His doctrines were considered a "threat to religion" and "orthodox beliefs."[62] Locke delved into the writing of lengthy responses to Stillingfleet.[63] According to Yolton:

58. Cranston, *John Locke*, 126.
59. Cranston, *John Locke*, 127.
60. Dunn, *Locke*, 19.
61. Dunn, *Locke*, 19.
62. Yolton, *Locke*, 4.
63. Locke, *Letter Concerning Toleration*.

Locke's doctrines were called most of the bad names of the day: sceptical, Socinian, Deist, Hobbist, even atheistical. His *Reasonableness of Christianity* was banned by the Grand Jury of Middlesex in 1697, and the Essay was censored by some of the Heads of Colleges at Oxford in 1703. As late as 1768, the Essay was placed on the Index of Prohibited Books by the Royal Censor Board in Portugal.[64]

While Locke was not the founder of deism, he was religiously a "deist."[65] His religious inclinations were natural, rationalistic, and material. According to Sahakian and Sahakian, "Inspired by the deistic movement and occasionally identified as a deist, Locke, who was negative toward traditional Christianity and an early adherent of theistic movement, nevertheless did endorse a number of Christian doctrines. Perhaps it would be more accurate to regard him as a forerunner of deism."[66]

In contrast to traditional faith, religious authority, and what deists called "religious dogmatism," deism represented the centralization of human reasoning rather than faith. In his own words Locke credits his belief in deism to the influence of Lord Herbert and the Cambridge Platonists. He writes, "When I had writ this, being informed that my Lord Herbert had in his book *De Veritate* assigned these innate principles, I presently consulted him, hoping to find, in a man of so great parts, something that might satisfy me in this point and put an end to my inquiry."[67] While they believe in the concept of creation, deists reject the role of God's direct intervention in world affairs. They believe that, after creation, God withdrew from the universe in order for natural law based on rationality to govern it.[68] In addition, deism rejects the standard doctrines of the church. Deism:

- Rejects the major doctrines of the church.
- Rejects the necessity of the creed.

---

64. Yolton, *Locke*, 4.
65. Reedy, "Socinians," 186.
66. Sahakian and Sahakian, *John Locke*, 34.
67. Locke, *Essay Concerning Human Understanding.*, bk. 1, chap. 3, sec. 15.
68. Syse, *Natural Law, Religion, and Rights*, 190. "Indeed, Locke uses as one of his authorities the Anglican divine Richard Hooker who was a Thomist and certainly no radical. Thus, it has been asserted that Locke's theory of natural law owes more to Thomism than to the emerging modern theory of rights found in, for instance, Thomas Hobbes."

- Rejects the traditional concept of salvation, miracles, and the inspiration of Scripture.[69]

According to Eldon Eisenach, Locke rejected the institutional church and argued instead for what he referred to as the "primitive church." The concept of the primitive church is associated with Locke's notion of "reasonable faith."[70] Referring to King Edward, Locke writes:

> He [Edward] does not observe the difference there is between what is necessary to be believed by every man to *make* him a Christian, and what is *required to be believed* by every Christian. The first of these is what, by the covenant of the Gospel, is necessary to be known, and consequently to be proposed to *every* man, to make him a Christian: the latter is no less than the whole revelation of God, all the divine truths contained in holy Scripture: which every Christian man is under upon his serious and constant endeavours, to enlighten his mind to understand them.[71]

It is argued that Locke wrote *The Reasonableness of Christianity* in order to create a distinction between Christianity as historical, mystical, institutional, and Christianity as rational and natural. Locke prefers philosophy, empiricism, and reason as the nucleus of Christianity. Thus, for Locke, deism became the most appealing religious belief and practice since it asserts a demystification and deinstitutionalization of Christianity. Eisenach notes, "The central argument of *The Reasonableness* transforms Christian faith into a rejection of the institutional history of the church and of the moral and political theories of which it was a part."[72] For the deist, God is no longer immanent but transcendent. Sahakian and Sahakian note:

---

69. Reedy, "Socinians," 285.
70. Eisenach, *Two Worlds of Liberalism*, 97.
71. Locke, *Second Vindication*, 352; italics original.
72. Eisenach, *Two Worlds of Liberalism*, 86–88. "Philosophy, by itself, is as impotent as the law of nature so long as supernatural religion defines men's moral opinions. Exactly paralleling Hobbes's argument, Locke argues that Christ's coming divorced religion from this history even though Christ's followers soon made the church an engine of earthly advantage and morality a servant of priestly and despotic interest. Locke explicitly places both himself and the task of philosophy within the time frame of sacred history. When mankind was under the sway of false religious doctrine, philosophers were shouting to the winds. Only *now*, when religious reformation is ushering in a new age does it become the task of the philosopher to outline the entire set of duties appropriate for men. Only *now* is a willing audience assembled to listen, for only now does reformed religion support the conclusions of true moral philosophy."

This view of a transcendent God who remains absent or beyond his universe is grounded on nature, reason, and morality. Nature reveals God through human reason. By ascertaining the laws of nature through the human intellect, mankind can discern the will of God and fend for himself. The deist rejects belief in miraculous or in supernatural intervention because it implies the disruption of natural laws.[73]

An important aspect of Locke's view of religion is the negation of the church as an institution and its ecclesiastical structure.

Locke: Religion and Civil Government

In his essay *A Letter Concerning Toleration*, Locke claims that "the only business of the Church is the salvation of souls, and it no way concerns the commonwealth or any member of it."[74] It can be argued that here we see Locke establishing the argument for the separation of church and state; his claims became pivotal to Thomas Jefferson's arguments for the separation of church and state in the United States. Locke begins by defining religion and Christianity through a specific notion of "toleration." He writes, "Since you are pleased to inquire what are my thoughts about the mutual toleration of Christians in their different professions of religion, I must needs answer you freely that I esteem that toleration to be the chief characteristic mark of the true Church."[75] Christianity is not about institutional structures, titles, positions, building, designation or "of the pomp of their outward worship; others, of the reformation of their discipline: all, of the orthodoxy of their faith—for everyone is orthodox to himself."[76] Locke was a rationalist and empiricist. He wanted that view to be reflected in his notion of religion and Christianity.

Locke's writings on religion often concerned the "toleration of those that differ from others in matters of religion."[77] Religion must be separated from the activities of civil government or loyalty to the prince or King of England. He writes:

---

73. Sahakian and Sahakian, *John Locke*, 34.
74. Locke, *Letter Concerning Toleration*, 23.
75. Locke, *Letter Concerning Toleration*, 3.
76. Locke, *Letter Concerning Toleration*, 3.
77. Locke, *Letter Concerning Toleration*, 6.

LOCKEAN RELIGION: BAPTISM AND DEISM

> I esteem it above all things necessary to distinguish exactly the business of civil government from that of religion to settle the just bounds that lie between the one and the other. If this be not done, there can be no end put to the controversies that will be always arising between those that have, or at least pretend to have, on the one side, a concernment for the interest of men's souls, and, on the other side, a care of the commonwealth.[78]

The above statement speaks to a fundamental problem that Locke sought to discuss in this letter. The problem is essentially Locke's negation of the authority of the Church of England to tell people what to do or interfere with an individual's right. According to Locke:

> The commonwealth seems to me to be a society of men constituted only for the procuring, preserving, and advancing their own civil interests. Civil interests I call life, liberty, health, and indolency of body; and the possession of outward things, such as money, lands, houses, furniture, and the like. It is the duty of the civil magistrate, by the impartial execution of equal laws, to secure unto all the people in general and to every one of his subjects, in particular, the just possession of these things belonging to this life. If anyone presumes to violate the laws of public justice and equity, established for the preservation of those things, his presumption is to be checked by the fear of punishment, consisting of the deprivation or diminution of those civil interests, or goods, which otherwise he might and ought to enjoy.[79]

In Locke's view, the church should not interfere in secular affairs. Furthermore, the church should not deprive citizens of any secular right. Locke believed that the magistrate and the court should legislate and punish, while the church should concern itself with the care of souls. He writes, "But seeing no man does willingly suffer himself to be punished by the deprivation of any part of his goods, and much less of his liberty or life, therefore, is the magistrate armed with the force and strength of all his subjects, in order to the punishment of those that violate any other man's rights."[80] The importance that Locke placed on the right to own private property and acquire private property was central to his rejection of church interference in judicial or secular affairs. In Locke's own case, this private property included slaves.

78. Locke, *Letter Concerning Toleration*, 6.
79. Locke, *Letter Concerning Toleration*, 6.
80. Locke, *Letter Concerning Toleration*, 6.

To reiterate, Locke was a slave trader while advancing the argument for private property as well as the rejection of the church in the affairs of commerce, state, and social concerns. For Locke, reason and rationality were the main ingredients to moral action, not religious constraints and their moral injunctions. Locke participated in the human trade because it made him wealthy. He considered slaves a part of his private property to be defended against the intrusion of the church or the state.

Locke does not hesitate in making clear the pursuit of capitalist interests and the marginalization of the church from the public sphere. In this regard Locke believed that religion was disrupting the public's freedom to own property, express their thoughts, and live their life as they chose. According to Henrik Syse:

> It is well known that Locke holds human beings to have a natural right to property arising from the need humans have for possessions in order to survive. He explains this right by describing how human beings "mix" their labor with something that is naturally common. This is repeatedly being pointed to as one of the most characteristically "capitalist" traits in Locke.... Property that is not owned by anyone is not for Locke, as it is for Grotius and Hobbes, no one's; rather, it is *everyone's*.[81]

Locke's distinction between the role of the church and the civil government is expressed through what he referred to as the "care of souls" defined under the "business of toleration."[82] Syse contends that Locke held "that land not in use is unproductive, whereas land in use produces more goods not only for the owner, but for all of mankind. Thus, Locke's well-known theory that private property arises when someone mixes his labor with something, does not contradict the common good, according to Locke, but rather serves everyone well."[83] Locke's defense of private property thus provides a philosophical and political defense for chattel slavery.

Fundamentally, "magisterial care," a phrase which describes the role of civil government, "consists in prescribing by laws and compelling by punishments"; it is distinguished from religious care of souls, "which consists in teaching, admonishing, and persuading" of souls.[84]

---

81. Syse, *Natural Law, Religion, and Rights*, 211.
82. Locke, *Letter Concerning Toleration*, 17.
83. Syse, *Natural Law, Religion, and Rights*, 214.
84. Locke, *Two Treatises of Government*, 17, 22. "These religious societies I call Churches; and these, I say, the magistrate ought to tolerate, for the business of these assemblies of the people is nothing but what is lawful for every man in particular to

This distinction explains his position on baptizing slaves. However, we are once again introduced to Locke's defense of religious individualism from a deistic perspective. He provides the following justification:

First, the church should concern itself with the care for souls, "because the care of souls is not committed to the civil magistrate, any more than to other men. It is not committed unto him, I say, by God; because it appears that God has ever given any such authority to one man over another as to compel any to his religion."[85]

Second, the church should concern itself with the soul, the mind, will, intellect, and emotions. He writes: "The care of souls cannot belong to the civil magistrate, because his power consists only in outward force." Locke wanted the church to concentrate on those aspects of human experience that largely concern the establishment and maintenance of religion. Locke did not believe that religion should usurp humanity's rational capacity.

Third, the church should care about the salvation of souls and not the civil government or the magistrate. Religion, Locke infers, is superstitious and the church is irrational. Locke here argues that rational individuals should not resign themselves to the irrationality of religion and the church. He writes, "Because, though the rigour of laws and the force of penalties were capable to convince and change men's minds yet would not that help at all to the salvation of their souls."[86] According to Locke, the civil government or the magistrate cannot legislate religion. Religion, he contends, is akin to a conscience, and it cannot be forced upon the rational mind. The authority of the civil government is restricted to civil matters. Similarly, the authority of religion or the church is not superior to the independence of reason. Locke provides a concise definition of the church: "A church, then, I take to be a voluntary society of men, joining themselves together of their own accord in order to the public

---

take care of—I mean the salvation of their souls; nor in this case is there any difference between the National Church and other separated congregations. But as in every Church there are two things especially to be considered—the outward form and rites of worship, and the doctrines and articles of things must be handled each distinctly that so the whole matter of toleration may the more clearly be understood. Concerning outward worship, I say, in the first place, that the magistrate has no power to enforce by law, either in his own Church, or much less in another, the use of any rites or ceremonies whatsoever in the worship of God."

85. Locke, *Letter Concerning Toleration*, Montuori, 17–25, 31–33, 45, 55, 65–69, 89, 91, 93.

86. Locke, *Letter Concerning Toleration*, Montuori, 17–25, 31–33, 45, 55, 65–69, 89, 91, 93.

worshipping of God in such manner as they judge acceptable to Him, and effectual to the salvation of their souls."[87] A particular point of interest here is Locke's emphasis on "voluntary." It is an essential element of Locke's individualistic interpretation of religion and the separation of church and state.

---

87. Locke, *Letter Concerning Toleration*, Montuori, 17–25, 31–33, 45, 55, 65–69, 89, 91, 93.

THE RELIGIOUS JUSTIFICATION

The sailing of ships to Africa to Islamize,
The sailing of ships to Africa to Christianize,
The sailing of ships to Arabicize
The sailing of ships to Westernize.

Gold and Ivory the Muslims sought.
In the depletion of their treasures,
Africans, their carriers, the Muslims sold.
To the West, Islam introduced its savage hosts.

In the Middle East, Africans they traded,
Perfect workers, the Arabs considered them to be.
Black pigmentation the Arabs saw beneath them,
But for economic reasons only of value.

Savage, they were in the Middle East.
Cheap labor to provide for their Islamic superiors.
For Islamization, Africans were perfect
Arabization in external reflection.

To Christianize the Africans, the Portuguese came.
They saw their hearts significantly transformed
Since the Africans are "notoriously religious."
But, to enslave them was their prudent choice.

To Christianize the absolute goal.
Christ the Messiah to bring to the weary.
But beneath the Holy Cross was the dungeon's way,
From Elmina Castle to the Middle Passage.[88]

GEORGE WALTERS-SLEYON

---

88. Walters-Sleyon, *Nuggets from the Night*, 117.

7

Lockean Philosophy: Empiricism

THIS CHAPTER PROVIDES AN ANALYSIS of Locke's philosophy in the context of his involvement with the slave trade. It contends that Locke's empiricist philosophy provided the justification for his racism against people of African descent. Locke's attack on innateness in the first book of the *Essay* was an attack on the theological and theistic concept of inherent dignity.[1] His goal was to dismantle it with every philosophical tool at his disposal.

By now, he had already rejected the offer of being a clergyman and the possibility of preaching a dogmatic Christian theology. According to Sterling P. Lamprecht, "Locke's dislike of innate ideas was clearly

---

1. Squadrito, "Racism and Empiricism." "According to both Chomsky and Bracken racism 'Is easily and readily stateable if one thinks of the person in accordance with empiricist teaching.' On the other hand, if one is a Cartesian, 'it becomes impossible to state a racist position.' The contention is that the Cartesian dualist model of the person provides 'a modest conceptual brake to the articulation of racial degradation and slavery,' whereas the empiricist model makes racism particularly easy to justify by 'providing us with ways of counting colour, head shape, language, religion, or IQ as essential properties' of man. Racism supposedly lies outside the context of Cartesianism because one is not permitted to count accidental properties as essential. Descartes, for example, regards the person as a thinking substance. Since the essence of human beings is mental, we cannot regard color, shape, sex, etc., as properties of the mind; these properties must be given an accidental status only. . . . In essence, Chomsky and Bracken are arguing that empiricism reduces the human person to a machine, an alienated, unproductive being that lacks freedom. Both suggest that a return to Cartesianism would alleviate many social injustices and oppressive institutions. Traditionally, empiricism has been associated with progressive social thinking. However, according to Chomsky, it involves a philosophy of man which does not provide a framework for the growth of moral consciousness, cultural achievement, and participation in a free and just community."

due above all else to the dogmatism which the assertion of such ideas involved."[2] Locke saw the foundation of innate ideas as antithetical to the foundation of empiricism and its verifications.

LOCKEAN TABULA RASA

By 1650, rationalism, with its emphasis on the mind, had been replaced in British philosophy by empiricism, which focused on the senses and perception. Locke was the most prominent advocate for sensual perception as a way to obtain knowledge. Cranston argues that "when he [Locke] looked back on the troubled history of this country, Locke saw two particularly potent sources of human error. One was unreflective adhesion to tradition ... the other was 'enthusiasm' or the reliance on emotional conviction as a basis of truth, the fault especially of Puritans and dissenters."[3] Locke responded with investigative analysis of the problem with his attention on "experience as a guide," and a reliance on reason in contrast to emotionalism and enthusiasm. The emphasis on reason is central to Locke's theoretical foundation. In Locke's view, the knowledge that reason uncovers is not innate. Furthermore, reason is associated with natural revelation. He writes, "There is a great deal of difference between an innate Law, and a Law of Nature; between something imprinted on our Minds in their very original, and something that we being ignorant of may attain to the knowledge of, by the use and due application of our natural faculties."[4] Reason serves as the light of nature and natural revelation, which humans comprehend through their five senses. For Locke, the mind is a "blank slate" or "tabula rasa" upon which the senses project their experiences, perceptions, concepts, and ideas. With his rejection of innate ideas that we are born with, Locke rejects the notion of "universal truth" as that which cannot be experienced. Experience is the absolute means of deriving knowledge and truth, thus his categorization of ideas into two segments: simple ideas and complex ideas.[5]

2. Lamprecht, "Locke's Attack Upon Innate Ideas," 145, 149.
3. Cranston, *John Locke*, 40.
4. Locke, *Essay Concerning Human Understanding*, 13.
5. Paeth, "Empiricism," 80. "Simple ideas are the basic sensations that enter our consciousness through the senses, things like color, sound, sensation, and taste. These simple ideas combine within our minds in order to enable us to develop more complex ideas, about are what he calls 'substances' on the one hand and 'modes' on the other. Substances are, essentially, objects and being in the world. Humans, rocks, houses, and

Locke attempts to ground moral laws in reason rather than religion. He believed that while "the law of nature, positive law and rules for ethical actions" may be established by God, they are certainly "discovered by reason" because reason is the fundamental means by which they are known.[6] "The light of reason or nature not only knows that there is a God who is supreme lawmaker; it knows very specific rules as derivable from the law of nature."[7] According to Syse, Locke's distinction between the law of nature and the light of reason presented a problem: why could the light of reason itself not be considered a revelation? "The *Essay*, which was meant to ground morality and religion in epistemology, failed. The conclusion that Locke had planned concerning the law of nature as the basis for all morality, was never written. Instead, natural law and divine law were for all practical purposes identified with each other and the matter was left with that."[8] Locke's assertion of empiricism knows no limit; God does not escape Locke's empiricist razor.

Locke argued that God's existence can be predicated on looking at the world. While this argument may seem akin to the cosmological argument about the existence of God, Locke's empiricism categorically rejects any knowledge of God, or the establishment of God's existence based on innateness and revelation. Furthermore, in Locke's argument, God is considered one of the "substances" in the world.[9] It is important to note that Locke rejects dogmatic Christianity. He did not believe in the Trinity or the divinity of Jesus Christ as the Son of God or God. For Locke, knowledge is derived through the senses, perception, and experience, not revelation. According to Locke:

> Had the poor Indian philosopher (who imagined that the earth also wanted something to bear it up) but thought of this word substance, he needed not to have been at the trouble to find an elephant to support it, and a tortoise to support his elephant:

---

even God are considered substances by Locke. Modes, on the other hand, are ideas that are constructed within the mind itself, such as moral precept or mathematical concepts. A third category Locke addresses is what he calls 'relations,' specifically the relationship between substances and modes. Thus, unlike the rationalists, Locke believes that our knowledge is, as it were, constructed from the ground up. We decorate the blank salve of our consciousness with experience and thus come to understand the world one step at a time."

6. Yolton, *Locke*, 48.
7. Yolton, *Locke*48.
8. Syse, *Natural Law, Religion, and Rights*, 224.
9. Paeth, "Empiricism," 80–82.

the word substance would have done it effectually. And he that inquired, might have taken it for as good an answer from an Indian philosopher, that substance, without knowing what it is, is that which supports the earth; as we take it for a sufficient answer, and good doctrine, from our European philosophers, that substance, without knowing what it is, is that which supports accidents. So that of substance, we have no idea of what it is, but only a confused obscure one of what it does.[10]

Cranston contends that Locke's goal was to "investigate the foundations of empirical knowledge. By the 1650s Locke had concluded that empiricism and reason were the foundation of knowledge. He was advancing toward the problems which were to be the subject of his masterpiece, the *Essay Concerning Human Understanding*."[11]

It is argued that Locke's *Essay Concerning Human Understanding* (1690)[12] marked the beginning of the Enlightenment period.[13] However, at Oxford, Locke initially espoused Descartes' rationalism in contrast both to any form of religious dogmatism and to the prevailing interpretation of Aristotelianism and scholasticism.[14] Aristotle and Descartes would

10. Locke, *Essay Concerning Human Understanding*, II, 13, 19, 175.

11. Cranston, *John Locke*, 41.

12. Cranston, *John Locke*, 224–25. "In it (*The Reasonableness of Christianity*) Locke gives his understanding of the essence of the Christian faith: that Jesus is the Christ, i.e., that Jesus is the Messiah. A minimalistic theology, devoid of any substantial dogmatism, is presented. But, more importantly for our purpose, the true effect of the Christian faith is shown to be moral. It is by the revelation of God through Jesus Christ that man is shown how to act morally. In passages that sound very much Socinian, Locke stresses how all men are the children of God, and how Christ teaches us, by instruction and by example, how to show love, respect, and care for our fellow human beings. Indeed, the law of nature is just this: the teaching of Christ on how to love our neighbor as ourselves."

13. Sahakian and Sahakian, *John Locke*, 13.

14. Cranston, *John Locke*, 274–75. Locke's "distinction between intuitive, demonstrative and sensitive *knowledge* comes straight from Descartes. The view that knowledge begins with intuitive relations between ideas is Locke's version of Cartesian intuition of relation between simple natures. He adds the thesis that abstract ideas are derived from ideas of sense to give an empiricist flavour to this particular *réchauffé*, but it falls short of a consistently empirical analysis. Locke claims that we have intuitive knowledge of our own existence: 'we perceive it so plainly . . . that it neither needs nor is capable of any proof,' (*Essay*, IV, ix, 3.). David Hume, who more or less adopted the Lockean doctrine of ideas, disputed this on the grounds that he had no perceptual experience which conveyed to him the idea of a self: 'For my part, when I enter most intimately into what I call *myself*, I always stumble on some particular perception or other, of heat or cold, light or shade, love or hatred, pain or pleasure. I never can catch myself at any time without a perception, and never can observe anything but the

eventually become the two major influences on Locke's philosophical development. Dunn notes, "As [Locke] told Lady Masham, it was those of Descartes which first strongly attracted him to philosophy to the attempt to understand very precisely and systematically what knowledge man 'was capable of.'"[15] Cartesian skepticism became a more attractive means of the pursuit of truth. According to Sahakian and Sahakian, "The Cartesian dictum *Cogito, ergo sum* ('I think therefore I am'), postulating the certain consciousness of one's own existence, the awareness of one's own consciousness, was for Descartes the only basis on which to find a philosophy issuing in certitude."[16] For Locke, the commencement of knowledge is intuitive. The basis of this intuition is experience—the concrete experience of a table, chair, flight, etc. The basis of knowledge is not abstract or *a priori* in the heavens.

To flee from the concepts of scholasticism, Descartes constructed his philosophical empiricism on experience and what is revealed in consciousness. However, Locke was conscious of the limitations of Descartes' empiricism.[17] For Locke, the acquisition of knowledge concerning truth is the ultimate expression of both human happiness and liberty. The human capacity to reason is established by the quest for truth, liberty, and happiness. Locke's pursuit of truth is experiential. What is truth must be experienced. According to Graham Faiella, "The only authority he respected was the evidence of his own experience of the world. . . . They were simply experiences that his own reason processed to come to his own conclusion about truth. Everything Locke experienced or learned was an influence that advanced his philosophy."[18] Like the empiricists of the Enlightenment, Locke believed that the acquisition of knowledge is based on the following: experience, reason as the ground of authority, the centralization of human potential to control nature, and the establishment

---

perception' (*Treatise of Human Nature*, Book One, IV, #6). Critics generally have taken Hume's side on this matter, but my own view is that Hume's account of the self is no more accurate than Locke's; What Hume does show is that commonsense certainty of one's own existence cannot be reconciled with the Lockean doctrine of ideas. But this only proves, I think, that the doctrine of ideas is wrong."

15. Dunn, *Locke*, 10.

16. Sahakian and Sahakian, *John Locke*, 20.

17. Sahakian and Sahakian, *John Locke*, 20. For Locke, knowledge involves two kinds of ideas: simple or elementary ideas derived from experiences or reflection about them, and complex ideas created by our minds as they abstract, compare, and combine the simple elementary ideas. True knowledge discloses the relationships between ideas and reality.

18. Faiella, *John Locke*, 55.

of rational methods to derive truth claims. He believed that ethics, like knowledge, is derived from experience. Experience is the "fountain" out of which knowledge springs and provides the basis upon which "all of our knowledge is founded, and from which it ultimately derives itself."[19] Locke's empiricism was also central to his interpretation of natural rights and his "personalism," or notion of what constitutes a person.[20] Like knowledge, experience serves as the basis for defining a person.

LOCKEAN ETHICS

Locke's philosophical themes are underscored by his distinction between faith and reason; the difference that emerges between faith and works is part of his central theological claim.[21] Locke's moral theory and theory of ethics are based on reason. In the *Essay Concerning Human Understanding*, Locke argues that the root of morality is "the *Divine* law."[22] However, he believed that divine laws require a human reason to complete the establishment of moral truths.[23] Does the will play a pivotal role in Locke's ethics? Indeed, it does. Eisenach notes that "Locke's epistemology rests on pleasure and pain. He who has power to enforce rules defines what is good and evil. Opinions of good and evil determine our will and our actions. Will is the power to act or to refrain from acting. Action, in turn, is motivated by a desire to seek pleasure or avoid pain."[24] Locke defines the will as:

---

19. Locke, *Essay Concerning Human Understanding*, 2.1.2.
20. Syse, *Natural Law, Religion, and Rights*, 226.
21. Eisenach, *Two Worlds of Liberalism*, 89.
22. Locke, *Essay Concerning Human Understanding*, 2.28.8.

23. Yolton, *Locke*, 43. "Locke has distinguished two kinds of truths, *truths of the world* and *systemic truths*. The first kind depend for their truth on the world. The second depend upon the system to which they belong, whether it be the system of Euclidean geometry or the system of the Christian religion. To discover the truth of a claim about the world requires that we use experience and observation, aided in more complex science by hypothesis and reasoning. To discover a systemic truth, we need only use reason alone, either to get clear about the ideas and concepts involved in the claim or to trace out the connection between those ideas and concepts. The two examples Locke uses of systemic truths are geometrical and moral truth. Systemic truths lay down standards which anything in the world must meet if it is to be an instance of, e.g., a triangle or a square, an act of murder or of homicide."

24. Eisenach, *Two Worlds of Liberalism*, 90.

> A power to direct the operative faculties to motion or rest in particular instances is that which we call the will. That which in the train of our voluntary actions determines the will to any change of operations is some present uneasiness, which is, or at least is always accompanied with, that of desire.[25]

However, reason provides the platform for the evaluation of ideas. For Locke, we arrive at ethical principles based on the available empirical data. In this process, human understanding plays a vital role since moral ideas serve as "real essences" concerning sense experience. Locke defines moral truths as "speaking things according to the persuasion of our own minds, though the proposition we speak agrees not to the reality of things."[26]

From this, Locke concludes that, like mathematics, ethical principles can be subjected to rational proofs. He writes:

> Upon this ground it is that I am bold to think that morality is capable of demonstration, as well as mathematics; since the precise real essence of the things moral words stand for may be perfectly known, and so the congruity or in congruity of the things themselves be certainly discovered, in which consist perfect knowledge. . . . Moral ideas are commonly more complex than those of the figures ordinarily considered in mathematics.[27]

Lockean empiricism provides the basis for his personalism. As a major characteristic of Lockean empiricism, innateness does not largely pertain to the nature of a person. Locke asserts a natural and materialist notion of the person. Having philosophically dismissed the notion of innateness, Locke is left with the assertion that the person is simply a natural and material being. In the following section, I advance the argument that Locke's notion of "person" as simply natural must be understood in the context of his position on race, property, religion, and the slave trade. Locke's concept of a person provides a window into his perception of the humanity of the African—simply as a slave and not a real person. Real persons in his view are rational and of European descent.

---

25. Locke, *Essay Concerning Human Understanding*, 11.21.71.
26. Locke, *Essay Concerning Human Understanding*, 4.5.11.
27. Locke, *Essay Concerning Human Understanding* (1975) bks. 3/4, chaps. 11, & 3, secs. 16 & 18.

LOCKEAN PHILOSOPHY: EMPIRICISM

THE LOCKEAN PERSON

Locke's concept of a person is materialist. As an empiricist, he denies the person any semblance of innateness. The Lockean person has no inherent dignity or immaterial worth. In contrast to Descartes' *cogito, ergo sum*, which refers to the metaphysical identity of the person, Locke reduces personhood to the senses, experience, and perception. According to Adam Grzelinski: "Locke's position on the issue of personal identity is completely opposite to Descartes'. The reasons are obvious: Locke makes the analysis of personal identity independent of substantialist metaphysics in its traditional, rationalistic version, and should there still be any reasons suggesting that one should refer to metaphysics, the solution he presents is closer to materialism than to dualism of thinking and extension."[28]

For Locke, the following properties provide the inherent foundation of a person:

1. A face usual to that species which though consisting of many particular Ideas for brevity's sake and the thing being obvious I take for one.
2. Two hands with five fingers on each.
3. Two legs.
4. Upright posture.
5. Living.
6. A power of laughing.
7. A power of speaking.
8. Of reasoning, i.e., knowing the consequences of words or propositions one to another.
9. Of judging, i.e., guesses at the truth of words or being of things.[29]

Locke argues that thinking is accompanied by our sense of "awareness."[30] According to Yolton,

> His point throughout *Essay* 2.27 is to emphasize that "person" is properly a first-person term. *I* come by my concept of person

---

28. Grzelinski, "Cartesianism and Anti-Cartesianism," 198.
29. Locke, *Early Draft of Locke's Essay*, 27.
30. Yolton, *Locke*, 30.

through *my* acts of perceiving, including the act of being aware that *I* am perceiving. Moreover, if I am to accept full responsibility for what I do, I *must* have that awareness of what I have done, know that those acts were mine. It is this first-person awareness of my actions which is the basis of moral responsibility. That awareness, too, constitutes my identity as a person, my personal identity, my "personal self" (*Essay* 11). A self can only be personal.[31]

A person is only that which can be perceived with the eyes. Locke does not subscribe to the notion of inherent dignity and innateness as the basis for personhood. According to Jonathan Lamb, Locke uses "person" as "the representation of the self that secures its identity by means of extended consciousness of its action.... 'The same Person,' the one responsible for owning the actions of the thinking thing—i.e., the self—actions which cannot be owned until the person is invented by blending self with consciousness."[32] According to Locke, we cannot know the "essence" of a person. However, a person as a "personification" is strictly defined by their "function."[33] Locke reduces the person to their function, and their acts to the embodiment of their identity.

For Locke, there are two kinds of persons: a mere biological person and a biological person who is cognitively, rationally, and intellectually superior to other biological persons. The biological person is no different from the irrational state of animals. Locke argues for a gradation of the human being from a mere biological being to a "moral man" based on "education," "understanding," and "cognitive acuteness." Thomas Jefferson, as we shall see, will adopt Locke's concept of personhood to argue that people of African descent are biologically and intellectually inferior to Whites.

Locke's hierarchy of humanity contains three forms of humans. The first is a natural human. This refers to an uncultivated human who shares almost identical qualities with nature and other natural beings—sharing the "basic human nature."[34] The second is a moral human. The moral human is a human being cultivated through education, who exhibits elements of rationality that produce "a responsible, self-conscious person."[35]

31. Yolton, *Locke*, 30.
32. Lamb, "Locke's Wild Fancies," 195.
33. Lamb, "Locke's Wild Fancies," 195.
34. Yolton, *Locke*, 25.
35. Yolton, *Locke*, 25. "The term 'person' is for us a very ordinary one, but for Locke

For Locke, this human has "thoughts."[36] He explains, "We know certainly by Experience, that we sometimes think, and thence draw this infallible Consequences, that there is something in us, that has a Power to think."[37] Yolton is not comfortable with Locke's transition from "we sometimes think" to "something in us thinks" because he thinks Locke cannot technically justify such a transition. Locke posited the separation of the soul and the body. The soul is the thinking part within the body that remains independent of the body. The body is the non-thinking part with the soul within it, which does not participate in the thinking process. Locke asserts a notion of two living beings in one person—"two persons in one man."[38] The soul is that part of the person that "thinks" while the body denotes the sleeping part of the human being. The soul is "awake" and the body is "sleeping": they are not the same.[39] The body does not understand the happiness of the soul like two persons.[40] Locke writes, "Whether Castor and Pollux, thus, with only one Soul between them, which thinks and perceives in one, what the other is never conscious of, nor is concerned for, are not two as distinct Persons, as Castor and Hercules; or, as Socrates and Plato were"?[41] The soul and the body are like Castor and Pollux or Socrates and Plato.

Locke's notion of a person is compartmentalized and consists of the soul, thinking soul, body, and non-thinking body. He writes, "Whether the Soul, when it thinks thus apart, and as it were separate from the Body, acts less rationally than when conjointly with it, or no; If its separates Thoughts be less rational, then these Men must say, that the Soul owes

---

it became a specialized and almost technical term. There are in the *Essay* some ordinary uses of that term (e.g. 1.3.3; 1.4.22; 2; 2.25.5). Even the discussion of the question, 'does the soul always think?', uses 'person' in the non-technical sense (2.1.9–21). This passage does, however, raise some of the questions and puzzlements which are elaborated in the later chapter on 'Identity and Diversity,' where Locke presents his specialized sense of the term 'person.' What is interesting about this 2.1.9–21 passage is the way Locke presents the puzzlements about personal identity in the traditional language of 'soul' as a metaphysical entity."

36. Yolton, *Locke*, 25. Locke's *Essay*: 2.1.9. As a Cartesian, Locke is also extrapolating from Descartes' dualism. "Descartes has talked of two substances, *res extensa* (body or matter) and *res cogitans* (minds or soul)."

37. Yolton, *Locke*, 25; Locke, *Essay Concerning Human Understanding*, 2.1.10.

38. Yolton, *Locke*, 26.

39. Yolton, *Locke* 26; Locke, *Essay* (11 and 12).

40. Yolton, *Locke*, 26; Locke, *Essay* (12).

41. Yolton, *Locke*, 26.

the perfection of rational thinking to the Body."⁴² The Lockean soul is responsible for thinking and has nothing to do with the body because the body does not think. The soul is the rational part of a person. In separating the soul from the body, Locke established the body as fundamentally material. The logical conclusion for Locke's argument is the claim for some kind of socially constructed humanity since he rejects the concept of innateness and inherent dignity of every human being—White body, White soul, Black body, Black soul. It is a philosophical argument for racism and racialized slavery. Yolton notes, "The process of education, of growing up in a family, is a progression from man to moral man. The goal is to bring into existence a responsible, self-conscious person."⁴³ Locke's use of "person" implies a "thinking being," albeit one that is racialized.

Finally, for Locke, "person" and "man/human being" are not the same. The word "person" is for Locke "a Forensick Term appropriating Actions and their merit."⁴⁴ A person exhibits rationality, action, intellectual capacity, and reasoning.⁴⁵ Furthermore, "in this personal identity is founded 'all the Right and Justice of Reward and Punishment.'"⁴⁶ According to Yolton, Locke viewed the "transgressor" of the law harshly. "The transgressor is not portrayed as breaking some minor law rule or law; he 'becomes dangerous to Mankind'; he has 'trespassed against the whole Species, and the Peace and Safety' of the species. One wonders what example Locke has in mind. Surely, no minor crime. 'A crime against mankind' is strong language."⁴⁷

According to Locke, the person who breaks the law is "irrational." Rational people do not break the laws. Furthermore, the one who breaks the law has committed a crime against the rest of humanity and deserves the severest punishment. Locke's notion of punishment is retributive—an eye for an eye. However, Locke was a slave trader and defender of the institution of slavery. While arguing for the harshest punishment for

---

42. Yolton, *Locke*, 27. "Locke's account of man, especially of moral man, of the man trained to virtue by the educator, is not yet complete. That he wants to use the term 'person' in a specialized sense is perhaps first indicated in *Essay* 2.27.7, where, speaking of the general concept of identity, he remarks that to explicate this concept, he need only be clear about the referent of that word or idea. Does it stand for or refer to the same substance, the same man, or the same person?"

43. Yolton, *Locke*, 25.

44. Yolton, *Locke*, 28; Locke, *Essay Concerning Human Understanding*, 2.27.26.

45. Yolton, *Locke*, 28; Locke, *Essay Concerning Human Understanding*, 2.27.25.

46. Yolton, *Locke*, 28; Locke, *Essay Concerning Human Understanding*, 2.27.18.

47. Yolton, *Locke*, 60; Locke, *Essay Concerning Human Understanding*, 10.

the transgressor of the law, Locke had no problem breaking the laws of humanity, as President Madison asserts in his condemnation of the slave trade.

Locke associated rationality with the soul and not the body. He advanced a clear distinction between the body and soul, which opens the door for some to argue for superior and inferior bodies and souls. Neither does he advance any argument for a holistic being, or the inherent dignity and worth of every person, body and soul. Locke's empiricism, his personalism or theory of a person, and his theory of knowledge/epistemology are disturbing and inherently racist. Proslavery advocates in the United States including Thomas Jefferson were quick to use the various strains of Locke's arguments (the separation of soul and body, rejection of inherent dignity; the rejection of innateness and religion; deism; and punitive harshness) to destroy the humanity of Black Africans.

THE COLORIZATION OF PEOPLE

White people!
Black people!
Yellow people!
Brown people!

The process of imposition,
The start of stigmatization,
The concept of conscription,
The making of marginalization.

Yellow eyes!
Brown eyes!
Green eyes!
Black eyes!

In the label, identity is concrete
In the label, ideas are confused.
In the label, humanity is dying.
In the label, humanity is dead.[48]

GEORGE WALTERS-SLEYON

---

48. Walters-Sleyon, *Nuggets from the Night*, 110.

CHATTEL SLAVERY

1779–1865

8

Lockean Slavery to Jeffersonian Slavery

Jefferson was, after all, the man who in the Declaration of Independence rewrote Locke's "life, liberty, and property" into "life, liberty and the pursuit of happiness."[1]

THIS CHAPTER DEMONSTRATES THE TRANSITION from Lockean slavery to Jeffersonian slavery. It explores the political, economic, and philosophical influences of Locke on Jefferson, as well as their contextual distinctions. This chapter is about the transition from the United Kingdom's justification of slavery to America's defense, perpetuation, and perfection of the industrial slave trade and chattel slavery. Furthermore, it is about Thomas Jefferson—the third president of the United States—and his enablement of the industrial slave trade and the institution of chattel slavery in the United States.

When Jefferson became president in 1801, he was not coming into the position as a political neophyte. Jefferson had been an active and consummate politician for close to fourteen years. He had served as governor of Virginia from 1779–81, as the United States ambassador to France from 1785–89, as the United States secretary of state from 1790–93, and as vice president of the United States from 1797–1801. These positions came with much political clout and influence and allowed Jefferson to

---

1. Katz, "Thomas Jefferson."

mold the political, penal, sociocultural, religious, and economic consciousness of the United States as an emerging nation.

On February 17, 1801, Jefferson became the third president of the United States. He came into the presidency with over 150 slaves as part of his property even while he wrote the Declaration of Independence. According to Finkelman, "Rather than the precursor of the antebellum abolitionists, Jefferson was the intellectual godfather of the racist pseudoscience of the American school of anthropology.... Jefferson's theories about race 'became indisputable dogma within a decade after his death.'"[2] Jefferson also emerged as an immediate facilitator of Lockean ideology in the American political, social, economic, and religious sphere. In July 1800, Jefferson solidified his position when he published the *Manual of Parliamentary Practice*. It would become a major procedural handbook for the senate of the United States after the death of Jefferson in 1826. Furthermore, Finkelman contends, "The traditional image of Jefferson is that of a slaveholder valiantly trying to come to terms with the inherent contradictions between slavery and the philosophy of the American Revolution. This image will not hold up under careful scrutiny."[3]

THE LOCKEAN PRESIDENCY IN THE UNITED STATES

Thomas Jefferson was the most efficient disciple of John Locke in American politics. As a Lockean, Jefferson used his positions, economic interests, and Enlightenment prowess to advance the religious, political, philosophical, and economic ideologies of Locke in the United States. Willard Sterne Randall notes,

> Jefferson bought John Locke's 1693 treatise, *Some Thoughts Concerning Education*, which advised young gentlemen to read works on international law and legal philosophy by Grotius and Pufendorf, two jurists very popular in Virginia. Jefferson owned Locke's *Education* with this much-read passage: "It would be strange to suppose an English gentleman should be ignorant of the law of his country. This, whatever station he is in, is so requisite that, from a justice of the peace to a minister of state, I know no place he can well fill without it."[4]

---

2. Finkelman, *Slavery and the Founders*, 110.
3. Finkelman, *Slavery and the Founders*, 110.
4. Randall, *Thomas Jefferson*, 45, 166. "Among his earliest recorded philosophical

This chapter explores Jefferson's "relationships" with Locke as the "Lockean" in the White House. It shows how Jefferson appropriated Locke's theories and put them into practice. In earnest, it shows how Jefferson used his political platform to sustain the institution of chattel slavery concerning the external and internal slave trades in the United States.

Locke's economic, political, philosophical, and religious claims were pivotal to the development of the Declaration of Independence. Furthermore, Locke's support of private property, the separation of church and state, human rights, and a government based on the consent of the people became the bedrock of the American Revolutionary War. According to Merle Curti,

> [America's] political thought both before and during the American Revolution was profoundly affected by the *Two Treatises on Civil Government*. Otis, John and Samuel Adams, and other leading revolutionists quoted "the great Mr. Locke" reverently; Franklin, Hamilton, and Jefferson read and praised him. His natural-rights philosophy, including the doctrine that all government rests on the consent of the governed and may be overthrown by revolution if it persistently violates individual life, liberty, and property, was incorporated in the Declaration of Independence itself.[5]

Locke was a prominent politician of the British Empire and a major philosophical theorist. Jefferson was a prominent American politician, political theorist, and philosopher. But Jefferson was a staunch admirer and copyist of Locke. In essence, one may argue that Jefferson was the political and philosophical pragmatist of Locke in the United States.

Locke's concepts of religious tolerance, natural theology/deism, and the separation of church and state were influential to the Founding Fathers. Jefferson relied on Locke's concepts of religious tolerance to construct and advance his argument for religious tolerance and the separation of church and state. He read Locke's *A Letter Concerning Toleration* to develop the "essence" of his argument for constructing the framework for his *Bill for Establishing Religious Freedom*.[6] According to S. Gerald

---

jottings, they are reflected the writing of Pufendorf, Hume, Montesquieu, Locke."

5. Curti, "Great Mr. Locke," 107.

6. Sandler, "Lockean Ideas," 110. "While the influence of John Locke on religious thinkers in America during the eighteenth and nineteenth centuries was considerable, there is probably no single document in American religious history which exemplifies this influence more clearly than Thomas Jefferson's *A Bill for Establishing Religious Freedom*. This bill, presented to the House of Delegates of Virginia in 1779, contains

Sandler, there are five areas that demonstrate Jefferson's direct paraphrasing of Locke's *A Letter Concerning Toleration*:

1. True belief is inspired by reason, not force.[7]
2. That civil magistrates may be fallible in religious matters is justified in history.[8]
3. Because the domains of church and state are separate, a citizen's (religious) opinions should have no effect upon his civil capacities.[9]
4. Civil government must interfere, however, when principles break out into overt acts against peace and good order.[10]
5. Truth, unaided, has sufficient power to prevail over error.[11]

Jefferson's politics was inherently Lockean, as was his Enlightenment philosophy m ore generally, which was highly tinted with Lockean

---

not only a Jeffersonian interpretation of Locke's theory of religious toleration, but also a discernible paraphrasing of several passages from Locke's *A Letter Concerning Toleration*. Scholars may question the extent to which Jefferson is indebted to Locke for his political theory and for the Declaration of Independence, but there can be little doubt of his indebtedness to Locke for his ideas on religious toleration."

7. Sandler, "Lockean Ideas," 111.

8. Sandler, "Lockean Ideas," 112. "In tracing the development of this idea from Locke to Jefferson, it will be helpful once more to distinguish its two components: first, that civil magistrates 'being themselves but fallible and uninspired men' know no more of 'true' religion than do other citizens, and second, that this assertion has been proven in many instances throughout the history of the world. The origin of the first part of the argument lies in Locke's definition of the limits of human capability which he claims applies equally to civil magistrates as well as to all other persons."

9. Sandler, "Lockean Ideas," 113. "At the heart of Jefferson's Bill is the doctrine of the separation of the church and state, and although the fact that Jefferson employs the doctrine is not in itself evidence of an indebtedness to Locke, the similarity of his supporting arguments to their counterparts in Locke's *Letter* is striking."

10. Sandler, "Lockean Ideas," 115. "Aware that faction and private meetings represent a potential danger to civil interests, both Locke and Jefferson concede that unlimited religious freedom is not practical from the standpoint of protecting civil liberties. Thus, in Locke's *Letter*, as well as in Jefferson's Bill, one finds the provision for civil intervention wherever sedition or other acts threatening the general peace and good order of society are perceptible."

11. Sandler, "Lockean Ideas," 115. "While the previous comparisons have relied primarily upon a similarity of ideas rather than of specific phraseology, the evidence seems to be conclusive that Jefferson's commentary on the power of truth has at least one sentence paraphrased directly from Locke's *A Letter Concerning Toleration*."

Enlightenment positions.[12] And like Locke, Jefferson was a slave trader and slave holder.

> He bought and sold slaves, punished them, and hunted them down when they escaped. He advised his friends and relatives about purchasing slaves and gave them as gifts. He sold slaves away from their families to punish them and to make examples of them in "terrorem to other." Throughout his life, he sold large number of slaves to raise cash.[13]

Exploring the intersections of slavery, race, and equality in Jefferson's works and personal life, John P. Diggins highlights an essential similarity between Jeffersonian and Lockean ethics. "Jefferson's definition of 'virtue' as 'utility,' his worship of nature and facticity, his instrumentalist approach to religion, and his Lockean materialist epistemology coupled with a contrary belief in an innate 'moral sense' is confident assumptions that are not seriously questioned."[14]

Locke influenced many Founding Fathers beyond Jefferson. His *Thoughts Concerning Education* and his *Sketch of an English School* influenced Benjamin Franklin.[15] Curti notes:

> He was indirectly among the fathers of both English and American deism. In various writings, notably in *The Reasonableness of Christianity* and in *An Essay for the Understanding of St. Paul's Epistles* as well as in his *Letters on Toleration*, Locke subjected the tenets of Christian theology to reason and maintained that natural knowledge was more certain than miracles and revelation.[16]

This influence manifested in the founding documents of America. According to Graham Faiella, "In the first draft of the Declaration, Jefferson copied Locke's phrase 'life, liberty, and property.' This was later changed to 'life, liberty, and the pursuit of happiness.'"[17] On the question of Jefferson's appropriation of Locke's "Life, Liberty, and Property" to "Life, Liberty and the Pursuit of Happiness," Willard Sterne Randall contends that "his choice of words 'pursuit of happiness' over John Locke's 'property'

---

12. See Koch, *Philosophy of Thomas Jefferson*, which explores the nature and essence of Jefferson's Enlightenment philosophy.
13. Finkelman, *Slavery and the Founders*, 110.
14. Diggins, "Slavery, Race, and Equality," 208.
15. Curti, "Great Mr. Locke," 111.
16. Curti, "Great Mr. Locke," 114.
17. Faiella, *John Locke*, 19.

marked a sharp break with the Whig doctrine of English middle-class property rights. It was a felicitous, memorable turn of phrase, the most succinct expression ever of American political philosophy."[18] This book differs from Randall's interpretation of Jefferson's appropriation of Locke's "Life, Liberty, and Property." It argues that the fundamental property in question was slaves. Furthermore, Jefferson's use of "pursuit of happiness" was a reference to the Lockean notion of property. Jefferson was aware that Locke was referring to the right to slaves as property.

The transition from Lockean slavery to Jeffersonian slavery is also enacted by the governorship and presidency of Jefferson.[19] This transition continues to influence the contemporary penal system of the United States and the United Kingdom. Jefferson copied Locke's arguments regarding private property. The adaptation can be seen in Jefferson's approach to land ownership and those who cultivate the land. In one of his letters to John Jay written in 1785, Jefferson wrote:

> Cultivators of the earth are the most valuable citizens. They are the most vigorous, the most independent, the most virtuous, and they are tied to their country and wedded to its liberty and interests by the most lasting bands. As long, therefore, as they can find employment in this line, I would not convert them into mariners, artisans or any thing else.[20]

Jefferson was directly quoting and paraphrasing Locke's theory of private property. As previously analyzed, Locke argues that God has given the earth to mankind but particularly to those who till it with their labor. According to Locke,

> The Earth, and all that is therein, is given to Men for the Support and Comfort of their being. And though all the Fruits it naturally produces, and Beasts it feeds, belong to Mankind in common, as they are produced by the spontaneous hand of Nature, and no body has originally a private Dominion, exclusive of the rest of Mankind, in any of them, as they are thus in their natural state: yet being given for the use of Men, there must of necessity be a means to appropriate them some way or other before they can be of any use, or at all beneficial to any particular Man. Whatsoever then he removes out of the State that Nature

---

18. Randall, *Thomas Jefferson*, 275.
19. Chaudhuri, "Jefferson's Unheavenly City," 207, 397.
20. Jefferson, "Letter from Thomas Jefferson to John Jay, Aug. 23, 1785," in *Jefferson Papers*, 426–28.

hath provided, and left it in, he hath mixed his Labour with it, and joyned to it something that is his own, and thereby makes it his Property.[21]

Jefferson provided a practical and public policy argument for the established racialization of slavery in the United States. Finkelman notes, "By the end of the Revolution, when he was just forty years old, Jefferson commanded a 'miniature state,' with some 10,000 acres of land and nearly 200 slaves. The only 'citizens' in this 'state' were Jefferson, his white relatives, and perhaps a few white employees."[22] Blacks in Monticello were not citizens; they were slaves. The Apostle of American liberalism, like his mentor Locke, was a typical slave trader and slave master. Jefferson was not only "a man of his time," he was a man defining his time for generations of Whites to come. Jefferson promoted his ideas through public policies, the law, and philosophy; as governor and later president, he helped establish the sociocultural norms regarding race, racism, and the treatment of Blacks in the new United States.[23]

SLAVERY AND THE DECLARATION OF INDEPENDENCE

The United States began as a "slave holders' republic."[24] While its founders appropriated the rationale of the Enlightenment to create a "more perfect union," they were practicing and developing a counter-narrative for the people of African descent as slaves in the United States. In describing the 1787 Constitution and the reference to slavery, Finkelman writes, "The word 'slavery' appears in only one place in the Constitution—in the Thirteenth Amendment, where the institution is abolished. Throughout the main body of the Constitution, slaves are referred to as 'other person,' 'such person,' or in the singular as a 'Person held to Service or Labour.'"[25] The Constitution of the United States otherizes Black people as a legal statement. The mention of slavery is almost totally

21. Locke, *Two Treatises of Government*, 185.
22. Finkelman, *Slavery and the Founders*, 110.
23. Campbell, *Middle Passages*, 40. "Jefferson's racial beliefs have lately become a subject of considerable popular interest, in the wake of DNA test of descendants that appear to confirm (as some political opponents alleged at the time) that he fathered children by an enslaved woman, Sally Hemings."
24. Finkelman, *Slavery and the Founders*.
25. Finkelman, *Slavery and the Founders*, 3.

absent because the northerners and the southerners in Congress at the time agreed on it. There were five provisions in the Constitution acting on the issue of slavery:

- *Article 1, Section 2, Paragraph 3*
- *Article 1, Section 9, Paragraph 1*
- *Article 1, Section 9, Paragraph 4*
- *Article 3, Section 2, Paragraph 1:* This clause made it explicit that Blacks—slave or free—could not have access to federal courts to hear their cases.[26]
- *Article 5, Section 2, Paragraph 3*

Article 5, Article 1, Section 2, Paragraph 3 dealt with the political and economic expediency of the "three-fifth clause" but not its moral and ethical implications.[27]

Neutrality in any of the articles of the Constitution was considered and interpreted in favor of slavery and the proslavery interests. Locke and Jefferson were advocates of liberty for all. Unfortunately, when it came to people of African descent, it was liberty for only those of European heritage. Furthermore, Locke and Jefferson were overt slave traders and slave holders. According to Finkelman, "American slavery was an essential form of race control. Most argued that slavery was a positive good and that it was a necessary, even essential, institution for a successful society. They were certain that whites constituted a superior race and that blacks were members of an inferior race. This was a central theme of almost every proslavery argument."[28] The neutrality and proslavery sentiments of the United States Constitution are demonstrated in the negotiation of the three-fifths clause.

THE SLAVE IS "THREE-FIFTHS" OF A HUMAN BEING

On July 9, 1783, William Paterson stood in Congress and repeated the following argument. "Negroes slaves in no light but as property. They are

---

26. Finkelman, *Slavery and the Founders*, 9. "The proslavery implications of this clause did not become fully apparent until the Supreme Court issued its opinion in *Dred Scot v. Sandford*, 19 How. (U.s) 393 (1857). There the Court held that even free blacks could not sue in diversity in federal courts."

27. Finkelman, *Slavery and the Founders*, 9.

28. Finkelman, *Defending Slavery*, 4.

no free agents, have no personal liberty, no faculty of acquiring property, but on the contrary are themselves property, & like other property entirely at the will of the master."²⁹ Chattel slavery existed throughout the world and was practiced by the British, the Scots, the Dutch, the French, the Portuguese, the Belgians, the Spaniards, the Germans, and the Americans.³⁰ T. M. Devine describes it as follows:

> The system of bondage practised was chattel slavery, where the enslaved became the property of their masters until death, like their beasts of the field or their household plenishings, with no legal right to be treated as humans and with all the potential for exploitation and degradation which could accompany that helpless condition. The progeny of enslaved women also became the property of their masters at birth, either to be sold on from the plantation where they had been born or to spend their lives in hard labour within its bounds in perpetual servitude.³¹

Chattel slavery in the United States was codified into law. Defenders of chattel slavery were vociferous in practice and politically clamorous in Congress. Thomas Jefferson and the Jeffersonians—including the proslavery activists in Congress and political positions across America concluded that slaves were property and not human beings or persons of inherent worth and dignity.³² At the Constitutional Convention of 1787, Thomas Lynch of South Carolina argued that slaves were property and should not be taxed any further. "Our slaves being our property why should they be taxed more than the land, sheep, cattle, horses."³³

However, Lynch and his fellow Southerners (including Jefferson) made a dramatic shift at some point during the debate—from arguing that slaves were "property" to arguing that slaves were "persons." It was a strategic political move. Slaves would still be considered property and less than human beings, in theory, practice, and economics. But politically, slaves were now counted as "three-fifths of all other persons."³⁴ This

29. Finkelman, "Garrison's Constitution," para. 41.
30. Devine, *Recovering Scotland's Slavery Past*, 7–8.
31. Devine, *Recovering Scotland's Slavery Past*, 1.
32. Finkelman, "Slavery in the United States," 115.
33. Finkelman, "Slavery in the United States," 116. *Journals of the Continental Congress* 6:1079–80 (debate of July 30, 1776).
34. Finkelman, "Slavery in the United States," 117. See the United States Constitution, Art. I, Sec. 2, Cl. 3: "Representatives and direct Taxes shall be apportioned among the several States which may be included within this Union, according to their respective Numbers, which shall be determined by adding to the whole Number of free

shift on the part of the Southerners at the Convention to count Blacks and slaves as three-fifths of a person was based on political expediency that "representation in the new Congress would be based on population," and not land, sheep, cattle, horses, or property as the Jeffersonians had argued—thus the three-fifths clause in the United States.[35] Finkelman notes:

> The three-fifths clause provided for counting three-fifths of all "other Persons"—slaves—for purposes of representation in Congress. This clause also provided that if any "direct tax" was levied on the states, it could be imposed only proportionally, according to population, and that only three-fifths of all slaves would be counted in assessing what each states' contribution would be.[36]

Southerners in particular used slaves to inflate their political clout at the same time denying slaves the right to vote. The three-fifths clause was a result of the political compromise at the Constitutional Convention of 1787. Leah Sakala explains:

> The three-fifths clause had the effect of using slave population numbers to artificially beef up the political power of the Southern, white, property-owning voters who were invested in maintaining and expanding the slave system. But the problem with the three-fifths clause wasn't that the slaves were counted as only a fraction of a person. After all, since their "political clout" went right into the hands of the very people who exploited them, the

---

Persons, including those bound to Service for a Term of Years, and excluding Indians not taxed, three-fifths of all other Persons."

35. Finkelman, "Slavery in the United States," 117. "Throughout the Constitutional Convention, slavery bedeviled the delegates. The call for population-based representation led to vitriolic debates over whether slaves were part of the population or merely property. The Three-Fifths Clause was formal recognition that they were persons, although as slaves, persons of a diminished capacity or value. Some Northern delegates could not stomach giving the South extra seats and thus power in Congress by counting slaves for representation. William Paterson of New Jersey complained that everyone knew that slaves were to be seen 'in no light but as property. They are no free agents, have no personal liberty, no faculty of acquiring property, but on the contrary are themselves property, and like other property entirely at the will of the Master.' Pointing to the apparent absurdity of allocating representation by counting slaves, he sarcastically asked, 'Has a man in Virga. a number of votes in proportion to the number of his slaves?' Paterson's complaints, however valid, could not prevent the Convention from giving political power to the South for its slave property. Part of this compromise was to try to hide what was really happening, by referring to the slaves as 'other persons.'"

36. Finkelman, *Slavery and the Founders*, 3.

political distortion would have been even greater had they been counted as full people.[37]

General Charles Cotesworth Pinckney of the House of Representatives of South Carolina had this to say about the three-fifth clause: "In short, considering all circumstances, we have made the best terms for the security of this species of property it was in our power to make. We would have made it better if we could; but on the whole, I do not think them bad."[38] The property in question were slaves or people of African descent.

The three-fifth clause, Sakala contends, is similar to the contemporary penal practice of prison-based gerrymandering. Prison-based gerrymandering is a political means of "stripping" prisoners of their political rights. The prisoners' "political clout is essentially handed through the bars to the real residents of the community that contains the prison, giving certain people more political say simply by their residential proximity to a large prison."[39] Thus, prison-based gerrymandering manipulates communities and enforces the concepts of civil death in civil society.[40]

Du Bois notes that, on the one hand, the opponents to the slave trade and its transition to the institution of chattel slavery were often disappointed. On the other hand, while one may have been known to oppose the slave trade and chattel slavery in theory, such opposition did not often translate into practical opposition. Jefferson's position is an established example of this race-based hypocrisy. Proslavery advocates included both White men and White women. Regardless of whether they voted or not, some White women were not reticent or shy about their proslavery campaigns and support of chattel slavery.[41]

Here is Lucy Kenney, a prominent lady of Southern heritage but a vociferous proslavery advocate and White supremacist. With scriptural and religious appropriations, she employs a copious number of biblical texts to defend the existing race-based chattel slavery: Genesis 11:25;

---

37. Sakala, "Prison-Based Gerrymandering's Striking Resemblance," para. 4.

38. Finkelman, *Slavery and the Founders*, 7–9. "The evolution of the three-fifth clause during the Convention show that the clause was not essentially a compromise over taxation and representation as historians have traditionally claimed and as the structure of Article 1, Section 2, Paragraph 3 implies. Rather, it began as a compromise between those who wanted to count slaves fully for purposes of representation and those who did want to count slaves at all."

39. Sakala, "Prison-Based Gerrymandering's Striking Resemblance," para. 5.

40. Skocpol, "Emerging Constitutional Law," 1489.

41. Finkelman, *Defending Slavery*, ix.

Exodus 21:20, 21; Leviticus 25:45, 46; Joel 3, 8; 1 Corinthians 7:23; Ephesians 6:5; and 1 Peter 2:18.[42] It must be acknowledged that her use of biblical passages is to overtly advance an anti-biblical concept of White supremacy. Nowhere in the Bible does the support for White-supremacist validation and practices exist. Kenney's use of these scriptures is to advance pseudo and anti-biblical interpretations that the enslavement of people of African descent is "divine" and "eternal." According to Kenney:

> No doubt they are of the seed of Cain; the word Nod implies that of drowsiness, dullness, stupineness, inertness, or want of ability, of body, of brightness, of intellect, or readiness of comprehension, or an enlargement of the faculties, a want of constant progression toward an improvement. We must observe what a vast difference there exists between their sensibilities and those of a white man. It might be advanced against those arguments, that God makes the back to bear the burden imposed on it, and, in mercy, has denied to them that refinement of mind and susceptibility which would constitute their misery. But could not God, if he had thought proper place them on an equality?[43]

Kenney argues that God has eternally separated Whites and Blacks by the color of their skin. She claims that the mandate to separate the races is divine in heaven and should be perpetuated on earth. Furthermore, she argues that Caine was a murderer who killed his brother and was given a black complexion from head to toe. Kenney claims that the black pigmentation, a mark of punishment and inferiority, became a part of his genetic makeup, and has been transmitted to his descendants—Africans. No matter how ridiculous and anti-Christian these claims are, they are still used to advance White-supremacist ideas and the physical and mental abuse of people of African descent.[44] Also, because of the mark of Blackness, Africans, Kenney argues, are intellectually inferior

---

42. Kenney, *Refutation of the Principles of Abolition*.
43. Kenney, *Refutation of the Principles of Abolition*, 5–6.
44. Finkelman, *Defending Slavery*, 32. "The punishment for adultery—that is, sexual relations with another man's wife—was execution of both parties. But sexual relations with another man's slave woman even if she were married, would not lead to any punishment for the man because the slave's marriage was not recognized by the law in the same way that a free person's marriage was. The slave woman would not be executed but only 'scourged' (whipped). This passage also assumed, without comment or explanation, that male masters were free to have sex with their female slaves. If God ordained slavery in the Old Testament—and even explained how to deal with sex between slave women and free men—then how, Southerners asked, could there be any moral taint from owning slaves?"

to Whites. Blacks must constantly exist under the power of Whites like slaves, children, and chattel property even reduced to the level of mere animals. Thus, Africans are black because Cain was their father who was cursed. Kenney's interpretation of the Bible, and like many of her White-supremacist community, is blatantly wrong and inherently racist. It is anti-Christian. But White supremacists have resorted to these pseudo-interpretations of the Bible to advance racism, White supremacy, and inhumane treatment against Black humanity with impunity. As we shall see, Jefferson did not shy away from these theories and practices. Finkelman notes: "Perhaps only when we fully understand the nature of proslavery thought can we finally come to terms with its legacy."[45]

Chattel slavery is about owning Black people, their labor, humanity, and products as the sole property of their slave master or property owner, even their bodies as sexual objects, economical and pleasurable interest. Lockean rights and thus Jeffersonian rights to own property entail arguments and justifications to own human beings as property. Their arguments were highly subjective regarding what could be owned, i.e., Locke and Jefferson's notions of right also consist of the right to own other human beings as property. It is chattel slavery embedded in the argument for private property.

In contrast to Stanley N. Katz's separation of Jefferson's economic and chattel slavery activities from his Enlightenment philosophy,[46] this book explores Locke and Jefferson's engagements in the slave trade and chattel slavery industry as central to their arguments for private property and Enlightenment philosophy. According to R. B. Bernstein, Jefferson was a "universalist." Bernstein contends that in Jefferson's Enlightenment philosophy and politics, he demonstrated a concept of "universalism." However, Jefferson's universalism only applied to people of European descent. As for the people of *Africa proper*, he relegated them to perpetual servitude. Bernstein writes, "Jefferson's universalism had its limits. He was not inclined to extend it to women, nor to Native Americans who insisted on following their traditional ways, nor to African Americans. Indeed, given his belief that freed slaves and free people of African descent

---

45. Finkelman, *Defending Slavery*, ix.

46. Katz, "Thomas Jefferson," 467. "My strategy is to isolate one theme in Jefferson's thought in order to blaze a tenuous trail through the richness of his mind and life and, at the same time, to try to show one of the ways in which Jefferson helped to shape the legacy of 1776: that theme is the right to property."

had to be exiled from America, the term 'African American' would have filled him with horror."⁴⁷

Locke and Jefferson's philosophical, economic, and political arguments are inextricable from their business engagements in the slave trade and chattel slavery. They contended that religion and government should not interfere in the acquisition and preservation of private property. These arguments were politically and philosophically expedient ways of protecting their business interests—the slave trade and chattel slavery. According to Paul Lucas,

> Locke had, therefore, a more important purpose. By insisting that men had a natural right to the land on which they had first laboured; by proving that their legitimate title to the land did not require the explicit consent of others, but was permitted by the law of reason; Locke made private property antecedent to government and divorced society from government, thereby allowing for limited revolutions: an alteration in government need not alter the existing property structure, the dissolution of government did not dissolve society.⁴⁸

Both Locke and Jefferson argued that God authorized them to acquire property. As such, the government was to simply stay out of the domain of private property.

LOCKEAN DEISM AND THOMAS JEFFERSON

Locke held the church and religious leaders in low esteem. He accused the church leaders of instability in their religious declarations and doctrinal pronouncements. He did not esteem the influence of the church upon his intellectual capacity, nor the influence of the church's ecclesiastical structures upon his activities. The "errors" of the church, he contended, are historic.

> How the Church was under the vicissitude of orthodox and Arian emperors is very well known. Or if those things be too remote, our modern English history affords us fresh examples in the reigns of Henry VIII, Edward VI, Mary, and Elizabeth, how easily and smoothly the clergy changed their decrees, their

---

47. Bernstein, *Thomas Jefferson*, xii.
48. Lucas, *Essays on the Margins*, 230–31.

articles of faith, their form of worship, everything according to the inclination of those kings and queens.[49]

Locke's critique of the church and orthodox Christian theology spread beyond Britain to the United States and greatly influenced the Founding Fathers. Benjamin Franklin experienced a similar deistic conversion, as described in his *Autobiography*:

> I was scarce fifteen when, after doubting by turns of several points, as I found them disputed in the different books I read, I began to doubt of Revelation itself. Some books against deism fell into my hands; they were said to be the substance of sermons preached at Boyle's Lectures. It happened that they wrought an effect on me quite contrary to what was intended by them; for the arguments of the deists, which were quoted to be refuted, appeared to me much stronger than the refutations; in short, I soon became a thorough deist.[50]

Franklin's deism contained aspects of polytheism. God, he argued, also created "many lesser gods."[51] Central to the deistic theology is the rejection of revelation or the innate capacity to derive knowledge outside of empirical experience. Like Locke, Franklin rejected revelation as a central means of deriving knowledge in Christianity. However, Franklin was not alone.

David L. Holmes refers to Jefferson as the embodiment of the American version called "the deist spectrum."[52] Jefferson read the works of Locke voraciously and was not shy of quoting and paraphrasing Locke. Donald Wayne Viney notes:

> Jefferson carefully read and made notes on Locke's *Letter on Toleration* in preparing for establishing freedom of worship in Virginia. However, he followed Voltaire and went further than Locke in extending toleration to atheists, and even to those with philosophies that seem contrary to republican government.[53]

In the second book Jefferson ever wrote, *The Moral Life and Morals of Jesus of Nazareth* (also called *The Jefferson Bible*), Jefferson presents a demystical Jesus. The book is a collection of passages from the first four

49. Locke, *Letter Concerning Toleration*, 20.
50. Franklin, *Autobiography*, 61.
51. Viney, "American Deism," 87.
52. Holmes, *Faiths of the Founding Fathers*, 44.
53. Viney, "American Deism," 93–94.

books of the New Testament: Matthew, Mark, Luke, and John. His goal is to mainly present an image of Jesus as a moral teacher rather than the Son of God, a divine person, or the redeemer of the world. In a more direct way, Jefferson claims that Christianity is a corruption, and it has imposed its corruption on Jesus to make him a mystical figure or God. He writes:

> To the corruption of Christianity, I am indeed opposed; but not to the genuine precepts of Jesus himself. I am a Christian in the only sense in which he wished any one to be; sincerely attached to his doctrines, in preference to all others; ascribing to himself every human excellence, and believing he never claimed any other.[54]

In the entire book, Jefferson refers to Jesus as "Jesus of Nazareth" and not Jesus Christ. Fundamentally for Jefferson, Jesus was not a part of the Godhead or the Trinity. For Jefferson, Jesus was a philosopher, but not a platonic philosopher who believes in the existence and reality of the immaterial world. Jefferson does not believe in Plato's philosophy. He contends that Platonic philosophy has "perverted" Christianity. He writes:

> They have been still more disfigured by the corruption of schematizing followers, who have found an interest in sophisticating and perverting the simple doctrines he taught, by engrafting on them the mysticisms of a Grecian Sophist (Plato), frittering them into subtleties and obscuring them with jargon, until they have caused good men to reject the whole in disgust, and to view Jesus himself as an impostor.[55]

With his focus on asserting a mere human Jesus with moral teachings, Jefferson accuses Christians of corrupting the minds of other people regarding the true identity of Jesus. For Jefferson, to attribute divinity, immortality and mysticism to Jesus is to be "an impostor." With extract from the four gospels, Jefferson refers to his book as the "Philosophy of Jesus." Jefferson explains:

> I, too, have made a wee-little book from the same materials (The Gospels) which I call the Philosophy of Jesus. It is a paradigms of his doctrines, made by cutting the texts out of the book and arranging them on the pages of a blank book, in a certain order of time or subject. A more beautiful or precious morsel of

---

54. Jefferson, *Life and Morals of Jesus of Nazareth*, 12.
55. Jefferson, *Life and Morals of Jesus of Nazareth*, 16.

ethics I have never seen. It is a document in proof that I am a REAL CHRISTIAN, that is to say, a disciple of the doctrines of Jesus, very different from the Platonists, who call ME infidel and THEMSELVES Christians and preachers of the Gospel, while they draw all their characteristic dogmas from what its author never said nor saw. They have compounded from the heathen mysteries a system beyond the comprehension of man, of which the great reformer of the vicious ethics and deism of the Jews, were he to return on earth, would not recognize one feature.[56]

The book concludes with passages on Jesus's crucifixion, his death, and burial but not Jesus' resurrection, post-resurrection appearances, or the ascension. In a direct way, Jefferson's book is saturated with deistic and Lockean religious assertions. As discussed earlier, deism:

- rejects the major doctrines of the church;
- rejects the necessity of the creed; and
- rejects the traditional concept of salvation, miracles, and the inspiration of Scripture.[57]

According to Viney, "Jefferson's deism, unlike that of Franklin and Paine, did not include belief in life after death. Jefferson accepted the materialist idea of death as the complete annihilation of consciousness.... Jefferson's attitudes about reason and its relation to religion were heavily deistic and Unitarian."[58] Like Locke, Jefferson emphasized reason over revelation. The rejection of revelation or innateness defines the framework of Jeffersonian deism. This can be seen quite explicitly in his statement to Peter Carr in 1787. "Fix reason firmly in her seat, and call to her tribunal every fact, every opinion. Question with boldness even the existence of God; because, if there be one, he must more approve the homage of reason, than that of blind-folded fear."[59] In words and arguments typical of a deist or latitudinarian, Jefferson refers to the Christian orthodox doctrines as "artificial systems."[60] He rejects the virgin birth of Jesus Christ and the

56. Jefferson, *Life and Morals of Jesus of Nazareth*, 18.
57. Reedy, "Socinians," 285.
58. Viney, "American Deism," 93–94.
59. Peterson, *Portable Thomas Jefferson*, 425.
60. Peterson, *Portable Thomas Jefferson*, 565. "The immaculate conception of Jesus [sic], His deification, the creation of the world by Him, His miraculous powers, His resurrection and visible ascension, His corporeal presence in the Eucharist, the Trinity, original sin, atonement, regeneration, election, orders of Hierarchy, etc."

legitimacy of his birth, his miracles, his resurrection, and his divinity. Instead, Jesus was a "great moral teacher."[61] For Locke and his disciples, it was theism versus deism.[62] Deism was triumphant. However, while the pioneers of deism claimed to championed concepts of the inherent dignity of all human beings, their interpretations of human dignity were highly racialized. Pioneers of deism were slaveholders and slave traders who saw the inherent dignity of people of African descent as inferior to those of European descent. They were White supremacists who advocated the establishment of a legitimate caste system consisting of Blacks as hierarchically inferior to Whites.

61. Viney, "American Deism," 94–95.

62. Hefelbower, "Deism Historically Defined," 223. "Deism, which was essentially non-philosophical, was the more radical application to religious problems of the rationalistic critical way of thinking, that characterized English thought in the seventeenth century, which resulted in the progressive depreciation of the supernatural, especially as it appeared in positive religion, and in magnifying the worth and authority of natural religion."

THE HETEROSEXUAL SLAVE MASTER

The master ran a harem of slave women.
The appealing slave girl was the masters' price.
For Thomas Jefferson, it was his right to rape Sally Hemings
and to birth six children.
Who dares to tell the master it was wrong to rape his slaves?

The notion of slave marriage was unthinkable.
The master owned the slaves, their sexuality, their labor
With absolute power, the master was the "husband."
With absolute power, he could rape, or sell, or kill his slave.

We must not forget the practice of slave breeding.
Congress ended the transatlantic slave trade in 1807,
But the Act left the domestic slave trade untouched.
This Congressional Act led to slave breeding farms for
the domestic slave markets.

The Bucks were used as stallions.
The Wenches were caged to produce babies.
The babies were made for the slave master.
He sold the babies when they were of age,
while the mothers were left in bleeding trauma.[63]

GEORGE WALTERS-SLEYON

---

63. Walters-Sleyon, *Nuggets from the Night*, 118.

9

Thomas Jefferson: The Slave Master

THE RUSH FOR BLACK DIAMONDS refers to the capturing, trading, and intentional acts of reducing Black people to thinghood and property. Thomas Jefferson inherited substantial wealth from his father Peter Jefferson, an Albemarle County planter and plantation owner. At fourteen, Jefferson received two-thirds of his father's estate, which was about 7,500 acres. His wife, a wealthy widow named Martha Wayles Skelton, inherited 11,000 acres of land and 135 slaves at the death of her father John Wayles. One of the slaves acquired by marriage was Sally Hemings—the half-sister of Martha Wayles Skelton. "By 1776 Jefferson managed three large plantations and several smaller ones (together they came to more than 10,000 acres) and he owned about over 180 slaves."[1]

Thomas Jefferson was an active participant in this dehumanization process of Black humanity and an essential philosophical, legal, political, and social architect of the institution of chattel slavery in the United States.

> Slaves were the most valuable form of privately held property in the United States at the end of the Revolution. A Number of slave owners attended the Constitutional Convention (1787). After the adoption of the Constitution, slave owners dominated the executive branch. Moreover, while the most important politician of the era—Thomas Jefferson, a slave owner—feared the

---

1. Katz, "Thomas Jefferson," 467.

negative effects that slavery had on his society, he feared emancipation and the presence of free blacks even more.[2]

Jefferson inherited slaves from his father and a bequest from his father-in-law. According to Bernstein, both acquisitions "made Jefferson one of the largest slaveholders in Virginia."[3] Finkelman notes:

> Jefferson's ideas about slavery and his relationships to the institution were complex and contradictory. A proponent of legal reform and humane criminal codes, he advocated harsh, almost barbaric, criminal punishment for slaves and free blacks; known for expensive views of citizenship, he nevertheless proposed legislation to make emancipated blacks "outlaws" in the land of their birth; opposed to "attainders for corruption of the blood," he proposed expelling from Virginia the children of white women and black men solely because they had "corrupt"—mixed—blood.[4]

THOMAS JEFFERSON: THE AVOWED WHITE SUPREMACIST

Jefferson's racist animus against Black people is quite explicit. He hated Black people. Jefferson made his hatred of Black people publicly explicit before and as the third president of the United States.

Like Locke's *Fundamental Constitutions*, Jefferson's first published book, *Notes on the State of Virginia* demonstrates Jefferson's attitude toward Blacks. It draws on pseudoscientific claims to argue for the "practical necessity" of chattel slavery. In the *Notes*, Jefferson contends that Blacks and Whites are "different." He writes: "The first difference which strikes is that of colour. Whether the black of the negro resides in the reticular membrane between the skin and scarf-skin, or in the scarf-skin itself; whether it proceeds from the colour of the blood, the colour of the bile, or from that of some other secretion, the difference is fixed in nature."[5] He thereafter goes into great detail to describe the differences between Black beauty and White beauty, concluding that Black women were bred from "Oranootan," something between apes and human beings. Black

2. Finkelman, *Slavery and the Founders*, ix–x.
3. Bernstein, *Thomas Jefferson*, 13.
4. Finkelman, *Slavery and the Founders*, 106.
5. Jefferson, *Notes on the State of Virginia*, 269.

men, he contends, prefer White women above Black women with a kind of animalistic sexuality as much as their humanity. He opines Black love is sensual, sexual, and undeveloped.[6] Blacks do not know how to love. He writes,

> They are more ardent after their female; but love seems with them to be more an eager desire, than a tender delicate mixture of sentiment and sensation. Their griefs are transient (what do you expect?) . . . In general, their existence appears to participate more of sensation than reflection. . . . Comparing them by their faculties of memory, reason, and imagination, it appears to me, that in memory they are equal to the whites; in reason much inferior, as I think one could scarcely be found capable of tracing and comprehending the investigations of Euclid; and that in imagination, they are dull, tasteless, and anomalous. It would be unfair to follow them to Africa for this investigation. . . . It is not their condition then, but nature, which has produced the distinction. . . . I advance it therefore as a suspicion only, that the blacks, whether originally a distinct race, or made distinct by time and circumstances, are inferior to the whites in the endowments both of body and mind. . . . The slave, when made free, might mix with, without staining the blood of his master. But with us a second is necessary, unknown to history. When freed, he is to be removed beyond the reach of mixture.[7]

Jefferson is vicious in his diatribes against people of African descent. He contends that people of African descent have not invented anything because it is not in their nature to invent. Finkelman explains that "President Jefferson was deeply hostile to the presence of free blacks in the United States. In a letter to Edward Coles, shortly after he left office, Jefferson referred to them as 'pests.'"[8] Furthermore, Blacks are holistically inferior to Whites. Considering the above, he concludes that Blacks should not

---

6. Finkelman, *Slavery and the Founders*, 265. The reality of Jefferson's statement is reflected in his action toward Joseph Fosset, a relative of Sally Hemings. "This view of Blacks were not merely theoretical. One of the great human tragedies of Jefferson's relationship to slavery occurred when he manumitted five of his male slaves in his will. One of those freed was Joseph Fosset. Revealing his utter inability to see slaves as people with human feelings, Jefferson did not free Fossett's wife and eight children, who were subsequently auctioned off 'to at least four different bidders.' This might be seen as a perverse kind of cruelty, to free Fossett but not his family. But Jefferson believed that blacks lacked the ability to love the way white people did."

7. Jefferson, *Notes on the State of Virginia*, 106.

8. Finkelman, *Slavery and the Founders*, 153.

be allowed to "mix" with Whites sexually. Jefferson was strongly against interracial marriage. Finally, he believed that Black people must be banished from the United States when free. They can only remain in the United States as slaves.

Although he is today considered an Enlightenment figure and advocate of equality for all, Jefferson refused to appropriate the values of his natural-law and natural-right arguments to address the plights of the slaves. If Locke was the Enlightenment theoretician of the defense of slavery and the slave trade, Jefferson was the political and social executive who ensured the survival of chattel slavery in the new nation of the United States. As a Lockean disciple, Jefferson wanted to establish slavery in perpetuity and as well as create a permanent and legitimate slave class in the United States. Jefferson and the Jeffersonians in Congress and the slave-holding states believed in the permanence of the institution of chattel slavery.[9]

A striking and disturbing inconsistency in Jefferson's views of people of African descent was his opposition to mixed-race relationships. His emphasis on the "expatriation" of free Blacks out of Virginia and the United States demonstrates his "paranoid fear of a 'mixture of colour here.'"[10]

According to Bernstein, "When Jefferson was elected to the Virginia House of Burgesses in 1768, he joined its radical bloc. . . . Gentlemen planters made up Virginia's governing class. Convinced that people of lower social status would defer to them automatically and understanding their political role as one of leadership by right of birth, they often saw legislature seats as their personal property."[11] Finkelman asserts that in the history of the United States Congress, most proslavery activists and political leaders were referred to as "Jeffersonians." "The Jeffersonians were also the most proslavery element in American politics."[12] The

---

9. Finkelman, *Slavery and the Founders*, 32.

10. Finkelman, *Slavery and the Founders*, 128. "Jefferson supported colonization even as he understood that the cost of moving so many people to Africa made it 'impossible to look at the enterprises a second time.' However, 'expatriation to the government of the W[est] I[ndies] of their own colour' was 'entirely practicable and greatly preferable to the mixture of colour here.' In 1824 gradual emancipation combined with colonization in St. Domingo seemed like the best solution. It was a reaffirmation of the plan Jefferson suggested in the *Notes* forty years earlier to ensure emancipated slaves were 'removed beyond the reach of mixture.'"

11. Bernstein, *Thomas Jefferson*, 15.

12. Finkelman, *Slavery and the Founders*, 121.

anti-slavery activists were known as the "Federalists." "The Federalists advocated some measure of racial equality, in contrast to the Jeffersonians, who fostered the emerging, racially based, proslavery argument and a concomitant attack on the rights of free blacks."[13] The Jeffersonians were blatant about selling slaves, holding slaves, viciously pursuing fugitive slaves, and supporting the fugitive slave laws and slave codes.[14]

In the 1790s Jeffersonians were known as slave traders, slave masters, and vehement proslavery activists.[15] It was common knowledge that Jefferson himself was vehemently "opposed to the 'liberty of negroes' under any circumstances" to the extent that "Jefferson wanted the British to return the former slaves who had gained their freedom by entering the British lines" after the Revolutionary War or compensate the slave masters, including himself.[16]

This conclusion from the third president of the United States was an indication of his decision to exclude Blacks from participating in the political, social, economic, and democratic life of the United States. Jefferson was excluding Blacks from participating in the "vision of equality" embedded in the Declaration of Independence and the institutions of the United States. He was consigning Blacks to a state of "permanent inequality."[17] Finkelman contends that "Jefferson's negrophobia was profound."[18] Jefferson harbored these negative feelings about Black people when Black people were cooking his food, cleaning his mansion in

---

13. Finkelman, *Slavery and the Founders*, 167.

14. Finkelman, *Slavery and the Founder*, 121.

15. Finkelman, *Slavery and the Founders*, 176–80. "Jefferson's was the party of slavery. The party leaders were Virginia masters. In the North, the party supported slavery and opposed black rights. 'Anti-Negro prejudice eventually became a test of party regularity for the New York Republican party.' Jefferson and his party wanted to destroy the 'black Republic' in Haiti. . . . When Federalists controlled the national government, trade with Haiti ballooned. 'Before Jefferson became president, the value of the American exchange with St. Dominique was perhaps seven times the value of the French commerce on the Island.' This ended with the end of Federalist rule, as Jefferson and his colleagues in the House and Senate imposed an embargo on the black republic."

16. Finkelman, *Slavery and the Founders*, 169–72; "Jefferson to William Gordon, July 16, 1788," in Boyd, *Papers of Jefferson*, 13:363–64; Peterson, *Jefferson and the New Nation*, 236, places the number of slaves taken at twenty-seven. In 1786 Jefferson told his Scottish creditor Alexander McCaul that 'Ld. Cornwallis's army took off 30 of my slaves, burnt one year's crop of tobacco in my houses' and destroyed other property 'to the amount of three or four thousand pounds.'" See "Jefferson to Alexander McCaul, Apr. 19, 1786," in Boyd, *Papers of Jefferson*, 9:389.

17. Finkelman, *Slavery and the Founders*, 108.

18. Finkelman, *Slavery and the Founders*, 109.

Monticello and the presidential mansion in Philadelphia, and tilling his land, among other things.

On September 14, 1769, Jefferson placed this ad regarding a runaway slave named Sandy who had fled from his plantation. Ten pounds was promised to the person who caught Sandy. To Jefferson's pleasure, Sandy was apprehended. Unfortunately for Sandy, Jefferson put him up on the auction block for sale. He was sold for 100 pounds. Finkelman explains, "As a slave owner, Jefferson sold scores of bonds people—at least eighty in one ten-year period ending in the early 1790s—all the while protesting that he had 'scruples about selling negroes but for delinquency or on their own request.'"[19]

Jefferson was also replicating the actions and perceptions toward Blacks of another prominent Virginian politician before him—George Mason. Mason was an avid slave trader. Through the human trade, he defined himself economically, politically, and socioculturally. It is recorded that "Mason sold men 'as you would do cattle at the market' to pay his debts and support his lifestyle."[20]

It was not the practice of Jefferson to free his slaves. There were states and jurisdictions where slaves could be free. Jefferson was never one to "voluntarily" free a slave. Thus, the fate of Sandy.[21] According to Finkelman,

> When Jefferson wrote Declaration, he owned over 150 slaves. Although many of his contemporaries freed their slaves during and after the Revolution, Jefferson did not. In the fight years from 1776 until his death in 1826, a period of extraordinary public service, he did little to end slavery or to disassociate himself from his role as the Master of Monticello. To the contrary, as he accumulated more slaves, he worked assiduously to increase the productivity and the property value of his labor force. Nor did he encourage his countrymen to liberate their slaves, even when they sought his blessing. Even at his death, Jefferson failed to fulfill the promise of his rhetoric. In his will he emancipated

---

19. Finkelman, *Slavery and the Founders*, 186.

20. Finkelman, *Slavery and the Founders*, 3rd ed., 147. "Letter from George Washington to Alexander Spotswood explaining that he would never sell slaves, like cattle (Nov. 23, 1794), in Fitzpatrick, *Writings of George Washington*, 47; see also Hirschfeld, *George Washington*, 16–17.

21. Finkelman, *Slavery and the Founders*, 115. He was a harsh slave master.

only five bondsmen, condemning some 200 others to the auction block.[22]

From 1776 to 1826, Jefferson acquired more slaves to increase the extent of his property. He was a brutal slave master who took no chance nor showed any latitude with his slaves.

There are two sides to Jefferson: the "public" side (the political hero) and the "private" side (the slave trader and slaveholder). These distinctions nonetheless collapsed into one person who was using his public and private persona to advance proslavery rhetoric and proslavery deeds as he engaged in selling his slaves to make ends meet. Finkelman explains that Jefferson even encouraged others to sell their slaves. He was insensitive to the concerns of "slaves as individuals even though they served him at home and in his fields and all too often became a ready form of capital to keep his creditors at bay. . . . Jefferson could not live without slaves. They built his house, cooked his meals, and tilled his fields. In contrast to George Washington, Jefferson failed to manage his lands and finances carefully and lived far beyond his means."[23] Jefferson believed the Black were intellectually and socially inferior to Whites as a fundamental "difference" between the races. "Between 1784 to 1794 alone, Jefferson sold at least eighty-five slaves. Jefferson could not maintain his extravagant lifestyle without his slaves, and to judge from his lifelong behavior, his grand style was far more important than the natural rights of his slaves."[24]

SLAVE BREEDING IN THE SLAVE TRADE AND CHATTEL SLAVERY

A disturbing and grossly ungodly phenomenon was also occurring during the slave trade and chattel slavery: slave breeding. This book argues that there were two kinds of slave breeding: domestic and commercial. Domestic slave breeding was done to increase the immediate plantation workforce. Commercial slave breeding was purposely designed as a commercial breeding farm of Black Africans to be sold at auctions to supply plantations.

Frederick Douglass articulates this travesty very well. The United States, he contended, is guilty of the cruelest maltreatment of human

---

22. Finkelman, *Slavery and the Founders*, 105.
23. Finkelman, *Slavery and the Founders*, 107.
24. Finkelman, *Slavery and the Founders*, 107.

beings. "Take the American slave trade, which we are told by the papers, is especially prosperous just now," he wrote in 1852.

> This trade is one of the peculiarities of American institutions. It is carried on in all the large towns and cities in one-half of this confederacy; and millions are pocketed every year by dealers in this horrid traffic. In several states, this trade is a chief source of wealth. It is called (in contradistinction to the foreign slave-trade) "the internal slave-trade." It is, probably, called so, too, in order to divert from it the horror with which the foreign slave-trade is contemplated.[25]

Douglass names the two forms of slave trade existing in the United States at the time: "the internal slave-trade"—the domestic slave trade, and the "foreign slave-trade""—the international slave trade. Du Bois has spoken particularly of the foreign slave trade as discussed in chapter 1. Douglass displays his disgust at the internal slave trade, which was sustained by the practice of breeding Black folks for sale. He writes:

> Behold the practical operation of this internal slave-trade, the American slave-trade, sustained by American politics and American religion. Here you will see men and women reared like swine for the market. You know what is a swine-drover? I will show you a man-drover. They inhabit all our Southern States. They perambulate the country, and crowd the highways of the nation, with droves of human stock. You will see one of these human flesh jobbers, armed with pistol, whip, and bowie-knife, driving a company of a hundred men, women, and children, from the Potomac to the slave market at New Orleans.[26]

In the domestic slave-breeding business, slave masters raped their female slaves to produce children to increase their slave populations. The slave masters' male children from his own marriage or designated workers might be involved but it was the slave masters' calling. While masters occasionally sold these children, the main purpose of this breeding was to increase the slave population for the immediate plantation. It was also done to gain wealth and social standing. The number of slaves one had contributed to one's social and political status, as well as wealth. Slaves were property —guaranteed wealth, the flow of income, and social status.

---

25. Douglass, "Meaning of July Fourth," 9.
26. Douglass, "Meaning of July Fourth," 10.

Associated with the practice of domestic slave breeding was also the practice of commercial slave breeding. The goal of the commercial slave breeders was strictly commercial. It was to supply the slave market with slaves. It was carried out directly by slave traders, who usually also had camps of slave dwellings under their control. While they were sexually involved in the breeding process, they were known for keeping and sorting out special male slaves to cohabitate with female slaves.

It was White folks as slave masters, slave traders, and slaveholders breeding Black people to increase their slave populations, to sell on the auction blocks, and to increase their revenue and social standing. And the governor of Virginia, senator of the United States Congress, a prominent Enlightenment philosopher, and third president of the United States, Thomas Jefferson, had no problem with it. He was also a prominent slave master and slave trader. If Africans were not captured with arms, inciting local conflict between tribes, villages, and towns, and brought into the United States, they were bred through slave masters' sexual use of female slaves and indiscriminately putting male slaves (bucks) and female slaves together to have children. The male and female slaves had no saying in the matter. They were slaves, rightless, and property of their masters who had absolute right over their humanity and labor.

> Durin' slavery if one marster had a big boy en 'nuther had a big gal de marsters made dem libe tergedder. Ef'n de 'oman didn't hab any chilluns, she wuz put on de block en sold en 'nuther 'oman bought. You see dey raised de chilluns ter mek money on jes lak we raise pigs ter sell.[27]

After 1820, restrictions on the international trade caused the breeding of domestic slaves. The end of the slave trade in Britain and the United States did not end the trade in practice. Slave masters and slave traders instead resorted to the breeding of Black people.

> Dey lots of places where de young massas has heirs by nigger gals. Dey sell dem jes' like other slaves. Dat purty common. It seem like de white women don't mind. Dey didn't 'ject [object], 'cause dat mean more slaves.[28]

Furthermore, it was common knowledge that the slave masters' wives consented to the slave masters' sexual seduction of their female

---

27. WPA Slave Narrative Project, "Interview with Sylvia Watkins."
28. WPA Slave Narrative Project, "Interview with Chris Franklin."

slaves. The slave master was simply increasing the number of his slaves—his human livestock. Whites were breeding Black folks for sale. According to Blackmon:

> During the 1850s, a man named J. M. Brown styled himself as "not a planter but a Negro raiser," growing no cotton on his Bibb County plantation but breeding slaves on his farm specifically for sale on the open market. On the courthouse steps, Bibb County sheriffs routinely held slave auctions to pay off the unpaid taxes of local landowners. County officials authorized holding the sales on either side of the Cahaba River for the convenience of potential buyers in each section of the county. The South's highly evolved system of seizing, breeding, wholesaling, and retailing slaves was invaluable in the final years before the Civil War, as slavery proved in industrial settings to be more flexible and dynamic than even most slave owners could have otherwise believed.[29]

Slave breeding was a common commercial practice even in the 1860s. As a form of "intensive commercial farming,"[30] slave breeding flourished in the interior of the southern states such as Mississippi and Alabama. Furthermore, slave breeding provided an immediate supply of slaves to the slave markets, farms, and companies requiring human labor in these southern parts.

Douglass describes the anguish of the slaves, bred for the market and driven in chains like cattle around from auction blocks to auction blocks with whips. The experience was horrible, the sight was tragic, the treatment was gross, and the experience wretchedly inhumane. He explains:

> These wretched people are to be sold singly, or in lots, to suit purchasers. They are food for the cotton-field and the deadly sugar-mill. Mark the sad procession, as it moves wearily along, and the inhuman wretch who drives them. Hear his savage yells and his blood-curdling oaths, as he hurries on his affrighted captives! There, see the old man with locks thinned and gray. Cast one glance, if you please, upon that young mother, whose shoulders are bare to the scorching sun, her briny tears falling on the brow of the babe in her arms. See, too, that girl of thirteen, weeping, yes! weeping, as she thinks of the mother from whom she has been torn! The drove moves tardily.[31]

---

29. Blackmon, *Slavery by Another Name*, 44.
30. Blackmon, *Slavery by Another Name*, 44.
31. Douglass, "Meaning of July Fourth," 10.

They were sold in droves, driven in sadness, and fettered; many of them were simply bred in slavery to be sold without the knowledge of any human relation and community. The inhumanity, shame, and disgrace they felt at the hands of other human beings were "more fiendish and shocking" to Douglass's imagination.

According to Du Bois, while the international slave trade formally ended in 1807, the local and internal slave trades in the United States continued unabated even after the Civil War ended in 1865. Slave traders could still be seen from farm to farm, village to village, town to town, and county to county exhibiting their goods for purchase—Blacks on display shackled in "droves" as slaves to be purchased in slave markets on auction blocks. Slave labor was legally available and cheap—oblivious to any angst or pain they were causing. The law legalized Black labor. Furthermore, religious and moral convictions were not the primary basis for stopping the breeding of Black human beings.[32]

JEFFERSON'S "CONGO HAREM"

In a letter written to Thomas Jefferson in 1808 entitled "A Slave," the writer, a slave, appeals to the conscience of Jefferson regarding the injustice of slavery.[33] On the maltreatment of female slaves and the appeal for the humane treatment of them, even if considered unworthy savages, he argues, they deserve a fair treatment as women. He writes:

> It is a mere state of barbarism, in which neither the delicacy and chastity of sex, nor the debility & ignorance of little children are regarded. The situation of the female slave is more deplorable & degrading than that of the untutored savage. For little as savages respect the rights of women & children, their women have exemption from labour, & protection from insult during those delicate & painful periods which are peculiar to their sex; & their children are instructed in all the knowledge which is by them deem either useful or ornamental. The degree of servitude to which savage women are bound, is trifling in comparison with the task of a female slave; and inasmuch as their husbands & children reap the fruits of their labour, & in some measure repay it by acquiring a superior skill in hunting & war their

---

32. Blackmon, *Slavery by Another Name*, 43.

33. Baker, "'A Slave' Writes Thomas Jefferson" (Thomas Jefferson to Joel Barlow, Oct. 8, 1809, in Looney, *Papers of Thomas Jefferson*, 1:589).

labour becomes rather a pleasure than a burden. But what is to mitigate the labour of the poor female slave, with the precious burden of her affections at her breast? Slavery is unjust, as [5r] it destroys all the physical & commercial distinctions of labour & property. It is a mere monopoly of labour men, and all their abilities and services.[34]

Unfortunately, Jefferson dismissed the letter as the incoherent ramblings of a slave and "a rhapsody of inconsistencies."[35] According to Thomas Baker, "Though Jefferson could brush aside the letter, modern readers need not (and should not) be so dismissive. For all the letter writer's intellectual inconsistency and rhetorical excesses, he was both consistent and insistent in his outrage against slaveholding as an inhuman and unrepublican practice."[36]

During the tenure of his presidency, Jefferson traveled to the presidential mansion with his "choice slaves" to serve him.[37] His travels to Philadelphia, France, and the rest of Europe were no exception.[38] By now, he had increased his slave holdings to about 500 slaves, a number that included men, women, and children.[39] Josiah Quincy the Federalist "mocked Jefferson's first inaugural; 'intimacy . . . with all the women—matrimonial alliance with none.'"[40] Finkelman writes, "Even if the Federalists could not prove that Jefferson was the father of the children of Sally Hemings, he nevertheless provided a convenient proxy for all southern white men who did father children with their slaves, in violation of Federalists' notions of morality and religion."[41] A prominent name that has come to be associated with Jefferson is Sally Hemings—referred to as his "African Venus."[42]

Sally Hemings was a "slave" girl Jefferson acquired through marriage. She was the slave daughter of Martha Wayles Skelton's father. Sally's mother was a slave named Elizabeth Hemings, affectionately called Betty. Betty's master was John Wayles, the father of Martha Wayles. Sally and

---

34. Baker, "'A Slave' Writes Thomas Jefferson," 144.
35. Baker, "'A Slave' Writes Thomas Jefferson," 129.
36. Baker, "'A Slave' Writes Thomas Jefferson," 139.
37. Finkelman, *Slavery and the Founders*, 174.
38. Finkelman, *Slavery and the Founders*, 129.
39. Finkelman, *Slavery and the Founders*, 128–29.
40. Finkelman, *Slavery and the Founders*, 175.
41. Finkelman, *Slavery and the Founders*, 175.
42. Finkelman, *Slavery and the Founders*, 174.

her brothers and sisters were relatives of Jefferson.[43] But it is of particular note that Sally was the half-sister of Jefferson's wife who was born to one of the slaves of his wife's father; thus Sally was the daughter of Jefferson's father-in-law. Sally Hemings was Thomas Jefferson's half-sister-in-law. Yet Jefferson decided to make Sally his slave mistress and had several children with Sally. "Sally's children," Finkelman notes, "as we now know, were also Jefferson's."[44] Furthermore, Sally traveled with Jefferson in order to serve him.[45]

Virginia law and the Constitution authorized Jefferson's treatment of Sally because Sally Hemings was simply a Black woman, a slave, and his chattel property. Finkelman notes that slaves' "masters would be the owners of their own children fathered with slave women and would treat them as property, to be bought, sold, used as collateral, and gifted. This law reduced the children of all slave women to property and, perversely, led generations of white Southern men to treat their own children as property."[46] Whatever he did to her was legal and right. Jefferson was not alone. What made the institution of chattel slavery also appealing to Whites was that slave masters could at any time legally rape their female slaves. Take for instance the following slave narratives from William Thompson, W. L. Bost, and Chris Franklin.

> I knew a man at the South who had six children by a colored slave. Then there was a fuss between him and his wife, and he sold all the children but the oldest slave daughter. Afterward, he had a child by this daughter, and sold mother and child before the birth. This was nearly forty years ago. Such things are done frequently in the South. One brother sells the other: I have seen that done.[47]

This example underscores the fact that slave masters were breeding children as slaves through their female slaves. It was not uncommon that

43. Finkelman, *Slavery and the Founders*, 218.

44. Finkelman, *Slavery and the Founders*, 218. "Even the Thomas Jefferson Memorial Foundation, which owns Monticello, has now accepted this result . . . there were three pieces of existing evidence to support this conclusion. First, that several of the children bore a striking physical resemblance to Jefferson. Second, that Sally's Fourth child, Madison, testified late in life that Sally had identified Jefferson as the father of her children,' and last, that 'Jefferson was in residence at his mansion in Monticello in Virginia at the time when each of the children was conceived.'"

45. Finkelman, *Slavery and the Founders*, 217.

46. Finkelman, "Slavery in the United States," 112.

47. Drew, "Interview with William Thompson."

slave masters were involved in breeding slaves. The children were also their "blood relatives," especially when the masters were the immediate males involved. Furthermore, it was not uncommon to see slave masters selling the children of their "blood," and keeping the mothers for more breeding. Similarly, it was not uncommon to see the mothers and the children sold together or selling the mothers when the babies were grown to break the connection between mothers and babies. "Plenty of the colored women have children by the white men. She knows better than to not do what he say."[48]

While these examples provide evidence consistent with human breeding, they also show the extent to which Whites engaged in acts of incest. The female slaves the slave masters were raping were also either their direct daughters or granddaughters by blood or step daughters or relatives by marriage born on the plantations. The female slaves had no choice. It was generally accepted that the female slaves and their children were simply economic units and property to sustain the family's wealth and social standing. As the governor of Virginia—a southern state—a congressman in the United States Senate, and the third president of the United States, Jefferson had political, sociocultural, and economic information about the practice of slave masters having sex with their female slaves to purposefully increase their slave populations. Furthermore, Jefferson was a slave trader and slave master.

At the end of his life, Jefferson had over 500 slaves, a phenomenal increase from the 180 slaves he inherited from his father and those his wife, Martha Wayles Skelton, brought into the marriage.[49] Was Thomas Jefferson subduing his female slaves to increase his slaveholding and population? Bernstein explains, "In 1795, Jefferson recorded in his firm book the first child born to Sally Hemings, who then was twenty-two years old. This daughter, Harriet, died two years later, in 1797. During the next fourteen years, Jefferson recorded the births of five more children to Sally Hemings, all but one of who grew to adulthood."[50]

48. WPA Slave Narrative Project, "Interview with W. L. Bost."
49. Katz, "Thomas Jefferson," 467.
50. Bernstein, *Thomas Jefferson*, 111. "William Beverly Hemings was born in 1798; another daughter [unnamed] was born in 1799 and died after later that year; a second Harriet was born in 1801; James Madison Hemings was born in 1805; and Thomas Eston Hemings was born in 1809. All of Sally Hemings's sons were known by their middle names: Beverly, Madison, and Eston."

We are only aware of Jefferson's affairs with Sally Hemings. However, what about the many female slaves that were at the Monticello slave plantation who might have been used to increase Jefferson's slave population and that of his father before Jefferson's marriage? Certainly, Jefferson did not own an all-male slave plantation. Slave breeding was a common practice and Jefferson engaged in it. Jefferson's affairs with Sally Hemings and the birth of six children was a form of slave breeding to increase the slave population of Monticello.

It is interesting to note that Jefferson freed only one female—his daughter with Sally Hemings: Harriet Hemings. "Seven of the eight were male; Jefferson seems to have had little regard for the liberty of his female relatives in bondage. Moreover, the three manumissions during his lifetime—including the one woman he freed—were not a result of philanthropic and humane instincts."[51] Jefferson, like the other slave masters, treated his slaves with complete, selective emotional and rational dissonance—separating his sexual affairs with slaves from any kind of emotional attachment. The slaves were simply property and animals to be used. Furthermore, to free a female slave was a grave economic risk. Male slaves could quickly be sold, dispensed with, and acquired, but female slaves were used to breed more slaves and they had to be kept close to the plantation.

Harriet ran away. Harriet's freedom was not voluntary or based on Jefferson's moral compunction, humanitarian instincts, ethical expedience, or simply a father's interest in the welfare of his daughter.[52] Like her mother, Sally Hemings, and the rest of her siblings, Harriet was a slave, a property like the other slaves. Finkelman notes, "The only woman Jefferson freed was Harriet Hemings, the twenty-year-old daughter of Sally. In 1822 she ran away with her brother Beverly. Jefferson freed Harriet while she was on the run, but not her twenty-four-year-old brother. Perhaps he blamed Beverly for the escape. Given the circumstances of Harriet's emancipation, it can hardly be called voluntary."[53] His children were fleeing perhaps because the only future they saw with him involved being sold on the auction block. They were his slaves with his blood and genes but not his children. Jefferson was breeding children with Sally Hemings to be sold as slaves and they could see it coming. And this is the saddest of all the commentaries on the life of the third president of

51. Finkelman, *Slavery and the Founders*, 129, 131.
52. Finkelman, *Slavery and the Founders*, 3rd ed., 218.
53. Finkelman, *Slavery and the Founders*, 220.

the United States of America: "Although he provided for the freedom of Madison and Eston Hemings when they turn twenty-one, Jefferson did not manumit their mother, Sally,"[54] the Black slave woman with whom he had about six children. It epitomizes his racial hatred for Black people even though she was his relative and half-sister-in-law, the half-sister of his wife Martha Wayles Skelton.[55]

Diggins describes Jefferson's relationship with slavery, race, and equality as a "blasphemous aberration."[56] Like Locke, it is one that further demonstrates Jefferson's inability to reconcile what he wrote in the Declaration of Independence and his slaveholding business practices. Jefferson engaged in a kind of racial cognitive dissonance in which the mind refuses to acknowledge what the body was involved with.

There were few prominent slave masters who freed their slaves and made provisions for them upon their death bed. One of those was Joseph Mayo of Powhatan. In 1785, long before Lincoln's Emancipation Proclamation in 1863, Mayo freed close to 170 slaves to the dislike and astonishment of Jefferson's colleagues. Another acquaintance of Jefferson, John Randolph of Roanoke, freed all of his slaves and provided money for them to buy lands.[57] Finkelman notes, "Had Jefferson freed his slaves, he would have given great impetus to this manumission movement."[58]

Thomas Jefferson died on July 4, 1826. Before he died, Jefferson only freed eight slaves during his entire "lifetime and in his will . . . two in the 1790s, one in 1822, and five by his will in 1826." The rest of the slaves he must have assigned to the horror of the auction block to either pay off his debt or to sustain the estate of Monticello in Virginia. Who were they? "All were members of the Hemings family and thus were Jefferson's relatives by marriage, blood, or both. Jefferson was never generous with freedom, even for his African American relatives."[59]

---

54. Finkelman, *Slavery and the Founders*, 131.

55. Finkelman, *Slavery and the Founders*, 3rd ed. "This brings us to Jefferson's posthumous manumission of five Hemings family members; Joe Fosset, the son of Sally's sister Mary; Burwell, the son of Sally's sister Bett; Sally's brother, John Hemings; and Sally's sons Madison and Eston Hemings" (220).

56. Diggins, "Slavery, Race, and Equality," 208.

57. Finkelman, *Slavery and the Founders*, 112.

58. Finkelman, *Slavery and the Founders*, 112.

59. Finkelman, *Slavery and the Founders*, 129. "The only woman Jefferson freed was Harriet Hemings, the twenty-year old daughter of Sally. In 1822 she ran away with her brother Beverley. Jefferson freed Harriet Hemings while her son was on the run, but not her twenty-four-year-old brother. Perhaps he blamed Beverley Hemings for the

What do we make of Jefferson's legacy? He was a universalist, a prophet of liberty, the third president of the United States, the writer of the Declaration of Independence, but also a slave master, a slave trader, and a public hater of Black humanity. The long-lasting impact of Jefferson's diatribes against Black humanity is reflected in the United States and White folks' inability to see Black people as equals. His "scientifically baseless conclusions and speculations undermined the concept of human equality" during his lifetime and thereafter.[60]

FREDERICK DOUGLASS: OPPRESSION IS MADDENING

Frederick Douglass's critique of the Fourth of July is also a critique of Jeffersonian slavery. Douglass speaks of the Fourth of July celebration as a day for Whites to celebrate but not Blacks. "This, for the purpose of this celebration, is the Fourth of July. It is the birthday of your National Independence, and of your political freedom."[61] Douglass contends that the Founding Fathers were keen to describe England as an oppressive colonial power: "They went so far in their excitement as to pronounce the measures of government unjust, unreasonable, and oppressive, and altogether such as ought not to be quietly submitted to."[62] However, Douglass's reference is a bit sarcastic. He explains, "To say now that America was right, and England wrong, is exceedingly easy. Everybody can say it; the dastard, not less than the noble brave, can flippantly discant on the tyranny of England toward the American Colonies."[63] Douglass notes that the Founding Fathers identified the American colony as a victim of the oppression of England. England is perceived as a diabolically oppressive nation, power, and people. The American colony had no choice but to rebel for freedom and independence. He writes, "Oppression makes a wise man mad. Your fathers were wise men, and if they did not go mad, they became restive under this treatment. They felt themselves the victims of grievous wrongs, wholly incurable in their colonial capacity."[64]

---

escape. Given the circumstances of this emancipation, it can hardly be called voluntary. None of Jefferson's biographers discusses manumission" (131).

60. Finkelman, *Slavery and the Founders*, 111.
61. Douglass, "Meaning of July Fourth," 1.
62. Douglass, "Meaning of July Fourth," 2.
63. Douglass, "Meaning of July Fourth," 2.
64. Douglass, "Meaning of July Fourth," 3.

The American colony had no choice but to rebel for freedom and independence. For Douglass, oppression is maddening. It was the fundamental reason for the strive for independence. The Revolutionary War was a resistance against the tyranny and oppression of the British Empire. With such consideration, the American Congress and its army were restless until they attained freedom and independence. He writes, "The 4th of July is the first great fact in your nation's history the very ringbolt in the chain of your yet undeveloped destiny. . . . I have said that the Declaration of Independence is the ringbolt to the chain of your nation's destiny; so, indeed, I regard it. The principles contained in that instrument are saving principles."[65]

While extolling America's resistance to British oppression, Douglass is careful to acknowledge the Founding Fathers' adherence to the principles of justice, equity, and fairness. These, he contends, were central to the Declaration of Independence. He interjects, "Fellow-citizens, pardon me, allow me to ask, why am I called upon to speak here to-day? What have I, or those I represent, to do with your national independence? Are the great principles of political freedom and of natural justice, embodied in that Declaration of Independence, extended to us?"[66] Douglass's eloquence and intelligence are on display as he establishes a pivotal distinction between himself, his race, his fellow former slaves and slaves, and the American enterprise of independence. He notes, "I am not included within the pale of this glorious anniversary! Your high independence only reveals the immeasurable distance between us."[67] He describes the richness of American justice but noted that it was not applied to the concerns of his people. "The rich inheritance of justice, liberty, prosperity, and independence, bequeathed by your fathers, is shared by you, not by me. . . . This Fourth July is yours, not mine. You may rejoice, I must mourn. . . . Do you mean, citizens, to mock me, by asking me to speak to-day? I can to-day take up the plaintive lament of a peeled and woe-smitten people!"[68] Douglass is describing the grave inconsistency between the founders' theory and practice. While appealing to God with "plaintive laments," he is also demonstrating the Founding Fathers' hypocrisy in accusing England of oppression while at the same time continuing to keep him and his people enslaved.

65. Douglass, "Meaning of July Fourth," 4.
66. Douglass, "Meaning of July Fourth," 6.
67. Douglass, "Meaning of July Fourth," 7.
68. Douglass, "Meaning of July Fourth," 7.

America jubilates over its independence even while keeping others in chains. Douglass writes:

> Whether we turn to the declarations of the past, or to the professions of the present, the conduct of the nation seems equally hideous and revolting. America is false to the past, false to the present, and solemnly binds herself to be false to the future. Standing with God and the crushed and bleeding slave on this occasion, I will, in the name of humanity which is outraged, in the name of liberty which is fettered, in the name of the constitution and the Bible which are disregarded and trampled upon, dare to call in question and to denounce, with all the emphasis I can command, everything that serves to perpetuate slavery—the great sin and shame of America! "I will not equivocate; I will not excuse"; I will use the severest language I can command; and yet not one word shall escape me that any man, whose judgment is not blinded by prejudice, or who is not at heart a slaveholder, shall not confess to be right and just.[69]

Douglass contends that he does not need any affirmation to declare that people of African descent are human beings, that in slavery in the independent United States they deserve liberty, that in the eyes of the Declaration of Independence, they ought to be treated as "equal" to all men and women. He writes:

> What, am I to argue that it is wrong to make men brutes, to rob them of their liberty, to work them without wages, to keep them ignorant of their relations to their fellow men, to beat them with sticks, to flay their flesh with the lash, to load their limbs with irons, to hunt them with dogs, to sell them at auction, to sunder their families, to knock out their teeth, to burn their flesh, to starve them into obedience and submission to their masters? Must I argue that a system thus marked with blood, and stained with pollution, is wrong? No! I will not. I have better employment for my time and strength than such arguments would imply. What, then, remains to be argued? Is it that slavery is not divine; that God did not establish it; that our doctors of divinity are mistaken? There is blasphemy in the thought. That which is inhuman, cannot be divine! Who can reason on such a proposition? They that can, may; I cannot. The time for such argument is passed.[70]

---

69. Douglass, "Meaning of July Fourth," 7.
70. Douglass, "Meaning of July Fourth," 8–9.

According to Douglass, the Fourth of July is antithetical to the Black experience. The celebration is the display of "a sham," "an unholy license," "heartless," "brass fronted impudence," and to God, "mere bombast, fraud, a nation of savages. There Is not a nation on the earth guilty of practices more shocking and bloody than are the people of the United States, at this very hour."[71] The American slavery and the American slave trade were industries of horror for Black humanity. Here Douglass describes the selling of Black people as "flesh-mongers" like fishmongers scrambled for the lives of Black people like cattle to buy and sell at a prominent slave market in Baltimore. He writes.

> I was born amid such sights and scenes. To me the American slave-trade is a terrible reality. When a child, my soul was often pierced with a sense of its horrors. I lived on Philpot Street, Fell's Point, Baltimore, and have watched from the wharves the slave ships in the Basin, anchored from the shore, with their cargoes of human flesh, waiting for favorable winds to waft them down the Chesapeake. There was, at that time, a grand slave mart kept at the head of Pratt Street, by Austin Woldfolk. His agents were sent into every town and county in Maryland, announcing their arrival, through the papers, and on flaming "hand-bills," headed cash for Negroes. . . The flesh-mongers gather up their victims by dozens, and drive them, chained, to the general depot at Baltimore. . .. In the deep, still darkness of midnight, I have been often aroused by the dead, heavy footsteps, and the piteous cries of the chained gangs that passed our door. The anguish of my boyish heart was intense.[72]

Douglass' speech demonstrates the inconsistency between the ideals and lofty principles of the Declaration of Independence and the state of his people in America's quest for freedom and independence from England. The breeding, selling, and ungodly practice of chattel enslavement of Black people by White people flourished with a socio-cultural, political, economic, and religious consensus. He writes:

> Your broad republican domain is hunting ground for men. Not for thieves and robbers, enemies of society, merely, but for men guilty of no crime. Your law-makers have commanded all good citizens to engage in this hellish sport. Your President, your Secretary of State, your lords, nobles, and ecclesiastics enforce, as

---

71. Douglass, "Meaning of July Fourth," 9.
72. Douglass, "Meaning of July Fourth," 10–11.

a duty you owe to your free and glorious country, and to your God, that you do this accursed thing.[73]

Under the shadows of the Northwest Ordinance[74] and the Declaration of Independence, Douglass explained the dilemma of being Black in the eyes of the law and the courts. To the American criminal justice system, even the "most pious" and "exemplary black man" is a suspect.[75] He writes:

> For black men there is neither law nor justice, humanity nor religion. The Fugitive Slave Law makes mercy to them a crime; and bribes the judge who tries them. An American judge gets ten dollars for every victim he consigns to slavery, and five, when he fails to do so. The oath of any two villains is sufficient, under this hell-black enactment, to send the most pious and exemplary black man into the remorseless jaws of slavery![76]

Justice is difficult to come by for the Black man in the courts of the United States. Judges are racist and deliberately partial. A Black man's testimony may even work against him because whatever he says is not fully respected, especially when it is against a White person. Justice in the United States courts is a "shameless" display and "disregard" for the law. He notes, "If any man in this assembly thinks differently from me in this matter, and feels able to disprove my statements, I will gladly confront him at any suitable time and place he may select."[77]

---

73. Douglass, "Meaning of July Fourth," 11.
74. Library of Congress, "Northwest Ordinance."
75. Douglass, "Meaning of July Fourth," 12.
76. Douglass, "Meaning of July Fourth," 12.
77. Douglass, "Meaning of July Fourth," 12.

THE HOMOSEXUAL SLAVE MASTER

Then there is the case of the homosexual slave master,
Not often talked about but indeed existed.
The slave master could publicly buck-break the arrogant Buck.
With the practice of buck-breaking, the master was in control.

Like the raping of the Wench, the Buck was subdued.
In public, the macho Buck was publicly humiliated.
Like the raping of the Wench, the Buck was humbled.
In the breaking of the Buck racial and sexual dominance, they perfected.

With impunity, the master could beat his slave to death.
With impunity, the master could starve his slave to death.
With impunity, the master could prosecute his slave to death.
To death, the slave was destined at the wimp of the master.

Sex and rape the slave masters used to intimidate.
Sex and rape the slave masters used to discipline.
Sex and rape the slave masters used to control.
Sex and rape the slave masters used as pleasure.[78]

GEORGE WALTERS-SLEYON

---

78. Walters-Sleyon, *Nuggets from the Night*, 120.

10

Emancipation
Toward the End of Chattel Slavery in the UK and the US

While I was at the hotel to-day, an elderly gentleman called upon me to know whether I was really in favor of producing a perfect equality between the negroes and white people. [Great Laughter.] While I had not proposed to myself on this occasion to say much on that subject, yet as the question was asked me I thought I would occupy perhaps five minutes in saying something in regard to it. I will say then that I am not, nor ever have been, in favor of bringing about in any way the social and political equality of the white and black races, [applause]— that I am not nor ever have been in favor of making voters or jurors of negroes, nor of qualifying them to hold office, nor to intermarry with white people; and I will say in addition to this that there is a physical difference between the white and black races which I believe will forever forbid the two races living together on terms of social and political equality. And inasmuch as they cannot so live, while they do remain together there must be the position of superior and inferior, and I as much as any other man am in favor of having the superior position assigned to the white race.[1]

---

1. Lincoln and Douglas, "Lincoln-Douglas Debates," para. 3.

My paramount objective in this struggle is to save the Union and is not either to save or destroy slavery. If I could save the Union without freeing any slave, I would do it, and if I could save it by freeing all the slaves I would do it, and if I could save it by freeing some and leaving others alone I would also do that. What I do about slavery, and the colored race, I do because I believe it helps to save the Union.[2]

IN THE UNITED STATES, SLAVERY did not end, it only mutated into penal slavery. For the rest of the non-European world, it mutated into full-blown colonialism.[3] The economic industry of the transatlantic slave trade and the institution of chattel slavery ended in theory in the United States with the Emancipation Proclamation in 1863. In 1833, the United Kingdom formally ended the human trade. However, the foundations for perpetual racial discriminations and assertions of White supremacy over Black humanity were set into motion. Europeans and White Americans will henceforth struggle in their conscience to accept Black people as equal human beings after Whites have subjected Black people with impunity to the horrors, cruelties, and ungodliness of the transatlantic slave trade and chattel slavery.

THE THEORETICAL END OF CHATTEL SLAVERY IN THE US AND THE BRITISH COLONIES

The Act of Parliament in 1807 made the importation of Africans[4]—the buying and selling of Africans in the slave trade into British territories—illegal.[5] In 1833/1834, the British Parliament outlawed slavery by

---

2. Lincoln, "Letter to Horace Greeley," para. 5.

3. Blackmon, *Slavery by Another Name*, 41. "In the first decades of that span, the intensity of southern whites' needs to reestablish hegemony over blacks rivaled the most visceral patriotism of the wartime Confederacy. White Southerners initiated an extraordinary campaign of defiance and subversion against the new biracial social order imposed on the South and mandated by the Thirteenth Amendment to the US Constitution, which abolished slavery. They organized themselves into vigilante gangs and militias, undermined free elections across the region, intimidated Union agents, terrorized black leaders, and waged an extremely effective propaganda campaign to place blame for the anarchic behavior of whites upon free slaves."

4. Eltis, "British Contribution."

5. Drescher, "Whose Abolition?"

passing the Slavery Abolition Act.[6] Notwithstanding these developments, the conditions of slavery remained well into the twentieth century in the British territories, including the Caribbean, and regions of the slave superpower nations, owned in Africa, Brazil, and the West Indies.[7] Furthermore, the post-1807 and 1833 slave-related Acts saw increased illegal slave trading and capturing of Africans in which the British Parliament and her allies were directly involved.[8] It was over a century after the death of John Locke[9] but only seven years after the death of Thomas Jefferson.[10]

The end of the slave trade[11] by the United Kingdom was not for ethical or humanitarian reasons.[12] As evident in the cases of Portugal, Spain, Netherlands,[13] and France, the slave trade and chattel slavery continued informally.[14] Furthermore, the transatlantic slave trade and the institution of chattel slavery intersected and mutated into full-blown empire-building, imperialism, and colonialism[15]—the British Empire[16] and the Commonwealth countries of Africa and the Caribbean;[17] the Portuguese Empire;[18] the Francophone countries of the French Empire[19] in Africa and the Caribbean;[20] the Spanish Empire and colonies of North America; and the Dutch Empire.[21] Fundamental to these empires and their current legacies are the human trade in Africans, the institution of slavery, and chattel slavery in which Africans were owned as property.[22] The institution of human trafficking and the reduction of human beings

---

6. Lowcountry Digital History Initiation, "Historical Context."
7. Landers, "Slavery in the Spanish Caribbean."
8. Head, "Slave Smuggling."
9. King, *Life of John Locke*.
10. Onuf, "Declare Them a Free and Independent People."
11. Jennings, "France, Great Britain."
12. Page, "Rational Dissent."
13. Weststeijn, "Republican Empire."
14. Viotti da Costa, "Portuguese-African Slave Trade."
15. Hatfield, "Slavery, Trade, War."
16. Wolff, "British Imperialism."
17. Lange, Mahoney, and Hau, "Colonialism and Development."
18. Rosenzweig and Tellis, "Portuguese Caravel."
19. Confer, "French Colonial Ideas."
20. Conklin, "Colonialism and Human Rights."
21. Ryckmans, "Belgian 'Colonialism.'"
22. Austen and Smith, "Images of Africa."

to mere property was immoral.[23] The slave trade and institution of chattel slavery demonstrate Europeans' and White Americans' inhumanity to Black Africans.[24]

In 1844, Kansas-Nebraska passed the Act of 1844, which made it possible for slavery and the slave trade to flourish in territories that were previously excluded from the slave trade. Furthermore, in the 1857 Supreme Court case of *Dred Scott*, chattel slavery or enslaved people as legal property received problematic recognition. According to Campbell, Chief Justice Roger Taney made it quite clear that it was not the intention to designate the individuals of the "African race" as "people" consistent with the meaning of the United States Constitution. He describes Black people as "beings of an inferior order, and altogether unfit to associate with the white race, either in social or political relations; and so inferior that they had no rights which the white man was bound to respect."[25]

Chief Justice Taney's statements were ladened with racial epithets and insinuations about Black humanity, not just about citizenship in the United States. He writes:

> The question is simply this: Can a negro, whose ancestors were imported into this country, and sold as slaves, become a member of the political community formed and brought into existence by the Constitution of the United States, and as such become entitled to all the rights, and privileges, and immunities, guaranteed by that instrument to the citizen? One of which rights is the privilege of suing in a court of the United States in the cases specified in the Constitution.[26]

Black people, he further argues, were enslaved people and property from the beginning and should always be regarded and treated as slaves in the United States of America. Since the Founding Fathers only held Blacks as slaves and property, they should be regarded as such and not as citizens with rights who ought to participate in the democratic process of the United States. Chief Justice Taney was advancing the argument for the perpetual enslavement of Black people and the support of a legitimate caste system on the state and federal levels. John Locke and Thomas Jefferson had advanced a similar argument as previously discussed. Taney's

---

23. Thomas and Bean, "Fishers of Men."
24. Deyle, "'Abominable' New Trade."
25. Campbell, *Middle Passages*, 69.
26. *Dred Scott v. Sandford* 1856, p. 408.

claims also underscore the argument that the United States Founding Fathers were staunch White supremacists and protectionists of Whiteness. Blacks, Taney contends:

> Are not included, and were not intended to be included, under the word "citizens" in the Constitution, and can therefore claim none of the rights and privileges which that instrument provides for and secures to citizens of the United States. On the contrary, they were at that time [1787] considered as a subordinate and inferior class of beings, who had been subjugated by the dominant race, and, whether emancipated or not, yet remained subject to their authority, and had no rights or privileges but such as those who held the power and the Government might choose to grant them.[27]

Based on Jefferson's dictum, Southern states immediately began to enact laws that forbid the mixing of the races and the reenslavement of Blacks through the penal system. As a scapegoat for the South's anger for losing the war, Blacks were treated horribly.[28]

Unlike the United Kingdom, it took a civil war in the United States to end the industrial slave trade and chattel slavery on the state and federal levels. Besides the quest to save the Union, as demonstrated in Lincoln's debate with Douglas above, the crux of the problem was also the attempt to end the ungodly and sinful practice of breeding and selling Black people. The residues of these divisions concerning slavery and the humanity of Black people live on as part of the American racial consciousness toward Black humanity. And there is a similar consciousness regarding how Blacks exist in the former slave-trading nations of Europe, including England and Wales, Scotland, Spain, France, Denmark, and Portugal. In both the United States and Europe, racial discrimination and segregation against people of African descent became legislative.

In 1863 President Abraham Lincoln issued the Emancipation Proclamation. According to David Oshinsky, emancipation was met with rage and "anti-Black" resistance. A new kind of violence toward Blacks emerged. During slavery, slaves were protected investments. After emancipation, Blacks were free but faced violence, hatred, and threats. Oshinsky contends, "A federal official noted that blacks in Mississippi were now more vulnerable than mules because the 'breaking of the neck of the free

---

27. *Dred Scott v. Sandford* 1856, p. 404.
28. Oshinsky, *Worse Than Slavery*, 16.

negro is nobody's loss.'"[29] A culture of violence erupted.[30] Emancipation legally removed a massive source of free labor for Whites. Mississippi, like other Southern states, lost its workforce after the war. Furthermore, the price of citizenship for Blacks did not come entirely with the signing of the Emancipation Proclamation. According to James Campbell:

> The basic privileges of citizenship—the right to bequeath and inherit property, to testify in court, to sit on juries, and, most importantly, to vote—were sharply circumscribed. In New York, for example, the state constitution of 1821 imposed new franchise restrictions on free people of color even as it extended universal suffrage to white men; by 1825, only sixteen African Americans remained on the voters' rolls of New York City, out of a total of the black population of more than twelve thousand.[31]

Before and after emancipation, the price of citizenship for Blacks in the United States came at the cost of their mortality, blood, labor, and dignity. This mortal and existential price is mainly reflected in the political and criminal justice institutions of the United States. Campbell notes, "The legislative assault on people of color reached its logical conclusion in the era's frequent 'race riots,' essentially pogroms, in which mobs rampaged through black neighborhoods, beating residents, and looting and burning property. However, these mob actions against Black people date back to the pre-emancipation era. One historian has counted forty-one significant riots in the United States in the quarter century between 1824 and 1849."[32]

This book has argued that foundational to the post-emancipation treatment of Blacks were the legacies of Lockean slavery and Jeffersonian slavery. Lockean slavery to Jeffersonian slavery facilitated the socioeconomic, political, and penal structures that normalized racial and economic marginalization in the US. They prepared the ground for the appropriation of Black "labor power" after the Civil War in 1865 through the penal system.[33] According to Blackmon, "By the end of the 1880s, at least ten thousand black men were slaving in forced labor mines, fields, and work camps in the former Confederate state. The subjugation of

---

29. Oshinsky, *Worse Than Slavery*, 25.
30. Oshinsky, *Worse Than Slavery*, 24.
31. Campbell, *Middle Passages*, 59.
32. Campbell, *Middle Passages*, 59.
33. Bair, *Prison Labor in the United States*, 19.

black labor was a lucrative enterprise and critical to the industrialists and entrepreneurial farmers amassing capital and land."[34]

Before emancipation, Black people rarely served time in jail; as one freedman explains, "jails was all built for the white folks. There warn't never nobody of my color put in one of them. No time . . . to stay in jail; they had to work; when they done wrong they was whipped and let go."[35] However, this changed after emancipation; almost overnight jails and prisons in Mississippi became a "negro preserve."

According to Robert Perkinson, emancipation was an economic but also a sociocultural and political shift. A sense of "dispossession" took over immediately as we shall see in *The Rush for Black Diamonds, Volume Two*. Former slaves were kept in "unlawful bondage" or severely attacked, whipped, shot, or hanged by vigilantes. Perkinson explains:

> A former slave named Susan Merritt reported that in Rusk Country, where Texas' second walled penitentiary would go up years later, planters employed every means to keep their field hands at work. "You could see lots of niggers hangin' to trees in Sabine bottom right after freedom, 'cause they cotch 'em swimmin'" 'cross Sabine River and shoot 'em.[36]

In the Fundamental Constitutions, Locke asserts in several ways that Whites are the legal owners of Blacks' bodies and labor power; that Blacks are the property of Whites; that Black bodies are economic units; and that Black humanity is sociopolitically and economically constructed. Locke's arguments about Blacks' humanity became germane to the social consciousness of the United States and Western Europe, including his home country Britain. Locke provided a unique theoretical and conceptual premise for Whites' perception and treatment of Black people in relation to the slave trade and chattel slavery before and after the Civil War in the United States. Douglass exclaims:

> Americans! your republican politics, not less than your republican religion, are flagrantly inconsistent. You boast of your love of liberty, your superior civilization, and your pure Christianity, while the whole political power of the nation (as embodied in the two great political parties) is solemnly pledged

---

34. Blackmon, *Slavery by Another Name*, 90.
35. Ayers, *Vengeance and Justice*, 46.
36. Perkinson, *Texas Tough*, 86.

to support and perpetuate the enslavement of three million of your countrymen.[37]

Penal slavery developed after emancipation with the advent of the convict leasing system. It was just a matter of time before the United States and the United Kingdom returned to profiting from Black bodies. This time, poor Whites and other minority groups were included among the exploited population, who were mostly Blacks. *The Rush for Black Diamonds, Volume Two* argues that the post-1970 modern penal systems of the United States and the United Kingdom and the phenomenon of mass incarceration maintain the ethos and financial interests of the slave trade and the institution of chattel slavery.[38]

I define Lockean slavery as the policies and practices under which: (1) slaves are captives through "just war"; (2) slaves are made rightless property through conquest; (3) the value of the slave's humanity is strictly one of economic utility, and slaves are "wild beasts" that must be tamed by slavery; (4) the discretionary power of the slave master toward his slave is "absolute"; and (5) slaves are legally dead and only useful to their masters. The slave master has the right to determine the value of the slave's humanity.[39]

The definition above will help show the practical and conceptual influences of Lockean slavery on post–Civil War penal developments in the United States after emancipation in 1863 and the Thirteenth Amendment as discussed in *The Rush for Black Diamonds, Volume Two*. The formal passing of the Thirteenth Amendment marks the transition from Lockean slavery to the concept of Lockean punishment. According to Du Bois, "The slave went free; stood a brief moment in the sun; then moved back again toward slavery."[40] In his theory of punishment, Locke combines concepts of divine law, human laws, and natural laws. Douglas Blackmon suggests:

> Blacks could be excluded from the Enlightenment concept that every man was granted by God individual freedom and a right to the pursuit of happiness because colonial laws codified a less than full-human status of any person carrying even a trace of black or Indian blood. Instead of embracing the concept that

---

37. Douglass, "Meaning of July Fourth," 15.
38. Farrall et al., "Thatcherism."
39. Richards, Mulligan, and Graham, "Property and People," 50.
40. Du Bois, *Black Reconstruction in America*, 30–31.

regardless of color "All men are created equal," with no king or prince born to higher status than any other, colonial leaders extended a version of "royal" status to all whites.[41]

Central to the industrial slave trade and the institution of chattel slavery are the horrific death tolls of Africans. Africans and their descendants died in the fields, bushes, in confinement camps, and on the beaches of Africa, where they were captured, gathered for transportation, and loaded on ships to the West Indies, Brazil, Europe, and America. They died in the Middle Passage of the Atlantic Ocean. They died in the slave breeding houses, fields, slave plantations, and territories of the superpowers of the human trade and chattel slavery: Britain, the Netherlands, France, Germany, Belgium, Spain, Scotland, the United States, and Portugal. With impunity, these superpowers of the human trade sold, raped, dismembered, wiped, and killed Black Africans for economic, political, military, racial and socio-cultural dominance.

---

41. Blackmon, *Slavery by Another Name*, 40.

ABOLITION IN BRITAIN AND AMERICA

In 1833, the British ended the trade in human beings,
Wilberforce was an instrument with a Divine mandate.
In Amazing Grace, John Newton regretted,
The trader in humans who sinned against God and Africans.

The human trade and economic industry,
Understood by Locke and Ashford, and Tilton,
An economic means to generational prosperity,
Yet, in Wesley's advice, Wilberforce was victorious.

The trade in human beings ended in Britain,
But Americans demanded a civil war.
Abraham Lincoln could bear the guilt no more,
Yet, in the Thirteenth Amendment, slavery is preserved.

32 years later, the North and the South to war they went,
To end the human trade in 1863.
A military battle they ardently fought,
The desire for slave labor America could not shake off

Though slavery was moribund by the law,
Ipso facto every Whiteman was a law enforcement officer Du Bois explains.
Mob justice and vigilante justice in law enforcement were birth,
They used the Black Codes and Convict Leasing System
to recoup lost Black labor.[42]

GEORGE WALTERS-SLEYON

---

42. Walters-Sleyon, *Nuggets from the Night*, 121.

11

Walter Rauschenbusch: Sin

SIN IS SOCIOPOLITICAL, ECONOMIC, AND RACIAL EXPLOITATION

THE BIBLICAL DEFINITION OF SIN implies a spiritual fall.[1] But for Walter Rauschenbusch (1861–1918), sin is social. The transatlantic slave trade and chattel slavery were sinful laws, policies, and practices. According to Gary Dorrien "Rauschenbusch was an idealist with a strong awareness of the pervasive reality of personal and social evil; he was a moralist who understood that moralism alone will never gain social justice; he was both religiously devout and deeply politicised."[2] Rauschenbusch defines sin as sociopolitical, economic, and racial exploitations. For him, the transatlantic slave trade and chattel slavery are sinful policies and practices that the West engaged in. He writes:

> It is not easy to define sin, for sin is as elastic and complicated as life itself. Its quality, degree, and culpability vary according to the moral intelligence and maturity of the individual, according to his social freedom, and his power over others. Theologians have erred, it seems to me, by fitting their definitions to the most highly developed forms of sin and then spreading them over germinal and semi-sinful actions and conditions.[3]

---

1. Romans 3:23.
2. Dorrien, *Soul in Society*, 6.
3. Rauschenbusch, *Theology for the Social Gospel*, 45.

Rauschenbusch argues that sin is social "guilt." It is informed by a concentrated form of selfishness, self-love, and misanthropy that manifests itself into several forms of malicious actions. "Men press their covetousness to the injury of society. They are willing to frustrate the cause of liberty and social justice in whole nations in order to hold their selfish social and economic privileges."[4] Sin is "conflict between the selfish Ego and the common good of humanity."[5] A working definition of sin for Rauschenbusch is one that is broadly concrete rather than abstract. He explains that "sin is not a private transaction between the sinner and God. We must democratise the conception of God; then the definition of sin will be more realistic."[6] Sin is social. Sin is injustice. Sin is not individualistic but collective and generational.

Rauschenbusch provides a theological critique of historical forms of marginalization due to sociopolitical and economic policies created to marginalize racial and economically disadvantaged groups generationally. His definition of sin is informed by personal insights acquired in the late 1800s as a pastor.

In 1886, Rauschenbusch was appointed to his first long-term parish at the Second Baptist Church located in a poor neighborhood called Hell's Kitchen in New York City. Previously, he had served a small German Baptist church in Louisville. However, it was at Hell's Kitchen that Rauschenbusch saw the collateral consequences of concentrated poverty, gross forms of economic exploitation of the poor, deplorable living conditions, racial conflicts, and overt racism. He describes his motivation for that congregation and his enthusiasm to declare Christ to them in January 1913 in an address delivered to the YMCA entitled "The Kingdom of God." He writes:

> I wanted to do hard work for God. Indeed, one of the great thoughts that came upon me was that I ought to follow Jesus Christ in my personal life, and die over again his death. I felt that every Christian ought to participate in the dying of the Lord Jesus Christ, and in that way help to redeem humanity, and it was that thought that gave my life it's fundamental direction in the doing of Christian work.[7]

---

4. Rauschenbusch, *Theology for the Social Gospel*, 46.
5. Rauschenbusch, *Theology for the Social Gospel*, 46.
6. Rauschenbusch, *Theology for the Social Gospel*, 48.
7. Rauschenbusch, "Kingdom of God," 265.

Unfortunately, neither his little church in Louisville nor his heavenly-bound "individualistic" understanding of salvation prepared him for Hell's Kitchen. The congregation at Hell's Kitchen church was about 125 members. They provided an annual salary of nine hundred dollars a year for the pastor.[8] According to Benson Landis, Rauschenbusch pastored Hell's Kitchen for a long time but not because of the salary he was receiving. Landis explains, "Rauschenbusch saw at first hand the soul-destroying effects of destitution, overcrowded, crime-breeding tenements, and economic exploitation. For eleven years he carried on his ministry in Hell's Kitchen, and there was born the Walter Rauschenbusch who later challenged the American churches with his prophetic declaration of the social gospel."[9]

The early and late nineteenth century in the United States saw the influx of European immigrants, and both free and runaway slaves migrating to northern cities in fear of mob lynching from the American South. They formed the backdrop to Rauschenbusch's social gospel. According to Landis, "It came through personal contact with poverty. . . . And when I saw how men toiled all their life long, hard, toilsome lives, and at the end had almost nothing to show for it; how strong men begged for work and could not get it in hard times; how little children died—oh, the children's funeral!"[10] The experience was the beginning of Rauschenbusch's involvement in the Social Gospel movement. Rauschenbusch's involvement was profoundly religious and "more rooted in the church, and more burdened with oedipal weight."[11] His newfound conversion compelled him to look beyond the confines of liberal pietism. "It was an experience of creative dislocation."[12]

Rauschenbusch's major argument was that the church had forsaken its social mandate as enshrined within the scriptures, especially the teachings of Jesus. The Western Church has reduced Christianity to a kind of racial solipsism. Based on the prophetic mandate of Old Testament prophets, he defined his social gospel message as based on the will of God. Injustice and structural forms of social marginalization as a result of myopic political policies were catalysts for the promotion of ill social conditions. He notes:

8. Landis, *Rauschenbusch Reader*, xiv.
9. Landis, *Rauschenbusch Reader*, xv.
10. Landis, *Rauschenbusch Reader*, xiv.
11. Landis, *Rauschenbusch Reader*, 25.
12. Dorrien, *Soul in Society*, 25.

> Sin is essentially selfishness. That definition is more in harmony with the social gospel than with any individualistic type of religion. The sinful mind, then, is the unsocial and anti-social mind. To find the climax of sin we must not linger over a man who swears, or sneers at religion, or denies the mystery of the Trinity, but put our hands on social groups who have turned the patrimony of a nation into the private property of a small class, or have left the peasant labourer cowed, degraded, demoralized, and without rights in the land. When we find such in history, or in present-day life, we shall know we have struck real rebellion against God on the higher levels of sin.[13]

The theological understanding of sin in the church is distorted[14] when it talks about original sin. Rauschenbusch contends that original sin does not recognize the concept of social sin.[15] The church's approach to defining original sin is inconsistent with the existential experience of the poor and racially marginalized. "The doctrine of original sin has directed attention to the biological channels for the transmission of general sinfulness from generation to generation, but has neglected and diverted attention from the transmission and perpetuation of specific evils through the channel of social tradition."[16]

Rauschenbusch argues that the manner in which the church teaches the doctrine of original sin has, to a large extent, helped to perpetuate the "social idealizations of evil." This is done, he contends, by the church not addressing the production of evil by the sociopolitical and economic institutions, thus leading to the "perpetuation of antiquated wrongs in society." Sin is promoted from generation to generation. Sin is personal but deeply social and generational. He writes, "The statistics of social morality are the pulse-beat of the social organism. The free and unrelated acts of individuals are also the acts of the social group. When the social group is evil, evil is overall."[17] The concept of original sin tends toward "individualistic conservatism" and undermines any coherent and active social endeavor. According to Rauschenbusch, injustice is the "corruption of justice."[18] Similarly, injustice is associated with the production

---

13. Rauschenbusch, *Theology for the Social Gospel*, 50.
14. Beach and Niebuhr, *Christian Ethics*, 460.
15. Rauschenbusch, *Theology for the Social Gospel*, 60.
16. Beach and Neibuhr, *Christian Ethics*, 458.
17. Beach and Niebuhr, *Christian Ethics*, 460.
18. Rauschenbusch, *Theology for the Social Gospel*, 252.

of evil. This is especially evident when associated with profiteering and exploitation associated with the slave trade and chattel slavery.

Rauschenbusch argues that original sin was meant to elicit a sense of guilt and remorse but which have not been fully understood in light of its distortion by the church.[19] Redemption is sociopolitical and economically defined through personal and collective repentance.[20] He writes:

> The idealization of evil is an indispensable means for its perpetuation and transmission. But the most potent motive for its protection is its profitableness. Ordinarily, sin is an act of weakness and side-stepping, followed by shame the next day. But when it is the source of prolific income, it is no longer a shame-faced vagabond slinking through the dark, but an army with banners, entrenched and defiant. The bigger the dividends, the stiffer the resistance against anything that would cut them down. When fed with money, sin grows wings and claws.[21]

Sin is social. Sin is political. Sin is racial. Sin is economic exploitation and human trafficking. Sin is injustice. Sin is collective, generational, and national. Sin is the transatlantic slave trade and the institution of chattel slavery that Rauschenbush was conversant with in the 1800s.

Born in 1861, Rauschenbusch provides a theological critique of historical forms of marginalization because of laws, policies, racism, greed, and militancy. Intergenerational evil, he argues, is self-perpetuating with the slave trade and chattel slavery in the background of his mind. Oppression perpetrated by one generation is quickly adopted by the next generation, especially where power, privilege, and prosperity are involved. Rauschenbusch notes:

> Our Italian immigrants are what they are because the church and the land system of Italy have made them so. The Mexican peon is ridden by the Spanish past. Capitalistic Europe has fastened its yoke on the neck of Africa. When Negroes are hunted from a Northern city like beasts, or when a Southern city degrades the whole nation by turning the savage inhumanity of a mob into public festivity, we are continuing to sin because our fathers created the conditions of sin by the African slave trade

---

19. Beach and Niebuhr, *Christian Ethics*, 460. "The doctrine of original sin was meant to bring us all under the sense of guilt . . . but the conscience of mankind has never been convinced. Partakers in his wretchedness we might well be by our family coherence, but guilt belongs only to personality, and requires will and freedom."

20. Beach and Niebuhr, *Christian Ethics*, 470.

21. Rauschenbusch, *Theology for the Social Gospel*, 66.

and by the unearned wealth they gathered from slave labour for generations.[22]

For Rauschenbusch, the church in the United States was an accomplice in the transatlantic slave trade and the institution of chattel slavery, the post-emancipation lynching and mob violence against Blacks, as well as the prevailing race-based consciousness of the American criminal laws. Rauschenbusch saw these acts of cruelty perpetrated against Black humanity, and the church was complacent. Thus, there is a divide between the White church and the Black church in the United States.[23] The church's individualistic interpretation of salvation has made it almost impossible for it to derive a concept of salvation that is adequately holistic. He indicts the church for its theological individualism and argues that "sin is not a private transaction between the sinner and God. . . . We rarely sin against God alone."[24] Sin is generational, he contends. It is reflected in the sociopolitical and economic exploitation of the weaker class. Generations perpetuate sin as it becomes socioculturally normative and entrenched.

The distortion of sin in the church has also distorted the concept of human solidarity. Rauschenbusch argues, "Our theological conception of sins is but fragmentary unless we see all men in their natural groups bound together in solidarity of all times and all places, bearing the yoke of evil and suffering."[25] Salvation, he contends, should be defined in relation to the end goals of justice—the common good.

> When we submit to God, we submit to the supremacy of the common good. Salvation is the voluntary socializing of the soul. . . . The three forms of sins—sensuousness, selfishness, and godlessness—are ascending and expanding stages, in which we sin against our higher self, against the good of men, and against the universal good.[26]

The sinful mind, then, is the mind that enacts and supports policies that undermine human flourishing and well-being. The sinful mind portrays

---

22. Beach and Niebuhr, *Christian Ethics*, 458.
23. Mohamed et al., "Faith Among Black Americans." "Most Black worshippers attend predominantly Black congregations and see a role for religion in fighting racial injustice, but generational patterns are changing."
24. Beach and Niebuhr, *Christian Ethics*, 454.
25. Beach and Niebuhr, *Christian Ethics*, 460.
26. Beach and Niebuhr, *Christian Ethics*, 436.

the poor and racially marginalized as pathological objects that must be monetized, auctioned, raped, sold, and discarded. The evidence of sin in this context, Rauschenbusch contends, is not moral or immoral behavior but the economic manipulation and usurping of the common good to prevent others from accessing necessary life opportunities. For Rauschenbusch, there is a collective interpretation of sin and redemption. Sin is social, and redemption is social. Collective sin requires collective repentance. "To repent of our collective social sins, to have faith in the possibility and reality of a divine life in humanity, to submit the will to the purpose of the Kingdom of God, to permit the divine inspiration, to emancipate and clarify the moral insight—this is the most intimate duty of the religious man who would help to build the coming Messianic era of mankind."[27]

Rauschenbusch's sinners are also European nations and the United States as slave traders, exploiters of poor nations, perpetuators of racial marginalization, and the reduction to economic units of the humanity of Africans that verges on narcissism. He notes:

> Our consciousness of sin deepens as our moral insight matures and becomes religious. When we think on the level of law or public opinion, we speak of crime, vice, bad habits, or defective character. When our minds is in the attitude of religion, we pray: "Create in me a clean heart, O God, and renew a right spirit within me...." To lack the consciousness of sin is a symptom of moral immaturity or of an effort to keep the shutters down and the light out.... By our very nature, we are involved in tragedy.[28]

Rauschenbusch's reflection on the social construction and definition of the Christian doctrine of original sin is poignant. With the slave trade, chattel slavery, and the post-emancipation cruelties of the Black Codes, lynching, mob violence, the convict-leasing system, and the Ku Klux Klan[29] in the background, he provides a salient critique of the prevailing sociopolitical and economic norms of White supremacist consciousness against Black humanity, also influenced by Lockean slavery and Jeffersonian slavery.

---

27. Rauschenbusch, *Theology for the Social Gospel*, 352.
28. Rauschenbusch, *Theology for the Social Gospel*, 31.
29. Parsons, "Ku Klux Klan."

TAKE YOUR ISSUES TO THE LORD IN PRAYER

I have issues that I struggle with.
Overwhelming, they are my human issues,
Issues I have acquired along the way.

The implications of my issues I sometimes dread,
They are issues that won't go away,
Yet they are issues I take to the Lord.

On the altar of prayer, these issues I submit.
My issues I present earnestly to God,
Unto God, I declare my imperfections.

In the name of Jesus Christ, I declare my faith.
The search for freedom I request in prayers,
Deliverance from my issues, the Lord is aware.

Take your issues to the Lord I hear,
He hears the silent cries of human issues.
The quiet tears He always dries.

The feeble knees He always strengthens,
Your issues Jesus Christ will resolve.
Take your issues to the Lord in prayer!

My issues at the altar I therefore offer.
In God's intervention, I relinquish my issues.
On the altar, I deposit my human issues.

My issues I relinquish on the divine altar.
Although their return I am conscious of, in God, I trust to keep them safe.
In the Lord, my issues are dealt with.

Take your Issues to the Lord in Prayer.[30]

GEORGE WALTERS-SLEYON

---

30. Walters-Sleyon, *Nuggets from the Night*, 186.

12

Is Locke a Racist?

THIS RESEARCH HAS ARGUED THAT John Locke and Thomas Jefferson were not simply men of their time. Locke and Jefferson provided the intellectual, political, administrative, and racial paradigms for the ripening of the industrial transatlantic slave trade and the economic institution of chattel slavery. They were the conscience and intellectual facilitators of their time in theory and in practice.[1] Locke and Jefferson's sociopolitical, economic, and philosophical theories and practices became the national standards for Britain, including Scotland, and subsequently the United States consecutively. Their constructive involvements and defenses created the intellectual conditions and lenses for subsequent interpretations of the humanity of Black people and their treatments in Europe and the United States. For Jefferson, his advancement of pseudoscientific beliefs regarding the humanity and intellectual ability of Black people provided a public political platform for proslavery activists who became known as Jeffersonians.

> Jefferson's views on race are embarrassing, not just by the standards of our age but by the standards of his own age. When corresponding with people of different views, Jefferson purposely misled them as to his true beliefs about race. He gave them "a soft answer." Tragically, Jefferson's pseudoscientific proclamations fostered the subsequent development of proslavery science, which led to scientific racism. Jefferson helped invent racism as an intellectually credible viewpoint. . . . The very importance of Jefferson ot the founding era . . . helped

1. Cranston, *John Locke*, 111.

make racism respectable in antebellum America. Racism might have developed without his support for it in the Notes, but it is nevertheless a legacy of Jefferson.²

Locke's participation in the slave trade and defense of chattel slavery have raised a lot of questions about the objectivity of his political, philosophical, and religious theories. Was he also a White supremacist and a racist who saw people of non-European origin humanly and intellectually inferior, and especially Black people who must be perpetually enslaved in civil society? A reflection of Locke's notion of racial distinction is found in the following examples he gave about a child's definition of a man.

> First, a child having framed the Idea of a Man, it is probable, that his Idea is just like that Picture, which the Painter makes of the visible Appearances joyned [joined] together; and such a Complication of Ideas together in his understanding, makes up the single examples Idea which he calls Man, whereof White or Flesh-colour in England being one, the Child can demonstrate to you, that a Negro is not a Man (Locke & (ed), 1975, p. 4.7.16).³

A child knows who a man is based on what his environment points to as a man. If society and the parents point to a man who is Black and call him a Negro with all of its negative connotations, or a devil, the child immediately knows that real men are White men and that any man that is not White is not a man but a Negro and Negro men are not real men. In another example, Locke contends that, "'The Child certainly knows, that the *Nurse* that feeds it, is neither the *Cat* it plays with, nor the *Blackmoor* it is afraid of' (1.2.25) (as well as in Draft A). 'A child unused to that sight & having had some such descriptions of the devil would call a Negro a devil rather than a Man & at the same time call a dryl a man.'"⁴

It is one thing to refer to Locke's consistent racial statements as "minor lapses." But it is another thing when such lapses have become the window through which Blacks are often perceived. According to Glausser, "Locke's choice of examples can make modern readers uneasy, especially those aware of his slavery connections. To Poliakov they 'suggest a prejudice already well rooted in English society,' and compatible with

---

2. Finkelman, *Slavery and the Founders*, 268.
3. Glausser, "Three Approaches to Locke," 213.
4. Nidditch, *Draft A of Locke's Essay*, 33.

Locke's empiricist theories."[5] Locke's strange silence is worth investigating in light of his involvement and participation in the transatlantic slave trade. Could it also be that Locke was justifying a political consciousness and doctrine that was inherently racist?[6] Locke refuses to categorically condemn slavery even though he was familiar with the work of Aphra Behn who cast a Black man in her work *Oronooko*. According to Farr, "Now, to say the least, Locke never criticised Afro-American slavery, despite his familiarity with Behn's classic."[7]

So, if Locke escapes the charge of being an explicit racist, he cannot avoid being a White supremacist. His writings and economic activities remain major causal conditions to the nineteenth, twentieth, and twenty-first centuries' perceptions of people of African descent in Europe and the United States.[8] According to Farr:

> If Locke was not guilty of racism, he most certainly was guilty of avoiding the moral issues raised by the enslavement of black Africans. He averted his eyes from the glaring contradiction between his theories and Afro-American slavery. . . . He invested alongside his patrons and contributed to the steady development of the old colonial system. Given the depth of his involvement, we are forced to conclude with John Dunn that "what we confront here is not an example of bland but deliberate moral rationalization on Locke's part but merely one of moral evasion."[9]

As one of the colonial masters to the Carolinas and profiteers, Locke constructed the Fundamental Constitutions with the full awareness that he was writing to define, defend, and put into perspective the existing norms of economic engagements. Richards et al. and Farr's contentions

---

5. Glausser, "Three Approaches to Locke," 213. "In *The Aryan Myth: A History of Racist and Nationalist Ideas in Europe*, 145, Poliakov cites two of the three passages mentioned in this essay, as well as an additional one (2.25.1), in which Locke's deep-rooted prejudice, according to Poliakov, accompanies defective logic."

6. Farr, "So Vile and Miserable an Estate," 277. "As argued by Rracken, 'Essence, Accident, and Race,' and Popkin, 'Philosophical Bases of Modern Racism.' Seliger, too, notes that Locke may have argued for hereditary slavery 'in virtue of natural predispositions' in *The Liberal Politics of John Locke*, 119n."

7. Farr, "So Vile and Miserable an Estate," 278.

8. Farr, "So Vile and Miserable an Estate," 279 "Historically, there have been two kinds of empirical theories put forward to explain racial differences. Polygenists have asserted that blacks and whites were created as different species (with blacks being naturally inferior)."

9. Farr, "So Vile and Miserable an Estate," 280.

that Locke must be exonerated because he was acting according to his time is a bit disingenuous. Locke was fully aware of the implications of his political arguments and slave-trading practices. Locke was in the process of constructing his political and economic theories also as a justification for the slave trade and the perpetual enslavement of Africans in civil society.[10] According to Farr, "In short, Locke justified Afro-American slavery by a racist political doctrine."[11] If Locke had a more extensive and universal meaning of property and social inclusion as Richards et al. have argued, Locke's trading practices and the inconsistency in his political and economic theories undermine that claim. Unfortunately, what is evident in Locke's arguments and his economic practices are the assertions of a caste system for Black people. Richards et al. argue that "although his signification of property was not invariably consistent, he interspersed reminders of this wider meaning throughout the rest of the *Second Treatise*. In Section 171, Locke reiterated that the function of political authority was 'to preserve the Members of that Society in their Lives, Liberties and Possessions.' In Section 173, he again asserted his definition of property."[12]

Locke's influence was not lost immediately after the Civil War. The preservation of cheap labor through Black labor and a racial caste system was fundamental to the post–Civil War era in the United States. Locke influenced the United States' political and economic consciousness. Peardon argues that Jefferson was accused of copying Locke's *Second Treatise*.[13] With the coming into being of the modern industrial system after the Civil War and the new consciousness of freedom established by the Fourteenth Amendment, unwelcomed interference with "Life,

---

10. Richards, Mulligan and Graham, "'Property' and 'People,'" 40. "If one ventures beyond a discussion of some uses of property in Locke's time and compares other current political terms, Locke's sympathy for a radically wider membership of political society becomes even clearer. Historians have argued that Locke was not intending to describe a political membership as inclusive as his words suggest."

11. Farr, "So Vile and Miserable an Estate," 277.

12. Richards, Mulligan, & Graham, "'Property' and 'People,'" 38.

13. Locke, *Second Treatise*, xx. "The lineage is direct: Jefferson copied Locke and Locke quoted (Richard) Hooker. In political theory and in political practice the American Revolution drew its inspiration from the parliamentary struggle of the seventeenth century. The philosophy of the Declaration was not taken from the French. It was not even new; but good old English doctrine newly formulated to meet a present emergency. In 1776 it was commonplace doctrine, everywhere to be met with, as Jefferson said, 'whether expressed in conversation, in letters, printed essays, or the elementary books of public right.' And in sermons also, he might have added."

Liberty, and Property" gained recognition by all states. Locke became the intellectual apostle for the modern industrial system as his theory of property became enshrined in the United States Constitution. According to Walton H. Hamilton, "The modern industrial system came into being—and the most Lockian phrases in the Constitution were employed to guard its integrity."[14]

If Locke is not a racist in the contemporary sense of the word, the following conclusions are difficult to dismiss based on his political defense of the institution of slavery and his position as a slave master. One, there is no evidence that Locke associated with slaves or Africans in a friendly fashion other than owning them as property. Secondly, we have no evidence that Locke freed his slaves, which would have been the most courageous act in light of his political and philosophical assertions. Thirdly, Locke saw Africans as subhuman beings and crafted his political and economic theories to perpetuate the claims that Blacks are inferior human beings. Fourthly, as the architect of the Fundamental Constitutions, Locke categorically stipulated the perpetual enslavement of Africans and the absolute power of the slave master over his slave. Finally, Locke makes it entirely clear that a slave's conversion to Christianity does not in any way change their social status as a slave in the broader civil society. He repeats, "Yet no slave shall hereby be exempted from that civil dominion his Master hath over him but in all other things in the same state and condicion he was in before. . . .Every Freeman of Carolina shall have absolute power and authority over his Negro slaves of what opinion or Religion soever."[15] Locke had no problem granting absolute powers and immunity to slave masters to treat their slaves any way they desire with impunity. Slave masters were brutal, harsh, and cruel to their slaves to keep them subdued. Locke logically and practically understood the implications of granting such authority and immunity to slave masters particularly in Carolina, which had one of the highest number of slaves in the American colony of Britain. According to Armitage:

> Though none of his later detractors could have known it, Locke himself had augmented the slaveholder's "absolute authority" by adding that "power and" in the 1669 manuscript now among the Shaftesbury papers. Had they known, that fact would have only confirmed their suspicion that the most eminent Republican

---

14. Hamilton, "Property—According to Locke," 874.

15. National Archives, PRO 30/24/47/3, fols.58r, 59r-60r, 58-59r, 65r-66r, ptd. in Locke, *Locke: Political Essays*, 177, 178, 179–80.

> Writers, such as Locke, Fletcher of Saltown, and Rousseau himself, pretend to justify the making slaves of others, whilst they are pleading as warmly for Liberty for themselves.[16]

With the granting of absolute powers and authority to the slave masters, Locke was endorsing the brutalities of the slave masters against Black people because he was also a slave master and slave trader. Locke wanted absolute power over his slaves without any interference because they were his property. He had the absolute power to sell them at any time and subject them to any treatment possible, with impunity. Thus, Locke's rejection and resistance to the church/religion in politics or civil society.

As we shall see in *The Rush for Black Diamonds, Volume Two*, Locke was a pioneer and major founding father of the Enlightenment project. David Hume, Thomas Jefferson, and Immanuel Kant testified to the intellectual influences Locke had on the development of their own philosophical and political theories.

Furthermore, even after Locke had resigned his position as secretary to the proprietors in November of 1675, Locke continued his involvement with Carolina. When he went to France after 1675, Locke was looking for suitable crops to be grown by slaves in Carolina under the instructions of his former boss Shaftesbury.[17] Regarding Locke's investments in the slave trade and chattel slavery as a proprietor, Woolhouse notes that Locke invested a considerable amount of money in the ships and trade to warrant his concern even after he went to France and thereafter returned to England.

> At the beginning of September (1672) the lords proprietors of Carolina who two years earlier had been given the Bahamas by the King, made a grant land on New Providence to a "Company of Adventures," with a view that they would organize trade between there and England. Locke subscribed 100 Pounds toward

---

16. Armitage, "John Locke," 609.

17. Armitage, "John Locke," 611. "Throughout his journeys in France, Locke took special notice of viticulture, arborculture, and sericulture. He meticulously noted every variety of grape, olive, and fig. . . . His notebooks for 1677 to 1678 reveal that these were not disinterested inquiries but instead concerned whatever might be 'fit', 'good', or 'useful in Carolina'. The 'Observations' should thus be read as a sketch for a practical economic future for Carolina in the business of Mediterranean import-substitution growing fruit and producing wine, silk, and olive oil. Shaftesbury received Locke's manuscript in February 1680 'with great joy' and 'perused it greedily.'"

the required 1600 Pounds (shortly afterwards taking over the interest which Mapletoft had bought).[18]

Looking at Locke's level of involvement in the slave trade and the economic and sociopolitical status he attained, it is impossible to exonerate him from any association with racism. According to Woolhouse,

> A further colonial enterprise, in which Locke became involved toward the end of the month, was by way of an investment of 400 Pounds in the Royal African Company, a reconstituted company whose trade partly consisted in the transport of slaves from the Gold Coast for sale in the West Indies and by whose new charter Locke was incorporated as a Trader and Adventurer.[19]

Locke was a consummate slave trader and slave master. He intentionally refused to advocate for Black people because he saw them as racially and intellectually inferior to Whites. Furthermore, Locke saw Black people as economic units to be marketized and monetized for wealth and status acquisition. Black people were the *black diamonds* responsible for the building of Europe, and for the economic and political dominance of Locke's country—Great Britain. Thus, Locke's refusal to criticize the enslavement of Black Africans even to express an iota of sympathy for Black people. Locke's liberalism is racial, not humanitarian; his equalitarianism is Eurocentric, not international; his concept of right is particularly individualistic and not universally communitarian; and his concept of justice is sociocolonial and racially myopic, not ontological and unconditional.

According to Farr, Locke criticized Filmer's proposal for the monarch to have the power to enslave English men, but Locke "unfortunately does nothing to lessen the principal contradiction between his theory and his age's practice."[20] Locke was a slave trader at the same time writing about human rights. Farr concludes, "In the case of John Locke's theory of slavery, we find an embarrassment of riches, a tale of intimate and informed involvement with all manner of slavery. Indeed, so well and thoroughly informed was Locke that, when once we grasp his theory of slavery, we come to wonder what it was designed to explain at all."[21]

Locke's direct participation in the slave trade and his philosophical and political theories regarding slavery and natural rights implicate

18. Woolhouse, *Locke*, 110, 111.
19. Woolhouse, *Locke*, 110, 111.
20. Farr, "So Vile and Miserable an Estate," 264.
21. Farr, "So Vile and Miserable an Estate," 265.

him as a major intellectual architect of anti-Black racial consciousness in Europe and the United States. Locke was fully aware of his participation. Indeed, his engagements in the slave trade have undoubtedly cast an embarrassing light on his political and economic theories. Nevertheless, Farr still maintains that Locke's theory reflects a positive condemnation of "seventeenth-century slave practices and any ongoing institution of slavery whatsoever." He goes on to contend, "In particular, Locke was not a racist in the strong sense required to justify slavery."[22] Unlike Farr, Bernasconi and Mann contend that Locke was the mastermind behind the concept and development of "race-based slavery."

> We are disturbed by the ease with which some commentators excuse Locke of racism or minimize its significance. To be sure, there is something artificial in the application of this word to a man who lived at a time when the races were seen in very different terms than has been the case in the last two centuries. But to advocate, administer, and profit from a specifically racialized form of slavery is clear evidence of racism, if the word is to have any meaning at all.[23]

This research further concludes that Lockean politics, Lockean religion, and Lockean philosophy were inherently constructed with slavery and the status of Africans as slaves in mind. Jefferson appropriated Lockeanism. As a Virginian aristocrat, Jefferson was also a slave master and slave trader. Lockeanism provided the social, intellectual, political, and religious justifications for the indeterminate and perpetual enslavement of Black Africans. Furthermore, Locke's concept of natural law and rights negate the concept of objectivity when it comes to Africans.

Lockean and Jeffersonian rights are subjective and racially solipsistic. Jefferson was very public with his animus and White-supremacist claims against people of African descent. He refused to entertain any semblance of making even free Blacks citizens of the United States. Jefferson was specific in his declaration that any free Black should be shipped to Africa or decide to remain in the United States as a perpetual slave. Jefferson advocated the concepts and practices of indeterminate enslavement and a caste system for Black people in the United States.

According to Witte's definition of rights under classical Roman law, Locke and Jefferson intentionally refused to appropriate any legal benefit

---

22. Farr, "So Vile and Miserable an Estate," 264.
23. Bernasconi and Mann, *Thomas Jefferson*, 91.

of the law to people of African descent. If "Roman law gave each person a basic freedom from subjection or undue restraint or action from others who had no right to (*ius*) or possessory claim (*dominium*) over them,"[24] as Witte has claimed, then Locke and Jefferson violated the spirit and ethos of Roman law concerning Africans. The racial legacies of Locke and Jefferson live on in the United Kingdom and the United States as two intellectual fathers of British and American intellectual history, and political and social-cultural consciousness.

Locke and Jefferson gladly participated in and defended the industrial slave trade and the institution of chattel slavery. These two industrial events are fundamental to the economic development of the United States and the United Kingdom, including Scotland. The legacies of the industrial slave trade and chattel slavery transitioned into the strengthening of the colonial enterprises of the superpowers of the slave trade including the United Kingdom, the United States, France, Spain, Portugal, and Belgium. Fundamental to these transitions are the race-based treatments of Black people in the United States, which linger on in the present. According to Kaye, "In 1789, 7,000 posters were printed showing 482 slaves crammed on board. This picture shocked people at the time and remains one of the most enduring images associated with the transatlantic Slave Trade."[25]

Unfortunately, in the West, it seems people of African descent—*Africa proper*, according to Hegel the German—cannot be accorded the full "blessings of liberty." This hesitance on the part of the West to allow people of African descent to experience the full blessings of liberty, justice, fairness, and respect for human dignity, as discussed, is a racist decision with John Locke, Thomas Jefferson, David Hume, Immanuel Kant, Georg Hegel, and other prominent French intellectuals including Voltaire serving as the intellectual godfathers of Western racist and White-supremacist consciousness towards Black humanity. The people of *Africa proper* will always be *black diamonds*. Nothing will change it. In their ungodly acts of the transatlantic slave trade, the reduction of African humanity to chattel property, the breeding of Africans for their plantations and slave markets, the monetization of African humanity for wealth and racial dominance, the raping, beating to death of pregnant women because they are slaves, the selling of and having children with

24. Witte, *The Blessings of Liberty: Human Rights and Religious Freedom in the Western Legal Tradition*, 24.

25. Kaye, *1807–2007*, 12.

their own children because they are slaves, etc. Europeans and White Americans and their ancestors have sinned against the people and descendants of Black Africa.

Locke died in 1704. However, he left a political and philosophical legacy that is also inextricable from his White supremacist contentions. His intellectual legacies and involvements in the transatlantic slave trade established an attractiveness for those who wanted a philosophical and theological justification for the perpetuation of chattel slavery and the indeterminate enslavement and racial marginalization of people of African descent. Locke's political, philosophical, economic, and religious defenses for the slave trade, chattel slavery, individual rights to own slaves, individualism, and private property with Black people as chattel property did not die with him. The American Founding Fathers put them into practice, including the third president of the United States, writer of the Declaration of Independence, and the most prominent Lockean disciple in American politics: Thomas Jefferson. John Locke was a racist and a White supremacist, and Thomas Jefferson was his disciple in the White House.

THEY HAVE SINNED AGAINST GOD AND THE AFRICANS

They have sinned against God and the people of Africa!
The Arab slave traders have sinned!
The Muslim slave traders have sinned!
The Catholic Popes: Nicholas V and Alexander VI have sinned.

The Muslim traders stole African gold and African labor,
While Arabization and Islamification were their covering.
The Catholic papal bulls of 1452, 1455, and 1493 were racial,
Africans, they claimed, were beneath their Catholic Eurocentrism.

They have sinned! Repentance, Reparation they must offer!
They have sinned! Britain, Belgium, Holland, United States.
They have sinned! Portugal, France, Spain, Scotland,
They have sinned! Locke, Hume, Kant, Hegel, Jefferson,
Thomas Leyland, Sir. James Stirling Richard Oswald . . .

150 Ramadans for Muslims and Arabs with prayers,
The Islamic prayers of *Fajr*, *Dhuhr*, *Asr*, *Maghrib*, and *Isha'a*
For the Catholics, 150 *Our Fathers*, *Hail Mary*, and Rosaries.
They have sinned against God and the people of Africa.

For Britain, Belgium, Holland, and the United States,
For Portugal, France, Spain, Scotland, and Denmark,
Reparation and Repentance for their bloody wealth,
They have sinned against God and the people of Africa.

Repentance, Apologies, and Reparation:
For Africans thrown overboard during the Middle Passage
For Africans raped, murdered, babies bred and sold as slaves willy-nilly.
For Africans who built London, Liverpool, Bristol, the American
South, Washington DC, Paris, Oxford and Cambridge Universities, Harvard,
Yale, Princeton, Columbia Universities, etc.[26]

GEORGE WALTERS-SLEYON

---

26. Walters-Sleyon, *Nuggets from the Night*, 127.

Bibliography

Aaron, Richard. *John Locke*. Oxford: Oxford University Press, 1937.
Adamson, Christopher R. "Punishment After Slavery: Southern State Penal Systems 1865–1890." *Social Problems* 30.5 (1983) 555–69.
Adu-Boahen, Kwabena. "The Impact of European Presence on Slavery in the Sixteenth to Eighteenth-Century Gold Coast." *Transactions of the Historical Society of Ghana* 14 (2012) 165–99.
Albrecht, Gloria. "The Heresy of White Christianity." *CrossCurrents* 64.3 (2014) 346–52.
Ames, Paul. "Portugal Confronts Its Slave Trade Past." *Politico*, February 6, 2018. https://www.politico.eu/article/portugal-slave-trade-confronts-its-past/.
Amposah, David Kofi. "Christian Slavery, Colonialism, and Violence: The Life and Writings of an African Ex-Slave, 1717–1747." *Journal of Africana Religions* 1.4 (2013) 431–57.
Antonovich, Jacqueline. "White Coats, White Hoods: Physicians and the Medical Politics of the Ku Klux Klan in 1920s America." *Bulletin of the History of Medicine* 95.4 (2021) 437–63. doi: 10.1353/bhm.2021.0053.
Appel, Liz. "White Supremacy in the Movement Against the Prison-Industrial Complex." *Social Justice* 30.2 (2003) 81–88.
Armitage, David. "John Locke, Carolina, and the 'Two Treatises of Government.'" *Political Theory* 32.5 (2004) 602–27.
Armstrong, Marques, et al. "White Supremacy." In *Faith in Action: A Handbook for Activists, Advocates, and Allies*, by Sharon Betcher et al., 39–42. Philadelphia: Fortress, 2017.
Arneil, Barbara. *John Locke and America*. Oxford: Clarendon, 1996.
Ashcraft, Richard. *Revolutionary Politics and Locke's Two Treatises of Government*. Princeton: Princeton University Press, 1986.
Auer, J. Jeffery, ed. *Antislavery and Disunion, 1858–1861*. New York: Harper & Row, 1963.
Austen, Ralph A., and Woodruff D. Smith. "Images of Africa and British Slave-Trade Abolition: The Transition to an Imperialist Ideology, 1787–1807." *African Historical Studies* 2.1 (1969) 69–83.
Ayers, Edward. *The Promise of the New South*. New York: Oxford University Press, 1992.
———. *Vengeance and Justice: Crime and Punishment in the 19th-Century American South*. New York: Oxford University Press, 1984.

BIBLIOGRAPHY

Bailey, Ronald. "The Slave(ry) Trade and the Development of Capitalism in the United States: The Textile Industry in New England." *Social Science History* 14.3 (1990) 373–414.

Bair, Asata P. *Prison Labor in the United States: An Economic Analysis.* New York: Routledge, 2008.

Baker, Thomas N. "'A Slave' Writes Thomas Jefferson." *The William and Mary Quarterly* 68.1 (2011) 127–54.

Bales, Kevin. *Disposable People: New Slavery in the Global Economy.* Berkeley: University of California Press, 1999.

———. *Understanding Global Slavery.* Berkeley: University of California Press, 2005.

Balkin, Jack M., and Sanford Levinson. "The Dangerous Thirteenth Amendment." *Columbia Law Review* 112.7 (2012) 1459–99.

Barcia, Manuel. "White Cannibalism in the Illegal Slave Trade." *NWIG: New West Indian Guide* 96.1/2 (2022) 1–28.

Battle-Baptiste, Whitney, and Britt Rusert, eds. *W. E. B. Du Bois's Data Portraits: Visualizing Black America.* New York: Princeton Architectural, 2018.

Bay, Mia. "The World Was Thinking Wrong About Race: The Philadelphia Negro and Nineteenth-Century Science." In *W. E. B. Du Bois, Race, and the City: The Philadelphia Negro and Its Legacy*, edited by Michael B. Katz and Thomas J. Sugrue, 41–59. Philadelphia: University of Pennsylvania Press, 1998.

Beach, Waldo, and H. Richard Niebuhr. *Christian Ethics: Sources of the Living Tradition.* New York: Ronald Company, 1955.

Beck, E. M. "Guess Who's Coming to Town: White Supremacy, Ethnic Competition, and Social Change." *Sociological Focus* 33.2 (2000) 153–74.

Bennett, J. Harry, Jr. *Bondsmen, and Bishops: Slavery and Apprenticeship on Codrington Plantation of Barbados, 1710–1838.* Berkeley: University of California Press, 1958.

Bercaw, Nancy. "Slavery and Emancipation." In vol. 24 of *The New Encyclopedia of Southern Culture*, by Nancy Bercaw, 157–61. Chapel Hill: University of North Carolina Press, 2013.

Berlin, Ira. "American Slavery in History and Memory and the Search for Social Justice." *The Journal of American History* 90.4 (2004) 1251–68.

———. *Many Thousands Gone: The First Two Centuries of Slavery in North America.* Cambridge: Belknap of Harvard University Press, 1998.

Bernasconi, Robert, and Anika Maaza Mann. "The Contradictions of Racism: Locke, Slavery and the Two Treatises." In *Race and Racism in Modern Philosophy*, edited by Andrew Valls, 88–107. Cornell University Press, 2005.

Bernstein, R. B. *Thomas Jefferson.* Oxford: Oxford University Press, 2005.

Bethell, Leslie. "The Mixed Commissions for the Suppression of the Transatlantic Slave Trade in the Nineteenth Century." *The Journal of African History* 7.1 (1966) 79–93.

Bhopal, Kalwant. "White Privilege." In *White Privilege: The Myth of a Post-Racial Society*, by Kalwant Bhopal, 9–28. Bristol: Bristol University Press, 2018.

Biddle, John C. "Locke's Critique of Innate Principles and Toland's Deism." *Journal of the History of Ideas* 37.3 (1976) 411–22.

Blackburn, Robin. "The Old World Background to European Colonial Slavery." *The William and Mary Quarterly* 54.1 (1997) 65–102.

Blackmon, Douglas A. *Slavery by Another Name: The Re-Enslavement of Black People in America from the Civil War to World War II.* New York: Doubleday, 2008.

Blassingame, John W., and John R. McKivigan, eds. *The Frederick Douglass Papers.* Series One, *Speeches, Debates, and Interviews.* Vol. 4, *1864–1880.* New Haven: Yale University Press, 1991.

Blight, David W. *Frederick Douglass's Civil War: Keeping the Faith in Jubilee.* Baton Rouge: Louisiana State University Press, 1989.

Bobo, Lawrence. "Crime, Urban Poverty, and Social Science." *Du Bois Review: Social Science Research on Race* 6.2 (2009) 273–78.

Bolt, Christine. *The Anti-slavery Movement and Reconstruction: A Study in Anglo-American Co-operation, 1833–1877.* London: Published for the Institute of Race Relations by Oxford University Press, 1969.

Bourne, H. R. Fox. *The Life of John Locke.* Vol. 2. New York: New York, 1896.

Boxill, Bernard. "A Lockean Argument for Black Reparation." *The Journal of Ethics* 7.1 (2003) 63–91.

Boyce, Travis D., and Winsome M. Chunnu. "Toward a Post-Racial Society or a 'Rebirth' of a Nation? White Anxiety and Fear of Black Equality in the United States." In *Historicizing Fear: Ignorance, Vilification, and Othering,* edited by Travis D. Boyce and Winsome M. Chunnu, 122–54. Denver: University Press of Colorado, 2020.

Boyd, William M. "Southerners in the Anti-Slavery Movement, 1800–1830." *Phylon (1940–1956)* 9.2 (1948) 153–63.

Braithwaite, John B. "Challenging Just Deserts: Punishing White Collar Criminals." *Journal of Criminal Law and Criminology* 73 (1982) 723–63.

Brawley, Benjamin. *A Social History of the American Negro.* New York: Macmillan, 1921.

Breen, Patrick H. "The Female Antislavery Petition Campaign of 1831–1832." *The Virginia Magazine of History and Biography* 110.3 (2002) 377–98.

Brown, Ira V. "'Am I Not a Woman and a Sister?' The Anti-Slavery Convention of American Women, 1837–1839." *Pennsylvania History* 50.1 (1983) 1–19.

Browne, Jaron. "Rooted in Slavery: Prison Labor Exploitation." *Race, Poverty & The Environment* 14.1 (2007) 42–44.

Brubaker, Stanley C. "Coming into One's Own: John Locke's Theory of Property, God, and Politics." *The Review of Politics* 74.2 (2012) 207–32.

Bucy, Ellen. "The Transatlantic Slave Trade and American Slavery." *OAH Magazine of History* 17.3 (2003) 55–56.

Byrd, Alexander X. "Studying Lynching in the Jim Crow South." *OAH Magazine of History* 18.2 (2004) 31–36.

Cable, George W. "The Convict Lease System in the Southern States." *Century Illustrated Magazine,* 1884.

———. "The Silent South, Together with the Freedom's Case in Equity and the Convict Lease System." In *The Silent South,* by George Washington Cable, 105–73. New York: Scribner's, 1885.

Campbell, James. *Middle Passages: African American Journeys to Africa 1787–2005.* New York: Penguin, 2006.

Campbell, John. "Work, Pregnancy, and Infant Mortality among Southern Slaves." *The Journal of Interdisciplinary History* 14.4 (1984) 793–812.

Campbell, Michael C. "Politics, Prisons, and Law Enforcement: An Examination of the Emergence of 'Law and Order' Politics in Texas." *Law & Society Review* (2011) 631–65.

Campbell, Randolph B. *Gone to Texas: A History of the Lone Star State*. New York: Oxford University Press, 2003.
Campney, Brent M. S. "'Light Is Bursting Upon the World': White Supremacy and Racist Violence Against Blacks in the Reconstruction Kansas." *Western Historical Quarterly* 41.2 (2010) 171–94.
Carper, N. Gordon. "Slavery Revisited: Peonage in the South." *Phylon* 37.1 (1976) 85–99.
Carrington, Selwyn H. H. "Capitalism and Slavery and Caribbean Historiography: An Evaluation." *The Journal of African American History* 88.3 (2003) 304–12.
Chafe, William H., et al., eds. *Remembering Jim Crow: African Americans Tell About Life in the Segregated South*. New York: New Press, 2001.
Chaudhuri, Joyotpaul. "Jefferson's Unheavenly City: A Bicentennial Look." *The American Journal of Economics and Sociology* 34.4 (1975) 397–410.
Cheever, George. *Guilt of Slavery and the Crime of Slaveholding*. New York: Smith & McDougal, 1860.
Chin, William. "Legal Inequality: Law, the Legal System, and the Lessons of the Black Experience in America." *Hastings Race and Poverty Law Journal* 16.2 (2019) 109–40.
Christian, Mark. "An African-Centered Perspective on White Supremacy." *Journal of Black Studies* 33.2 (2002) 179–98.
Churchill, Ward, and Pierre Orelus. "Confronting Western Colonialism, American Racism, and White Supremacy." *Counterpoints* 430 (2012) 56–112.
Clemens, Paul G. E. "The Rise of Liverpool, 1665–1750." *The Economic History Review* 29.2 (1976) 211–25.
Cliff, Gerald, and Christian Desilets. "White Collar Crime: What It Is and Where It's Going." *Notre Dame Journal of Law, Ethics & Public Policy* 28 (2014) 481–523.
Cole, Ailsa. "Scotland's Slavery Silence: Have Recent Insights Into Scotland's Role in the Transatlantic Slavery Made Their Way into Heritage Presentations and If So, In What Way?" MA Thesis, Heritage and Memory Studies, University of Amsterdam, 2017.
Confer, Vincent. "French Colonial Ideas Before 1789." *French Historical Studies* 3.3 (1964) 338–59.
Conklin, Alice L. "Colonialism and Human Rights, a Contradiction in Terms? The Case of France and West Africa, 1895–1914." *The American Historical Review* 103.2 (1998) 419–42.
Cranston, Maurice. *John Locke: A Biography*. New York: MacMillan, 1957.
Crothers, A. Glenn. "Quaker Merchants and Slavery in Early National Alexandria, Virginia: The Ordeal of William Hartshorne." *Journal of the Early Republic* 25.1 (2005) 47–77.
Crouch, Barry A. "A Spirit of Lawlessness: White Violence, Texas Blacks 1865–68." *Journal of Social History* 18.2 (1984) 217–32.
Curti, Merle. "The Great Mr. Locke: America's Philosopher, 1783–1861." *The Huntington Library Bulletin* 11 (1937) 107–51.
Curtin, Philip D. *The Rise and Fall of the Plantation Complex: Essays in Atlantic History*. 2nd ed. Cambridge: Cambridge University Press, 1998.
Dal Lago, Enrico. "Slavery, Capitalism, and Emancipation: From the Antebellum South to the Confederate South." *Comtemporanea* 2 (2015) 319–29.

Darity, William Jr. "A Model of 'Original Sin': Rise of the West and Lag of the Rest." *The American Economic Review* 82.2 (1992) 162–67.

———. "The Numbers Game and the Profitability of the British Trade in Slaves." *The Journal of Economic History* 45.3 (1985) 693–703.

Daudin, Guillaume. "Profitability of Slave and Long-Distance in Context: The Case of Eighteenth-Century France." *The Journal of Economic History* 64.1 (2004) 144–71.

Davis, A. Y., et al. *The Prison Industrial Complex*. San Francisco: AK Press Audio, 1999.

Davis, David B. "Looking at Slavery from Broader Perspectives." *American Historical Review* 105.2 (2000) 452–66.

———. *The Problem of Slavery in Western Culture*. Ithaca: Cornell University Press, 1966.

DeBeer, E. S., ed. *The Correspondence of John Locke*. Vol. 1. Oxford: Oxford University Press, 1976.

DeCorse, Christopher. "Tools of Empire: Trade, Slaves, and the British Forts of West Africa." In *Building the British Atlantic World*, by Christopher DeCorse, 166–87. Chapel Hill: University of North Carolina Press, 2016.

Demos, John. "The Antislavery Movement and the Problem of Violent 'Means.'" *The New England Quarterly, Inc.* (1964) 501–26.

Desdunes, Rodolphe Lucien. "White Supremacy." *The Daily Crusader*, March 19, 1892.

Desrochers, Robert E. Jr. "Slave-for-Sale Advertisements and Slavery in Massachusetts 1704–1781." *The William and Mary Quarterly* 59.3 (2002) 623–64.

Devine, T. M. "Did Slavery Make Scotia Great?" *Britain and the World* 4.1 (2011) 40–64.

———. *Recovering Scotland's Slavery Past: The Caribbean Connection*. Edinburgh: Edinburgh University Press, 2015.

Deyle, Steven. "An 'Abominable' New Trade: The Closing of the African Slave Trade and the Changing Patterns of U.S. Political Power, 1808–60." *The William and Mary Quarterly* 66.4 (2009) 833–50.

Dickey, Laurence, and H. B. Nisbet, eds. *Hegel, G. W. F. Political Writings*. Cambridge: Cambridge University Press, 1999.

Diggins, John P. "Slavery, Race, and Equality: Jefferson and the Pathos of the Enlightenment." *American Quarterly* 28.2 Special Issue: An American Enlightenment (1979) 206–28.

Dilts, Andrew. "To Kill a Thief: Punishment, Proportionality, and Criminal Subjectivity in Locke's Second Treatise." *Political Theory* 40.1 (2012) 58–83.

Donnan, Elizabeth. "The New England Slave Trade After the Revolution." *The New England Quarterly* 3.2 (1930) 251–78.

Dorrien, Gary. *The New Abolition: W. E. B. Du Bois and the Black Social Gospel*. New Haven: Yale University Press, 2015.

———. *Soul in Society: The Making and Renewal of Social Christianity*. Minneapolis: Fortress, 1995.

Douglass, Frederick. *Life and Times of Frederick Douglass, Written by himself. His Early Life as a Slave, His Escape from*. Boston: De Wolfe Fiske & Co., 1892.

———. "The Meaning of July Fourth for the Negro." Speech Given at Rochester, New York, July 5, 1852. https://masshumanities.org/files/programs/douglass/speech_complete.pdf.

———. *Narrative of the Life of Frederick Douglass, an American Slave, Written by Himself (1845)*. Boston: Bedford, 1993.

———. "Speech on the Death of William Lloyd Garrison." 1879. http://www.ibiblio.org/ebooks/Douglass/Douglass_Garrison.pdf.
Drabble, John. "From White Supremacy to White Power: The FBI, Cointelpro-White Hate, and the Nazification of the Ku Klux Klan in the 1970s." *American Studies* 48.3 (2007) 49–74.
Draper, N. "The City of London and Slavery: Evidence from the First Dock Companies, 1795–1800." *The Economic History Review* 61.2 (2008) 432–66.
Drescher, Seymour. "People and Parliament: The Rhetoric of the British Slave Trade." *The Journal of Interdisciplinary History* 20.4 (1990) 561–80.
———. "Whose Abolition? Popular Pressure and the Ending of the British Slave Trade." *Past & Present* 143 (1994) 136–66.
Du Bois, W. E. B. *Autobiography of W.E.B. Dubois: A Soliloquy on Viewing My Life from the Last Decade of Its First Century.* New York: Intl Pub Co Inc., 1997.
———. *Black Radical Democrat.* Updated ed. New York: Routledge, 2004.
———. *Black Reconstruction in America.* New York: Harcourt, Brace, 1935.
———. "Bleeding Ireland." *The Crisis* (1921).
———. "Bound by the Color Line." *New Masses* (1946).
———. "The Conservation of Races." *The Occasional Papers of the American Negro Academy* 2 (1897).
———. *Darkwater: Voices from Within the Veil.* New York: Schocken, 1969.
———. *Dusk of Dawn: An Essay Toward an Autobiography of a Race Concept.* New York: Harcourt, Brace, 1940.
———. "Missions and Mandates." In *Color and Democracy,* by W. E. B. DuBois, 123–43. New York: Harcourt, Brace, 1945.
———. "The Negro and Crime." *Independent* 51 (May 18, 1899) 1355–57.
———. *The Negro Problem.* London: University of London, 1911.
———. *The Philadelphia Negro: A Social Study.* New York: Schocken, 1899.
———. *Prayers for Dark People (Correspondence of W.E.B. Du Bois).* Amherst: University of Massachusetts Press, 1980.
———. "The Problem of Amusement." In *On Sociology and The Black Community,* edited by Dan S. Green and Edwin D. Driver, 226–37. Chicago: University of Chicago Press, 1978.
———. "Reconstruction and Its Benefits." *The American Historical Review* 15.4 (1910) 781–99.
———. "The Relations of Negroes to Whites in the South." *Annals of the American Academy of Political and Social Sciences* 18 (1901).
———. "Segregation." *The Crisis* (1924).
———. "The Shape of Fear." *North American Review* 223 (1926) 291–304.
———. "The Study of the Negro Problems." *Annals of the American Academy of Political and Social Sciences* 568 (1898) 13–27.
———. *The Suppression of the African Slave-Trade to the United States of America 1638–1870.* New York: Longmans, Green, and Co., 1896.
———. *W. E. B. Du Bois: Biography of a Race 1868–1919.* New York: Henry Holt, 1993.
———. *The World and Africa and Color and Democracy.* The Oxford W. E. B. Du Bois. Oxford: Oxford University Press, 2014.
Dunn, John. *Locke: A Very Short Introduction.* Oxford: Oxford University Press, 1984.
Dunning, Wm, A. "The Constitution of the United States in Reconstruction." *Political Science Quarterly* 2.4 (1889) 558–602.

———. "Military Government in the South During Reconstruction." *Political Science Quarterly* 12.3 (1897) 381–406.Edmondson, Locksley. "Trans-Atlantic Slavery and the Internationalization of Race." *Caribbean Quarterly* 22.2 (1976) 5–25.

Edwards, Barrington S. "W. E. B. Du Bois: Between Worlds: Berlin, Empirical Social Research, and the Race Question." *Du Bois Review* 3.2 (2006) 395–424.

Eisenach, Eldon. *The Two Worlds of Liberalism: Religion and Politics in Hobbes, Locke and Mill.* London: The University of Chicago Press, 1981.

Elkins, Stanley M. *From Slavery to Freedom: A History of Negro Americans.* 3rd ed. New York: Alfred A. Knopf, 1967.

Eltis, David. "The British Contribution to the Nineteenth-Century Transatlantic Slave Trade." *The Economic History Review* 32.2 (1979) 211–27.

———. "The Economic Impact of the Ending of the African Slave Trade to the Americas." *Social and Economic Studies* 37.1/2 (1988) 143–72.

———. "Fluctuations in Mortality in the Last Half Century of the Transatlantic Slave Trade." *Social Science History* 13.3 (1989) 315–40.

———. "The Volume and Structure of the Transatlantic Slave Trade: A Reassessment." *The William and Mary Quarterly* 58.1 (2001) 17–46.

Eltis, David, and David Richardson. "Abolition and Suppression of the Transatlantic Slave Trade." In *Atlas of the Transatlantic Slave Trade*, by David Eltis and David Richardson, 271–90. New Haven: Yale University Press, 2015.

———. "Nations Transporting Slaves from Africa, 1501–1867." In *Atlas of the Transatlantic Slave Trade*, by David Eltis and David Richardson, 21–36. New Haven: Yale University Press, 2015.

Eltis, David, Frank D. Lewis, and David Richardson. "Slave Prices, the African Slave Trade, and Productivity in the Caribbean." *The Economic History Review* 58.4 (2005) 673–700.

Eltis, David, and Stanley L. Engerman. "The Importance of Slavery and the Slave Trade to Industrializing Britain." *The Journal of Economic History* 60.1 (2000) 123–44.

England, Lynn, and W. Keith Warner. "W. E. B. Du Bois: Reform, Will, and the Veil." *Social Forces* 91.3 (2013) 955–73. https://muse.jhu.edu/article/501445.

Equal Justice Initiative. "From Slavery to Segregation." In *Segregation In America*, by Equal Justice Initiative, 6–16. Montgomery: Equal Justice Initiative, 2018. https://segregationinamerica.eji.org/report.pdf.

———. "The Post-Slavery Experience." In *Slavery in America: The Montgomery Slave Trade*, by Equal Justice Initiative, 50–66. Montgomery: Equal Justice Initiative, 2018.

Ericson, David. *The Debate Over Slavery: Antislavery and Proslavery Liberalism in Antebellum America.* New York: New York University Press, 2000.

Evans, Curtis. "W. E. B. Du Bois: Interpreting Religion and the Problem of the Negro Church." *Journal of the American Academy of Religion* 75.2 (2007) 268–97. http://muse.jhu.edu/article/219096/pdf.

Eze, Emmanuel Chukwudi, ed. *African Philosophy.* Malden, MA: Blackwell, 1998.

———. *Race and the Enlightenment: A Reader.* Malden, MA: Blackwell, 1997.

Faiella, Graham. *John Locke: Champion of Modern Democracy.* New York: Rosen, 2006.

Farr, James. "Locke, Natural Law, and New World Slavery." *Political Theory* 36.4 (August 2008) 495–522.

———. "'So Vile and Miserable an Estate': The Problem of Slavery in Locke's Political Thought." *Political Theory* 14.2 (1986) 263–89.

Farrall, S., et al. "Thatcherism, Crime and the Legacy of the Social and Economic 'Storms' of the 1980s." *The Howard Journal of Crime and Justice* 56.2 (2017) 220–43.
Fee, John Gregg. *An Anti-Slavery Manuel*. New York: Arno, 1969.
Fierce, Milfred. *Slavery Revisited: Blacks and the Southern Convict Lease System, 1865–1933*. Brooklyn: City University of New York, 1994.
Filler, Louis. *The Crusade Against Slavery 1830–1860*. New York: Harper & Row, 1960.
———. "Liberalism, Anti-Slavery, and the Founders of the Independent." *The New England Quarterly* 27.3 (1954) 291–306.
———. "Parker Pillsbury: An Anti-Slavery Apostle." *The New England Quarterly* 19.3 (1946) 315–37.
Finkelman, Paul. *Defending Slavery: Proslavery Thought in the Old South: A Brief History with Documents*. 2nd ed. Boston: Bedford, 2020.
———. "The Founders and Slavery: Little Ventured, Little Gained." *Yale Journal of Law & the Humanities* 13.2/3 (2001) 413–49.
———. "Garrison's Constitution: The Covenant With Death and How It Was Made." National Archives, *Prologue Magazine* 32.4 (2000). https://www.archives.gov/publications/prologue/2000/winter/garrisons-constitution-1.
———. "Let Justice Be Done, Though the Heavens May Fall: The Law of Freedom." *Chicago-Kent Law Review* 70.2 (1994) 325–68.
———. "Race, Slavery, and Federal Law, 1789–1804: The Creation of Proslavery Constitutional Law Before Marbury." *University of St. Thomas Law Journal* 14.1 (2018) 1–26.
———. *Slavery and the Founders: Race and Liberty in the Age of Jefferson*. New York: M. E. Sharpe, 1996.
———. *Slavery and the Founders: Race and Liberty in the Age of Jefferson*. 3rd ed. New York: M. E. Sharpe, 2014.
———. "Slavery in the United States: Persons or Property?" In *The Legal Understanding of Slavery: From the Historical to the Contemporary*, edited by Jean Allain, 105–34. Oxford: Oxford University Press, 2012.
———. "Thomas Jefferson, Original Intent, and the Shaping of American Law: Learning Constitutional Law From the Writings of Jefferson." *New York University Survey of American Law* 62.45 (2006) 45–84.
———. "Thomas R. R. Cobb and the Law of Negro Slavery." *Roger Williams University Law Review* 5.1 (1999) 75–115.
First Annual Convention of the People of Colour. "Minutes and Proceedings of the First Annual Convention of the People of Colour." Philadelphia, June 6–11, 1831.
Fisher, Miles Mark. "Friends of Humanity: A Quaker Anti-Slavery Influence." *Church History* 4.3 (1935) 187–202.
Fitzpatrick, John C., ed. *The Writings of George Washington from the Original Manuscript Sources, 1745–1799*. Washington, DC: George Washington Bicentennial Commission, 1931–44.
Fogel, Robert William, and Stanley L. Engermann. *Time on the Cross: The Economics of American Negro Slavery*. Boston: Little, Brown, 1974.
Foner, Philip, ed. *Life and Writings of Frederick Douglass*. Vol. 1. New York: International Publishers, 1950.

Fortner, M. J. "The Silent Majority in Black and White Invisibility and Imprecision in the Historiography of Mass Incarceration." *Journal of Urban History* 40.2 (2014) 252–82.

Fout, John. "The Explosive Cleric: Morgan Godwyn, Slavery and Colonial Elites in Virginia and Barbados, 1665–1685." MA Thesis, Virginia Commonwealth University, 2005.

Franklin, Benjamin. *The Autobiography of Benjamin Franklin*. New York: Collier, 1962.

Franklin, V. P. "Introduction: Ending the Transatlantic Slave Trade: Bicentennial Research, Reflections, and Commemoration." *The Journal of African American History* 93.4 (2008) 471–73.

Fredrickson, George. *The Black Image in the White Mind*. New York: Harper, 1971.

Fryer, Peter. "Britain's Slave Ports." In *Staying Power: The History of Black People in Britain*, by Peter Fryer, 33–66. London: Pluto, 2010.

———. *Staying Power: The History of Black People in Britain*. London: Pluto, 1984.

Galenson, David W. "The Atlantic Slave Trade and the Barbados Market, 1673–1723." *The Journal of Economic History* 42.3 (1982) 491–511.

Garforth, Francis, ed. *John Locke's Of the Conduct of the Understanding*. New York: Teachers College Press, 1966.

Garrison, William Lloyd. *William Lloyd Garrison and the Fight Against Slavery: Selections from The Liberator*. Boston: Bedford Books of St. Martin's, 1995.

Geggus, David. "Racial Equality, Slavery, and Colonial Seccession During the Constituent Assembly." *The American Historical Review* 94.5 (1989) 1290–1308.

General Assembly. "An Act Declaring That Baptisme of Slaves Doth Not Exempt Them from Bondage." 1667. https://encyclopediavirginia.org/entries/an-act-declaring-that-baptisme-of-slaves-doth-not-exempt-them-from-bondage-1667/.

Gerbner, Katharine. "The Ultimate Sin: Christianising Slaves in Barbados in the Seventeenth Century." *Slavery and Abolition* 12.1 (2010) 57–73.

Ghali, Kamal. "No Slavery Except as a Punishment for Crime: The Punishment Clause and Sexual Slavery." *UCLA Law Review* 55 (2008) 607–42.

Gifford, Zerbanoo. *Thomas Clarkson and the Campaign Against Slavery*. London: Anti-Slavery International, 1996.

Gigantino, James J. "Trading in Jersey Souls: New Jersey and the Interstate Slave Trade." *Pennsylvania History: A Journal of Mid-Atlantic Studies* 77.3 (2010) 281–302.

Gilder Lehrman Institute of American History. "Frederick Douglass from Slavery to Freedom: The Journey to New York City." Gilder Lehrman Institute of American History, n.d. https://www.gilderlehrman.org/history-resources/online-exhibitions/frederick-douglass-slavery-freedom-journey-new-york-city.

Gillborn, David. "Rethinking White Supremacy: Who Counts in 'White World.'" *Ethnicities* 6.3 (2006) 318–40.

Gilmore, Kim. "Slavery and Prison—Understanding the Connections." *Social Justice* 27.3 (2000) 195–205.

Glausser, Wayne. "Three Approaches to Locke and the Slave Trade." *Journal of the History of Ideas* 51.2 (1990) 199–216.

Godinho, Vitorino Magalhaes. "Portugal and the Making of the Atlantic World: Sugar Fleets and Gold Fleets, the Seventeenth to the Eighteenth Centuries." *Review* 28.4 (2005) 313–37.

Godwyn, Morgan. *The Negro's & Indian's Advocate, Suing for Their Admission to the Church*. London: J. D. Printed for the Author, 1685.

Goluboff, Risa L. "The Thirteenth Amendment and the Lost Origins of Civil Rights." *Duke Law Journal* 50.6 (2001) 1609–85.

Goodman, R. David. "Expediency, Ambivalence, and Inaction: The French Protectorate and Domestic Slavery in Morocco, 1912–1956." *Journal of Social History* 47.1 (2013) 101–31.

Grassroots Leadership. *Locked Up and Shipped Away: Interstate Prisoner Transfer and the Private Prison Industry*. Grassroots Leadership: Helping People Gain Power, 2013.

Gross, Samuel R., et al. "Rate of False Conviction of Criminal Defendants Who Are Sentenced to Death." University of Michigan, University of Michigan Law School, Ann Arbor, 2014. https://repository.law.umich.edu/articles/1591/.

Grzelinski, Adam. "The Cartesianism and Anti-Cartesianism of Locke's Concept of Personal Identity." *Roczniki Filozoficzne/Annales de Philosopie/Annals of Philosophy* 68.2 (2020) 195–212.

Guy, Talmadge C., and Stephen Brookfield. "W. E. B. Du Bois's Basic American Negro Creed and the Associates in Negro Folk Education: A Case of Repressive Tolerance in the Censorship of Radical Black Discourse on Adult Education." *Adult Education Quarterly* 60.1 (2009) 65–76. https://eric.ed.gov/?id=ej860115.

Hall, Ronald E. "White Women as Postmodern Vehicle of Black Oppression: The Pedagogy of Discrimination in Western Academe." *Journal of Black Studies* 37.1 (2006) 69–82.

Hamilton, Walton H. "Property—According to Locke." *The Yale Law Journal Company* 41.6 (1932) 864–80.

Hartnett, S. J. *Challenging the Prison-Industrial Complex: Activism, Arts, and Educational Alternatives*. Urbana: University of Illinois Press, 2011.

Hasani, Alvaro. "'You Are Hereby Sentenced to a Term of . . . Enslavement?': Why Prisoners Cannot Be Exempt from Thirteenth Amendment Protection." *Barry Law Review* 18.2 (2013) 273–96.

Haslam, David. *Race for the Millennium: A Challenge to Church and Society*. London: Church House, 1996.

Hatfield, April Lee. "Slavery, Trade, War, and the Purposes of Empire." *The William and Mary Quarterly* 68.3 (2011) 405–8.

Head, David. "Slave Smuggling by Foreign Privateers: The Illegal Slave Trade and the Geopolitics of the Early Republic." *Journal of the Early Republic* 33.3 (2013) 433–62.

Hefelbower, S. G. "Deism Historically Defined." *The American Journal of Theology* 24.2 (1920) 217–23.

Hegel, G. W. F. *Element of the Philosophy of Right*. Edited by Allen Wood. Cambridge Texts in the History of Political Thought. Cambridge: Cambridge University Press, 1991.

———. *Lectures on the Philosophy of World History*. Translated by H. B. Nisbet. New York: Cambridge University Press, 1975.

———. *Phenomenology of Spirit*. Translated by A. V. Miller. New York: Oxford University Press, 1977.

Higginbotham, Michael F. "Maintaining White Dominance During Reconstruction." In *Ghosts of Jim Crow: Ending Racism in Post-Racial America*, by F. Michael Higginbotham 63–84. New York University Press, 2015.

Hinshelwood, Brad. "The Carolinian Context of John Locke's Theory of Slavery." *Political Theory* 41.4 (2013) 562–90.

Hirschfeld, Fritz. *George Washington and Slavery: A Documentary Portrayal.* Columbia: University of Missouri Press, 1997.

Hogendorn, Jan S. "The Economics of the African Slave Trade." *The Journal of American History* 70.4 (1984) 854–61.

Holmes, David L. *The Faiths of the Founding Fathers.* New York: Oxford University Press, 2006.

Holmes, William. *The White Chief: James Kimble Vardaman.* Baton Rouge: Louisiana State University Press, 1970.

Horton, James Oliver, and Lois E. Horton. *Slavery and the Making of America.* New York: Oxford University Press, 2005.

Hough, Joseph C. *Black Power and White Protestants: A Christian Response to the New Negro Pluralism.* New York: Oxford University Press, 1968.

Hough, Mike, Rob Allen, and Una Padel. *Reshaping Probation and Prisons: The New Offender Management Framework.* Bristol: Policy, 2006.

Howe, Scott W. "Slavery as Punishment: Original Public Meaning, Cruel and Unusual Punishment, and the Neglected Clause in the Thirteenth Amendment." *Arizona Law Review* 51 (2009) 983–1034.

Howell World History. "The Atlantic Slave Trade." https://howellworldhistory.wordpress.com/quarter-one/unit-3-european-global-interactions/the-atlantic-slave-trade-15-4/.

Hynes, Gerald C. "A Biographical Sketch of W. E. B. Du Bois." *W. E. B. Du Bois Learning Center* (2014). http://www.duboislc.org/html/DuBoisBio.html.

Imbua, David Lishilinimle. "Slavery and Slave Trade Remembered: A Study of the Slave History Museum in Calabar, Nigeria." *Journal of the Historical Society of Nigeria* 22 (2013) 112–36.

Inikori, Joseph E. "Market Structure and the Profits of the British African Trade in the Late Eighteenth Century." *The Journal of Economic History* 41.4 (1981) 746–76.

———. "Slavery and the Development of Industrial Capitalism in England." *The Journal of Interdisciplinary History* 17.4 (1987) 771–93.

Issacs, Caroline. "Treatment Industrial Complex: How For-Profit Prison Corporation Are Undermining Efforts to Treat and Rehabilitate Prisoners for Corporate Gain." American Friends Service Committee, 2014.

Itzigsohn, Jose, and Karida Brown. *The Sociology of W. E. B. Du Bois: Racialized Modernity and the Global Color Line.* New York: NYU Press, 2020.

Jaron, B., "Rooted in Slavery: Prison Labor Exploitation." *Race, Poverty & the Environment* 14.1 (2007) 42–44.

The JBHE Foundation, Inc. "The Nation's Hot Spots of White Supremacy." *The Journal of Blacks in Higher Education* 64 (2009) 49–50.

Jefferson, Thomas. *The Life and Morals of Jesus of Nazareth: Extracted Textually from the Gospel Together with a Comparison of His Doctrines with Those of Others.* New York: N. D. Thompson, 1902.

———. *Notes on the State of Virginia.* London, 1787.

Jennings, Lawrence C. "France, Great Britain, and the Repression of the Slave Trade, 1841–1845." *French Historical Studies* 10.1 (1977) 101–25.

Katz, Stanley N. "Thomas Jefferson and the Right to Property in Revolutionary America." *The Journal of Law & Economics* 19.3 (1776) 467–88.

Katz-Fishman, Walda, and Jerome Scott. "Diversity and Equality: Race and Class in America." *Sociological Forum* 9.4 (1994) 569–81.

Kaye, Mike. *1807–2007: Over 200 Years of Campaigning Against Slavery*. United Kingdom: Anti-Slavery International, 2005.

Kenney, Lucy. *A Refutation of the Principles of Abolition; By a Lady of Fredericksburg*. Washington, DC: Library of Congress, 1836.

Keren, Ella. "The Transatlantic Slave Trade in Ghanaian Academic Historiography: History, Memory, and Power." *The William and Mary Quarterly* 66.4 (2009) 975–1000.

Kharem, Haroon. "Internal Colonialism: White Supremacy and Education." *Counterpoints* 208 (2006) 23–47.

———. "White Supremacy's Politics of Culture and Exclusion." *Counterpoints* 208 (2006) 49–73.

King, Lord. *The Life of John Locke*. London: Henry Colburn and Richard Bentley, 1830.

Kishi, Roudabeh. "White Supremacy and White Nationalism." In *Far-Right Violence and the American Midterm Election*, by Roudabeh Kishi, 12–13. Armed Conflict Location & Event Data Project, 2022.

Klein, Herbert S. "The English Slave Trade to Jamaica, 1782–1808." *The Economic History Review* 31.1 (1978) 25–45.

Koch, Adrienne. *The Philosophy of Thomas Jefferson*. New York: Columbia University Press, 1943.

Kornweibel, Theodore, Jr. "Railroads and Slavery." *Railroad History* 189 (2003) 34–59.

Lamb, Jonathan. "Locke's Wild Fancies: Empiricism, Personhood, and Fictionality." *The Eighteenth Century* 48.3 (2007) 187–204.

Lamprecht, Sterling P. "Locke's Attack Upon Innate Ideas." *The Philosophical Review* 36.2 (1972) 145–65.

Landers, Jane. "Slavery in the Spanish Caribbean and the Failure of Abolition." *Review* 31.3 (2008) 343–71.

Landis, Benson Y. *A Rauschenbusch Reader: The Kingdom of God and the Social Gospel*. New York: Harper & Brothers, 1957.

Lange, Matthew, James Mahoney, and Matthew vom Hau. "Colonialism and Development: A Comparative Analysis of Spanish and British Colonies." *American Journal of Sociology* 111.5 (2006) 1412–62.

Levy, Claude. "Slavery and the Emancipation Movement in Barbados 1650–1833." *The Journal of Negro History* 55.1 (1970) 1–14.

Levy, Michael. "Eighth Amendment: United States Constitution." *Encyclopedia Britannica*, March 16, 2016. https://www.britannica.com/topic/Eighth-Amendment.

Lewis, David Levering. "W. E. B. Du Bois: The Fight for Equality and the American Century: 1919–1963." *Sociology of Religion* 63.2 (2002) 239–53.

Library of Congress. "Northwest Ordinance." *Primary Documents in American History*, n.d. https://www.loc.gov/rr/program//bib/ourdocs/northwest.html.

Lincoln, Abraham. "Abraham Lincoln Papers: Series 2. General Correspondence. 1858–1864: Abraham Lincoln to Horace Greeley, Friday, August 22, 1862." Clipping from August 23, 1862, *Daily National Intelligencer*, Washington, DC. Library of Congress. https://www.loc.gov/resource/mal.4233400/?st=text &r=-1.559,0,4.118,2.818,0.

———. "Letter to Horace Greeley, August 22, 1862." Lincoln as the Great Communicator, n.d. https://lincolnasgreatcommunicator.wordpress.com/public-letters/letter-to-horace-greeley-august-22-1862/.

Lincoln, Abraham, and Stephen A. Douglas. "The Lincoln-Douglas Debates, 4th Debate, Part I." Teaching American History, September 18, 1858. https://teachingamericanhistory.org/document/the-lincoln-douglas-debates-4th-debate-part-i.

Litwack, Leon F. "The Abolitionist Dilemma: The Antislavery Movement and the Northern Negro." *The New England Quarterly* 34.1 (1961) 50–73.

———. *North of Slavery: The Negro in the Free State, 1790–1860*. Chicago: University of Chicago Press, 1961.

Locke, John. *1823 Works*. 10 Vols. London: Scientia Verlag Aalen, 1963.

———. *An Early Draft of Locke's Essay Together with Excerpts from his Journal*. Edited by R. I. Aaron and Jocelyn Gibb. Oxford: Clarendon, 1936.

———. *An Essay Concerning Human Understanding*. Edited by Peter H. Nidditch. Oxford: Oxford University Press, 1975.

———. "Fundamental Constitutions of Carolina, 1669." *Fundamental Constitutions*, 1669. https://www.carolana.com/Carolina/Documents/fundamental_constitutions_1669.html.

———. "Fundamental Constitutions of Carolina 1670." *Fundamental Constitutions*, 1670. https://www.carolana.com/Carolina/Documents/fundamental_constitutions_1670.html.

———. "Fundamental Constitutions of Carolina Aug. 1682." *Fundamental Constitutions*, August 1682. https://www.carolana.com/Carolina/Documents/fundamental_constitutions_1682_august.html.

———. "Fundamental Constitutions of Carolina 1698." *Fundamental Constitutions*, 1698. https://www.carolana.com/Carolina/Documents/fundamental_constitutions_1698.html.

———. "Fundamental Constitutions of Carolina 1699." *Fundamental Constitutions*, 1699. https://www.carolana.com/Carolina/Documents/fundamental_constitutions_overview.html.

———. *John Locke Writings on Religion*. Edited by Victor Nuovo. Oxford: Oxford University Press, 2002.

———. *A Letter Concerning Toleration*. Edited by Oskar Piest. New York: The Liberal Arts, Inc., 1955.

———. *Locke: Political Essays*. Edited by Mark Goldie. Cambridge: Cambridge University Press, 1997.

———. *Of the Conduct of the Understanding*. Edited by Francis W. Garforth. New York: Teachers College Columbia University, 1966.

———. *Political Essays*. Edited by Mark Goldie. Cambridge: Cambridge University Press, 1997.

———. *Second Treatise of Civil Government*. 1690.

———. *Second Treatise of Government*. Adapted by Jonathan Bennett. 1660/2017.

———. *Second Treatise of Government*. Edited by Thomas P. Peardon. New York: Pearson, 1952.

———. *A Second Vindication of the Reasonableness of Christianity, &c, By the author of The Reasonableness of Christianity, &c*. London: Printed for A. and J. Churchill and Edward Castle, 1697.

---. *Some Thoughts Concerning Education; and On the Conduct of the Understanding*. Edited by Ruth Grant and Nathan Tarcov. Indianapolis: Hackett, 1996.

---. *A Third Letter for Toleration, to the Author of the Third Letter Concerning Toleration*. London: Printed for Awnsham and John Churchill, 1692.

---. *Two Treatises of Government*. Edited by Peter Laslett. Cambridge: Cambridge University Press, [1690] 1967.

---. *The Works of John Locke*. 10 vols. New York: Cosimo Classics, 2008.

---. *The Works of John Locke*. Vol. 1. London: Printed for Thomas Tegg, 1823.

Locke, John, George Berkeley, and David Hume. *The Empiricists: John Locke, George Berkeley, David Hume*. New York: Anchor, 1974.

Loewenberg, Robert J. "John Locke and the Antebellum Defense of Slavery." *Political Theory* 13.2 (1985) 266–91.

Looney, J. Jefferson, ed. *The Papers of Thomas Jefferson, Retirement Series*. Vol. 1. Princeton: Princeton University Press, 2004.

Lovejoy, Paul E. "The Upper Guinea Coast and the Trans-Atlantic Slave Trade Databased." *African Economic History* 38 (2010) 1–27.

Lovejoy, Paul E., and David Richardson. "British Abolition and Its Impact on Slave Prices Along the Atlantic Coast of Africa, 1783–1850." *The Journal of Economic History* 55.1 (1995) 98–119.

Lowcountry Digital History Initiation. "Historical Context: Abolishing the Trans-Atlantic Slave Trade." LDHI, Voyage of the Echo: The Trials of an Illegal Trans-Atlantic Slave Ship, n.d. https://ldhi.library.cofc.edu/exhibits/show/voyage-of-the-echo-the-trials/historic-context--abolishing-t.

Lowe, Richard G., and Randolph B. Campbell. "The Slave-Breeding Hypothesis: A Demographic Comment on the 'Buying' and 'Selling' States." *The Journal of Southern History* 42.3 (1976) 401–12.

Lucas, Paul. *Essays on the Margin of Blackstone's Commentaries*. Princeton: Princeton University Press, 1963.

Lundy, Benjamin. *The War in Texas; A Review of Facts and Circumstances, Showing That This Contest Is Crusade Against Mexico, Set on Foot and Supported by Slaveholders, Land-Speculators, Etc. In Order to Re-Establish, Extend, and Perpetuate the System of Slavery...* Philadelphia: Merrihew and Gunn, 1837.

Lydon, James G. "New York and the Slave Trade, 1700 to 1774." *The William and Mary Quarterly* 35.2 (1978) 375–94.

Maclachlan, Colin M. "Slavery, Ideology, and Institutional Change: The Impact of the Enlightenment on Slavery in Late Eighteenth-Century Maranhao." *Journal of Latin American Studies* 11.1 (1979) 1–17.

Mancini, Matthew J. *One Dies, Get Another: Convict Leasing in the American South, 1866–1928*. Columbia: University of South Carolina Press, 1996.

---. "Race, Economics, and the Abandonment of Convict Leasing." *The Journal of Negro History* 63.4 (1978) 339–52.

Mandel, Bernard. *Labor: Free and Slave; Workingmen and the Anti-slavery Movement in the United States*. New York: Associated Authors, 1955.

Matthews, Donald. "The Abolitionist on Slavery: The Critique Behind the Social Movement." *The Journal of Southern History* 33.2 (1967) 163–82.

Mayer, Henry. *All on Fire: William Lloyd Garrison and the Abolition of Slavery*. New York: St. Martin's, 1998.

McCord, Charles. *The American Negro as a Dependent, Defective, and Delinquent.* Nashville: Benson, 1914.

McCord, David J. *The Statutes at Large of South Carolina: Edited Under Authority of the Legislature.* Vol. 7. Columbia, SC: A. S. Johnston, 1840.

McFeely, William S. *Frederick Douglass.* New York: W. W. Norton, 1991.

McKelvey, Blake. "Penal Slavery and Southern Reconstruction." *The Journal of Negro History* 20.2 (1935) 153–79.

McLaughlin-Stonham, Hilary. "The Rise of White Supremacy the Road to Segregated Streetcars." In *On the Streetcars of New Orleans 1830s–Present,* by Hilary McLaughlin-Stonham, 83–122. Liverpool: Liverpool University Press, 2020.

McNeill, Fergus, et al. *How and Why People Stop Offending: Discovering Desistance.* Glasgow: University of Glasgow, 2012.

McPherson, James. *The Struggle for Equality: Abolitionists and the Negro in the Civil War and Reconstruction.* New Jersey: Princeton University Press, 1964.

Merk, Frederick. *Slavery and Annexation of Texas.* New York: Alfred A. Knopf, 1972.

Mills, Charles W. "Revisionist Ontologists: Theorizing White Supremacy." *Social and Economic Studies* 43.3 (1994) 105–34.

Minkema, Kenneth. "Jonathan Edwards on Slavery and the Slave Trade." *The William and Mary Quarterly* 54.4 (1997) 823–34.

Miura, Nagamitsu. *John Locke and the Native Americans: Early English Liberalism and Its Colonial Reality.* Cambridge: Cambridge Scholars, 2013.

Mohamed, Besheer, et al. "Faith Among Black Americans: Most Black Worshippers Attend Predominantly Black Congregations and See a Role for Religion in Fighting Racial Injustice, but Generational Patterns Are Changing." Pew Research Center, February 16, 2021. https://www.pewresearch.org/religion/2021/02/16/faith-among-black-americans/.

Morgan, Kenneth. "Bristol and the Atlantic Trade in the Eighteenth Century." *The English Historical Review* 107.424 (1992) 626–50.

Mtubani, C. D. Victor. "The Black Voice in Eighteenth-Century Britain: African Writers Against Slavery and the Slave Trade." *Phylon* 45.2 (1984) 85–97.

Muelder, Walters George. *Learning for Life Course: Essential Human Rights.* Chicago: Methodist Pub., 1948.

Nanasi, Mariel. "White Supremacy." *Off Our Backs* 20.10 (1990) 19–20.

The National Archives. "The Evil Trade: Olaudah Equiano and Abolition." n.d. https://cdn.nationalarchives.gov.uk/documents/education/this-evil-trade-pack.pdf.

———. "Slavery and the British Transatlantic Slave Trade." n.d. https://www.nationalarchives.gov.uk/help-with-your-research/research-guides/british-transatlantic-slave-trade-records/.

National Records of Scotland. "Slavery and the Slave Trade." n.d. https://www.nrscotland.gov.uk/research/guides/slavery-and-the-slave-trade.

The National Trust for Scotland. "Scotland and the Slave Trade." n.d. https://www.scottishopera.org.uk/media/4208/scotland-and-the-slavetrade-nts-pdf-schools-pack-1.pdf.

Neushouser, Frederick. *Foundation of Hegel's Social Theory: Actualizing Freedom.* London: Harvard University Press, 2000.

Nidditch, Peter H., ed. *Draft A of Locke's Essay Concerning Human Understanding: The Earliest Extant Autograph Edition.* Sheffield: University of Sheffield, 1980.

Nina, Bernstein. "VA: Death in Another ICE Jail." Real Cost of Prisons, January 28, 2009. http://realcostofprisons.org/blog/archives/2009/01/va_death_in_.

Nunn, Nathan, and Leonard Wantchekon. "The Slave Trade and the Origins of Mistrust in Africa." *The American Economic Review* 101.7 (2011) 3221–52.

O'Malley, Gregory E. "Beyond the Middle Passage: Slave Migration from the Caribbean to North America, 1619–1807." *The William and Mary Quarterly* 66.1 (2009) 125–72.

Onuf, Peter S. "'To Declare Them a Free and Independent People': Race, Slavery, and National Identity in Jefferson's Thought." *Journal of the Early Republic* 18.1 (1998) 1–46.

Oregon Historical Society. "White Supremacy & Resistance." *Oregon Historical Quarterly* 120.4 (2019) 380–81.

Orelus, Pierre W. "Black Masculinity Under White Supremacy: Exploring the Interpretation Between Black Masculinity, Slavery, Racism, Heterosexism, and Social Class." *Counterpoints* 351 (2010) 63–111.

Oshinsky, David M. *"Worse Than Slavery": Parchman Farm and the Ordeal of Jim Crow Justice*. New York: Free, 1996.

Osofsky, Gilbert, ed. *The Burden of Race: A Documentary History of Negro-White Relations in America*. New York: Harper and Row, 1966.

Otis, James. "The Rights of the British Colonies Asserted." *America's Heritage: Historical Documents of the United States*. 2009. http://ahp.gatech.edu/rights_brit_colonies_1764.html.

Paeth, Scott. "Empiricism." In *Philosophy: A Short Visual Introduction*, by Scott Paeth, 77–95. Minneapolis: Fortress, 2015.

Page, Anthony. "Rational Dissent, Enlightenment, and Abolition of the British Slave Trade." *The Historical Journal* 54.3 (2011) 741–72.

Parsons, Elaine Frantz. "Ku Klux Klan, Reconstruction-Era." In *The New Encylopedia of Southern Culture*, Vol. 24, *Race*, edited by Thomas C. Holt et al., 229–33. Chapel Hill: University of North Carolina Press, 2013.

Perkinson, Robert. *Texas Tough: The Rise of America's Prison Empire*. New York: Henry Holt, 2010.

Peterson, Merrill D. *Jefferson and the New Nation*. 1st ed. Oxford: Oxford University Press, 1975.

———. *The Portable Thomas Jefferson*. New York: Penguin, 1975.

Pettigrew, William. "Free to Enslave: Politics and the Escalation of Britain's Transatlantic Slave Trade 1688–." *The William and Mary Quarterly, Third Series* 64.1 (2007) 3–38.

Phillips, Wendell. *The Philosophy of the Abolition Movement*. New York: American Anti-slavery Society, 1860.

Pinar, William F. "White Women in the Ku Klux Klan." *Counterpoints* 163 (2001) 555–619.

Pope-Hennessy, James. *Sins of the Fathers*. London: Pan, 1988.

"Portugal." Port Cities Bristol, n.d. https://www.discoveringbristol.org.uk/slavery/routes/places-involved/europe/portugal/.

Posey, Walter Brownlow. "Influence of Slavery upon the Methodist Church in Early South and Southwest." *The Mississippi Valley Historical Review* 17.4 (1931) 530–42.

Post, David M. "Jeffersonian Revisions of Locke: Education, Property-Rights, and Liberty." *Journal of the History of Ideas* 47.1 (1986) 147–57.

BIBLIOGRAPHY

Proceedings of the Annual Congress of the National Prison Association of the United States: Held at Austin, Texas, December 26, 1897. London: Forgotten Books, 2018.
"Queen Elizabeth I's Sea Dogs." The History Press, September 26, 2017. https://thehistorypress.co.uk/article/queen-elizabeth-is-sea-dogs/.
Rabaka, Reiland. "The Souls of White Folks: W.E.B. Du Bois's Critique of White Supremacy and Contribution to Critical White Studies." *Journal of African American Studies* 11.1 (2007) 1–15.
Radburn, Nicholas. "Guinea Factors, Slave Sales, and the Profits of the Transatlantic Slave Trade in Late Eighteenth-Century Jamaica: The Case of John Tailyour." *The William and Mary Quarterly* 72.2 (2015) 243–86.
Raesly, Barboura. "Interview with William Thompson, April 3, 1974." University of Georgia, Oral History Collections. https://georgiaoralhistory.libs.uga.edu/RBRL216RBROH/RBRL216RBROH-101.
Randall, Willard Sterne. *Thomas Jefferson: A Life.* New York: HarperPerennial, 1993.
Randive, Mayur. "Case Study: Portugal and The Transatlantic Slave Trade." Human Rights Pulse, July 25, 2021. https://www.humanrightspulse.com/mastercontentblog/case-study-portugal-and-the-transatlantic-slave-trade.
Ransom, Roger, and Richard Sutch. "Capitalist Without Capital: The Burden of Slavery and the Impact of Emancipation." *Agricultural History* 62.3 (1988) 133–60.
Rauschenbusch, Walter. *Christianity and the Social Crisis.* New York: Macmillan, 1907.
———. *Christianizing the Social Order.* Waco: Baylor University Press, 2010.
———. "The Kingdom of God." In *The Social Gospel in America, 1870–1920*, edited by Robert T. Handy. New York: Oxford University Press, 1966.
———. *The Social Principles of Jesus.* New York: Association, 1918.
———. *A Theology for the Social Gospel.* New York: Abingdon, 1917.
Rawley, James A. *The Transatlantic Slave Trade.* New York: Norton, 1981.
Reddie, James. "Slavery." *The Anthropological Review* 2.7 (1864) 280–93.
Reedy, Gerard. "Socinians, John Toland, and the Anglican Rationalists." *The Harvard Theological Review* 70.3/4 (1977) 285–304.
Rhodes, James F. *History of the United States, from the Compromise of 1890.* New York: Cosimo Classic, 1928.
Richards, Judith, Lotte Mulligan, and John K. Graham. "'Property' and 'People': Political Usages of Locke and Some Contemporaries." *Journal of the History of Ideas* 42.1 (1981) 29–51.
Roberts, Derrell. "Joseph E. Brown and the Convict Lease System." *The Georgia Historical Quarterly* 44.4 (1960) 399–410.
Rodrigue, John. "'Repudiating the Emancipation Proclamation, and Re-establishing Slavery': The Abolition of Slavery in the Lower Mississippi Valley and the United States." *Louisiana History: The Journal of the Louisiana Historical Association* 58.4 (2017) 389–403.
Romanell, Patrick, et al. "Who Read John Locke?" *The American Scholar* 59.3 (1990) 475–78.
Rosenzweig, Stav, and Gerard J. Tellis. "Portuguese Caravel: Building an Oceanic Empire." In *How Transformative Innovations Shaped the Rise of Nations*, by Gerard J. Tellis and Stav Rosenzweig, 143–56. London: Anthem, 2018.
Ruchames, Louis. *The Abolitionists: A Collection of Their Writings.* New York: G. P. Putnam's Sons, 1963.

Ryan, James Gilbert. "The Memphis Riots of 1866: Terror in a Black Community During Reconstruction." *The Journal of Negro History* 62.3 (1977) 243–57.
Ryckmans, Pierre. "Belgian 'Colonialism.'" *Foreign Affairs* 34.1 (1955) 89–101.
Sahakian, Williams S., and Mabel Lewis Sahakian. *John Locke*. Boston: Twayne, 1975.
Sakala, Leah. "Prison-based Gerrymandering's Striking Resemblance to the Infamous Three-Fifth Clause." Prison Policy Initiative, September 9, 2011. https://www.prisonersofthecensus.org/news/2011/09/09/three-fifths/.
Sakala, Leah, Peter Wagner, and Drew Kukorowski. "Please Deposit All of Your Money: Kickbacks, Rates, and Hidden Fees in the Jail Phone Industry." Prison Policy Initiative, May 2013.
Salley, Columbus, and Ronald Behm. *Your God Is Too White: An Illustrated Documentary of Christianity and Race in America*. London: Lion, 1973.
Sallis, William C. "The Color Line in Mississippi Politics, 1865–1915." Dissertation, University of Kentucky, 1967.
Sandler, Gerald S. "Lockean Ideas in Thomas Jefferson's Bill for Establishing Religious Freedom." *Journal of the History of Idea* 21.1 (1960) 110–16.
Schlosser, Eric. "The Prison-Industrial Complex." *The Atlantic*, December 1, 1998. https://www.theatlantic.com/magazine/archive/1998/12/the-prison-industrial-complex/304669/.
Schmidt, James. "What Enlightenment Project." *Political Theory* 28.6 (2000) 734–57.
Schmidt-Nowara, Christopher. "Big Questions and Answers: Three Histories of Slavery, the Slave Trade and the Atlantic World." *Social History* 27.2 (2002) 210–17.
———. "Empires Against Emancipation: Spain, Brazil, and the Abolition of Slavery." *Review* 31.2 (2008) 101–19.
"Scotland and Black Slavery to 1833." The Scottish History Society, n.d. https://scottishhistorysociety.com/scotland-and-black-slavery-to-1833/.
Sellin, Thorsten. *Slavery and the Penal System*. New Orleans: Quid Pro Books, 2016.
Seltzer, Rick, and Grace M. Lopes. "The Ku Klux Klan: Reasons for Support or Opposition Among White Respondents." *Journal of Black Studies* 17.1 (1986) 91–109.
Shanks, Caroline. "The Biblical Anti-Slavery Argument of the Decade 1830–1840." *The Journal of Negro of Negro History* 16.2 (1931) 132–57.
Sharrow, Walter G. "John Hughes and a Catholic Response to Slavery in Antebellum America." *The Journal of Negro History* 57.3 (1972) 254–69.
Shelby, McCloy, T. *The Negro in France*. Black Studies 2. Lexington: University of Kentucky Press, 1961. https://uknowledge.uky.edu/upk_black_studies/2.
Sheldon, Randall G. "From Slave to Caste Society: Penal Changes in Tennessee, 1830–1915." *Tennessee Historical Quarterly* 38.4 (1979) 462–78.
Sheridan, R. B. "The Commercial and Financial Organization of the British Slave Trade, 1750–1807." *The Economic History Review* 11.2 (1958) 249–63.
Shyllon, Folarin. *Black People in Britain 1555–1833*. London: Oxford University Press, 1977.
Sinha, Manisha. "Did He Die an Abolitionist? The Evolution of Abraham Lincoln's Antislavery." *American Political Thought* 4.3 (2015) 439–54.
Sklar, Kathryn Kish. *Women's Rights Emerges within the Antislavery Movement, 1830–1870*. Boston: St. Martins, 2000.
Skocpol, Michael. "The Emerging Constitutional Law of Prison Gerrymandering." *Stanford Law Review* 69 (2017) 1473–1539.

Smallwood, Stephanie E. "Reflections on Settler Colonialism, the Hemisphere Americas, and Chattel Slavery." *The William and Mary Quarterly* 76.3 (2019) 407–16.
Snyder, Terri L. "Suicide, Slavery, and Memory in North America." *The Journal of American History* 97.1 (2010) 39–62.
Solow, Barbara L. "The Transatlantic Slave Trade: A New Census." *The William and Mary Quarterly* 58.1 (2001) 9–16.
Squadrito, Kay. "Racism and Empiricism." *Behaviorism* 7.1 (Spring 1979) 105–15.
Stampp, Kenneth M. *The Peculiar Institution: Slavery in the Ante-Bellum South*. New York: Random House, 1956.
Sundquist, Eric. *W. E. B. Du Bois Reader*. Oxford: Oxford University Press, 1996.
Sutherland, Edwin H. "Is 'White Collar Crime' Crime?" *American Sociological Review* 10.2 (1944) 132–39.
———. "White-Collar Criminality." *American Sociological Review* 5.1 (1940) 1–12.
Sweet, David G. "Black Robes and 'Black Destiny': Jesuit Views of African Slavery in 17th-Century Latin America." *Revista de Historia de America* 86 (1978) 87–133.
Syse, Henrik. *Natural Law, Religion and Rights*. South Bend, IN: St. Augustine, 2007.
Tannenbaum, Frank. *Slave & Citizen*. New York: Random House, 1947.
Taylor, Clare. *Women of the Anti-Slavery Movement*. New York: St. Martin, 1995.
Taylor, Elizabeth. "The Abolition of the Convict Lease System in Georgia." *Georgia Historical Quarterly* 26.3/4 (1942) 273–87.
Taylor, Rosser Howard. *Slaveholding in North Carolina: An Economic View*. New York: Negro Universities Press, 1969.
Thomas, Robert Paul, and Richard Nelson Bean. "The Fishers of Men: The Profits of the Slave Trade." *The Journal of Economic History* 34.4 (1974) 885–914.
Thompson, Heather Ann. "The Prison Industrial Complex: A Growth Industry in a Shrinking Economy." *New Labor Forum* 21.3 (2012) 38–47.
Tully, James. *A Discourse on Property: John Locke and His Adversaries*. Cambridge: Cambridge University Press, 1980.
Turner, Jack. "John Locke, Christian Mission, and Colonial America." *Modern Intellectual History* 8.2 (2011) 267–97.
Turner, Lorenzo Dow. "The Anti-Slavery Movement Prior to the Abolition of the African Slave-Trade (1641–1808)." *The Journal of Negro History* 14.4 (1929) 373–402.
"U.S. Constitutional Amendments." FindLaw, reviewed June 14, 2022. http://constitution.findlaw.com/amendments.html.
Uzgalis, William. "John Locke." *The Stanford Encyclopedia of Philosophy* (Spring 2020). https://plato.stanford.edu/entries/locke/.
Viney, Donald Wayne. "American Deism, Christianity, and the Age of Reason." *American Journal of Theology & Philosophy* 31.2 (2010) 83–107.
Vink, Markus. "'The World's Oldest Trade': Dutch Slavery and Slave Trade in the Indian Ocean in Seventeenth Century." *Journal of World History* 14.2 (2003) 131–77.
Viotti da Costa, Emilia. "The Portuguese-African Slave Trade: A Lesson in Colonialism." *Latin American Perspective* 12.1 (1985) 41–61.
Vogt, John L. "The Lisbon Slave House and African Trade, 1486–1521." *Proceedings of the American Philosophical Society* 117.1 (1973) 1–16.
Walters, Ronald W. "The Impact of Slavery on 20th- and 21st-Century Black Progress." *The Journal of African American History* 97.1/2 (2012) 110–30.

Walters-Sleyon, George. *God in the Name of Jesus Christ*. United States: Independent, 2022.

———. *Locked Up and Locked Down: Multitude Lingers in Limbo*. Rev. ed. United States: Lulu, 2013.

———. *Nuggets From the Night: An Anthology of Poetic Expressions*. United States: Independent, 2020.

———. *Prison Chaplains on the Beat in US and UK Prisons*. Parker, CO: Outskirts, 2021.

Waterman, Anthony M. C. "Property Rights in John Locke and in Christian Social Teaching." *Review of Social Economy* 40.2 (1982) 97–115.

Wehr, K., and E. Aseltine. *Beyond the Prison Industrial Complex: Crime and Incarceration in the 21st Century*. New York: Routledge, 2013.

Welchman, Jennifer. "Locke on Slavery and Inalienable Rights." *Canadian Journal of Philosophy* 25.1 (1995) 67–81.

Welie, Rik Van. "Slave Trading and Slavery in the Dutch Colonial Empire: A Global Comparison." *New West Indian Guide* 82.1/2 (2008) 47–96.

West, Cornel. *Black Prophetic Fire*. Boston: Beacon. 2015.

———. *The Cornel West Reader*. New York: Basic Civitas, 1999.

———. *Keeping Faith: Philosophy and Race in America*. London: Routledge, 1993.

———. *Race Matters*. New York: Vintage, 2001.

Weststeijn, Arthur. "Republican Empire: Colonialism, Commerce and Corruption in the Dutch Golden Age." *Renaissance Studies* 26.4 (2012) 491–509.

White, Eugene. "Anti-Racial Agitation in Politics: James Kimble Vardaman in the Mississippi Gubernatorial Campaign of 1903." *Journal of Mississippi History* 7 (1945).

Whitmore, William H. *A Bibliographical Sketch of the Laws of the Massachusetts Colony*. Boston: Rockwell and Churchill, 1890.

Williams, Eric. *Capitalism & Slavery*. Richmond: William Byrd, 1945.

Williams, James. *Letters On Slavery*. Miami: Mnemosyne, 1861.

Willis, Clive. "David Livingstone, Africa and the Portuguese." The British Historical Society of Portugal: Thirty Second Annual Report and Review, 2005.

Wilson, Charles Reagan. "Reconstruction." In vol. 3: *History of The New Encyclopedia of Southern Culture*, edited by Charles Reagon Wilson, 219–23. Chapel Hill: University of North Carolina Press, 2006.

Witte, John, Jr. *The Blessings of Liberty: Human Rights and Religious Freedom in the Western Legal Tradition*. Cambridge: Cambridge University Press, 2022.

Witte, John, Jr., and Frank S. Alexander. *Christianity and Law: An Introduction*. Cambridge Companion to Religion. Cambridge: Cambridge University Press, 2008.

Wolff, Richard D. "British Imperialism and the East African Slave Trade." *Science & Society* 36.4 (1972) 443–62.

Woodson, Carter G. *The History of the Negro Church*. Washington: Associated Publishers, 1945.

Woolhouse, Roger. *Locke: A Biography*. Cambridge: Cambridge University Press, 2007.

WPA Slave Narrative Project. "Interview by Chris Franklin." 1937.

———. "Interview with Sylvia Watkins." 1937.

———. "Interview with W. L. Bost." 1937.

Yarborough, Richard. "Frederick Douglass and Theology." *Nineteenth-Century Literature* 68.3 (2013) 287–91.

Yolton, John W. *Locke: An Introduction*. Oxford: Basil Blackwell, 1985.
Zanden, James W. Vander. "The Ideology of White Supremacy." *Journal of History of Ideas* 20.3 (1959) 385–402.
Zietlow, Rebecca. "Free At Last! Anti-Subordination and the Thirteenth Amendment." *Boston University Law Review* 90.1 (2010) 255–312.
Zimmerman, Jane. "The Convict Lease System in Arkansas and the Fight for Abolition." *The Arkansas Historical Quarterly* 8.3 (1949) 171–88.
Zuckerman, Phil. *The Social Theory of W.E.B. Du Bois*. London: Pine Forge, 2004.

Index

Abolition in Britain and America, author nugget, 185
abstract ideas, 123n14
Act Prohibiting Importation of Slaves of 1807, 42
"An Act to Prevent the People called Quakers from bringing Negroes to their Meeting," 104
adultery, punishment for, 146n44
"Adventurers to the Bahamas," Locke as one, 75
Africa, 4–5, 11, 12
African descent, people of, 146, 202
African slave trade, sin created by, 190
"African Slave-Trade," by W. E. B. Du Bois, 27–28
"African Venus," Sally Hemings as, 165
Africans. *See also* black people; slave(s)
  as black diamonds, 5
  hauling out of Africa, 36
  horrific death tolls of, 184
  hunted and captured like animals, 4
  importation of as slaves into America, 44
  as intellectually inferior to Whites, 22, 146–47
  Locke's perception of the humanity of, 126
  total number sold by the Royal Company, 35
  voluntarily submitted to slavery, 89
Africans on the Auction Block in Europe, author nugget, 97
"aggressors" in a "just war," Africans and American Indians as, 92

Alabama-Mississippi Territory Act of 1815, 43
Aldrich, Henry, 70
American Civil War, 36, 48–49, 180, 197
American colonies, no choice but to rebel, 170–71
American flag, immunity under, 44–48
American Indians, treatment of, 90
American racial consciousness, toward Black humanity, 94, 180
American Revolutionary War, 36, 39–40, 137, 171, 197n13
Americans, came to Africa highly weaponized, 36
Anstey, Roger, 20
anti-slavery activists, known as the "Federalists," 158
anti-slavery advocates, disgust for human trade, 105
Aquinas, Thomas, 82
Aristotle, 123–24
Armitage, David, on Locke, 64, 198–99
Lord Ashley, 52, 55–57, 58, 61, 62, 74
"Asiento," agreement with the Spanish colonies, 28
Asiento treaty, 34, 35
Atlantic slave trade, 22, 28–29
Aubrey, Walter, 100
Auker, Katherine, 100
author nuggets, 23, 50, 60, 77, 97, 119, 132, 153, 175, 185, 193, 204
authority of religion or church, reason superior to, 117

Baker, Thomas, 165

INDEX

Bancroft, George, 35
baptism, as not freedom from slavery, 100–108
Barbados, slave masters acted with cruelty, 104
Bean, Richard Nelson, 18
Beckford, William, 63
Behm, Ronald, 22
Behn, Aphra, 196
Bernasconi, Robert, 15, 75–76, 106, 201
Bernstein, R. B., on Jefferson, 147–48, 155, 157, 167
biblical claims, used by Locke, 84, 94
biblical definition, of sin, 186
Bill for Establishing Religious Freedom (Jefferson), 137, 137n6
biological person, 128
Black Africans, Hegel on, 12, 13
Black Codes, 21, 36
black diamond, defined, 67
black diamonds
    Black people as, 200
    foundation of Europe's financial dominance, 20
    people of Africa proper as, 202–3
    rush for, 27–50
    transatlantic slave trade as a rush for, 4
Black families, as economic units, 94
Black humanity, 15, 173, 179
Black love, 156
Black men, 155–56, 174
black of the negro, as fixed in nature, 155
Black people. *See also* Blacks
    argument for perpetual enslavement of, 179
    as economic units, 3, 94
    Jefferson's racist animus against, 155
    legal dehumanization of, 11
    Locke refusing to appropriate his argument for, 87
    Locke saw as racially and intellectually inferior, 200
    Locke's assertions of a caste system for, 197
    race-based treatments of lingering on, 202
    reducing to thinghood and property, 154
    regarded as slaves with no right in civil society, 94
    responsible for the building of Europe and for the dominance of Great Britain, 200
"black Republic" in Haiti, Jefferson and his party wanted to destroy, 158n15
Blackmon, Douglas A., 163, 181–84
Blacks. *See also* Black people
    after emancipation, 180
    Jefferson consigning to "permanent inequality," 158
    not allowed to "mix" with Whites sexually, 156–57
    not citizens in Monticello, 141
    robbed of their natural rights, 84
    second-class status of in Virginia, 10
    as slaves, 67, 102
    sold and exchanged in Virginia, 9
"blank slate" ("tabula rasa"), mind as, 121
Blomer, Thomas, 53
body (human), 129, 130
Boon, John, 91
Bounds, between Opinion and Knowledge, 99n3
Boyle, Robert, 54, 58
Brazil, 28, 29
Bristol, slave trade and, 16, 21
Britain. *See also* England; United Kingdom
    abolition in, 185
    Black people responsible for the building of, 200
    collected taxes on slaves imported, 74
    legal justification for slavery in, 63
    monopoly of the slave trade in 1713, 34
    pushing out Dutch and Spanish from the slave trade, 4
    slave trade, 31–36, 162
    slavery generated capital for development of cities, 16
    slaves seeking baptism in, 100

INDEX

treaty granting mutual limited
  Right of Search, 49
British Parliament, 31, 33, 35, 177–78
Brown, J. M., breeding slaves on his
  farm, 163
brutality of slavery, Locke had seen and
  endorsed, 85
President Buchanan, 46
Burnet, Gilbert, 111
Burwell (son of Sally's sister Bett),
  169n55
Busby, Richard, 52
business interests, Locke and Jefferson
  protecting, 148

Caine, given a black complexion, 146
Cambridge Platonists, 111
Campbell, James, 181
Can a Man Declare Himself Innocent?
  author nugget, 60
"capitalist" traits, in Locke, 116
capture, methods of, 93
care of souls, 116, 117
Carolina (colony of), 62, 63, 89, 198
Cartesian dualist model, 120
Cartesian intuition, 123n14
Cartesian skepticism, 124
Cary, Lucius, 109
caste system of Black people, perpetual,
  93
Censor of Moral Philosophy at Christ
  Church, Locke's position of, 54
chattel slavery
  of Black people by White people,
    173
  codified into law in the United
    States, 143
  deaths through, 21
  as distinct from the international
    slave trade, 5
  embedded in the argument for
    private property, 147
  end of in the UK and US, 176–85
  existed throughout the world in
    1783, 143
  Jefferson and Jeffersonians on, 157
  Locke a theorist of, 7
  Lockean slavery as, 93–96

Locke's defense of private property
  and, 116
mutated into forms of racialized
  bondage, 14
political and philosophical
  justifications for, 7
"practical necessity" of, 155
religious and philosophical
  validations for, 15
as sinful, 186
transitioned into strengthening of
  colonial enterprises, 202
cheap labor, preservation of as
  fundamental, 75, 197
children, as the responsibility of
  enslaved women, 10
children of God, all men as, 123n12
Chillingworth, William, 109
Christian baptism. *See* baptism
Christian doctrines, Socinians rejected
  standard, 110
Christian faith, moral effect of, 123n12
Christianity
  as "artificial systems" for Jefferson,
    151
  Locke rejecting dogmatic, 122
  not changing slaves' legal status,
    107, 198
  "perverted" by Platonic philosophy,
    150
  Western Church reduced to a racial
    solipsism, 188
Christianization of slaves, as a major
  challenge to slave traders, 101
Christians, not enslaving Christians, 102
church
  as an accomplice in the slave trade,
    191
  concerning itself with the care of
    souls, 115, 117
  dogmas, intentional disintegration
    of, 110
  Locke's definition of, 117–18,
    117n84
church and state, separation of, 8, 82,
  114, 138
Church of England, 109, 111, 115
"citizens," in the Constitution, 180

INDEX

citizenship, price of for Blacks, 181
civil government, religion and, 115, 117
civil magistrates, 116n84, 117, 138, 138n8
civil society, enforced the law against Black family structure and relationships, 94
Civil War. *See* American Civil War
Clemens, Paul G. E., 17
cogito, ergo sum, 127
collective sin, requiring collective repentance, 192
Colleton, John, 64
Colleton, Peter, 64, 91n51
colonies, laws of before 1774, 39
colonists, slaves and, 33, 91
The Colorization of People, author nugget, 132
commercial slave breeding. *See* slave breeding
"commercial supremacy," of the slave trade, 32
common good, 191, 192
"common-law criminal homicide," slave masters and, 68
companies, slave trading, 30, 74
Company of Royal Adventurers Trading to Africa, 30, 32, 35, 75, 199
competitive market, 19
complex ideas, 124n17
"congo harem," Jefferson's, 164–70
Congress of Verona in 1822, 44
Connecticut, ending the slave trade, 39
consciousness, 128, 192
Constitution of the United States, 141, 142, 177n3, 197, 198
Constitutional Convention of 1787, 143, 154
Convict Lease System, 21
Cooper, Anthony Ashley. *See* Lord Ashley
corruption, of Christianity seen by Jefferson, 150
Council of Trade and Foreign Plantations, Locke as secretary of, 70
Cranston, Maurice

account of Lord Ashley, 56
on Latitudinarianism, 109–10
on Locke, 121, 123
on Lord Ashley getting Locke involved in the transatlantic slave trade, 59
on the Lords Proprietors, 62
refutation of Filmer, 86
on Socinianism, 111
on Tyrrell and Locke meeting, 85–86
on Westminster purging Locke of Puritan faith, 52
on the work of the Council, 74n47
crime, against mankind as strong language, 130
Culverwel, Nathanael, 80n7
Cumberland, Richard, 80n7
Curti, Merle, 137, 139
custom duties, on slave grown imports, 75

Davis, David B., 101
death
  from the human trade, 21–22
  in Middle Passage, 33
  of the slave at the hand of the master, 67
  tools of Africans, 184
Declaration of Independence
  Douglass' speech on, 173
  as good old English doctrine, 197n13
  Jefferson as writer of, 8, 169
  Locke's claims pivotal to, 137
  saving principles of, 171
deism
  Locke and, 109–14
  origins of, 109n50
  rejecting doctrines of the church, 112–13
  tenets of, 151
  Thomas Jefferson and Lockean, 148–52
deist(s)
  denied the possibility of any religious truth, 109n51, 112, 114
  Locke and Jefferson as, 8, 79

230

INDEX

Scripture and, 98n2
Descartes, 120n1, 123–24, 129n36
Devine, T.M., 143
diatribes against Black humanity, impact of Jefferson's, 170
Diggins, John P., 139, 169
dignity, Locke's rejection of the concept of, 99
divine law, 81, 125
divine Original, 99
divine right of kings, theory of, 86
DNA testing, of descendants of Sally Hemings, 141n23
doctrine of ideas, of Locke, 124n14
Dorrien, Gary, 186
Dorset slave ship, 44–45
Douglass, Frederick, 160–61, 163, 170–74, 182–83
Drake, Francis, 32
Dred Scot v. Sandford Supreme Court case, 142n26, 179
Du Bois, W. E. B., 27–50, 145, 164, 183
dualism, of Descartes, 129n36
Dunn, John, 52, 87, 111, 196
Dutch, slavery and, 30, 31, 32
The Dutch West India Company, 30

Earl of Shaftesbury, as Locke's patron, 63n10
economic importance, of the slave trade in the US, 48
economic units, slaves as, 75
Edwards, John, 111
egalitarianism, Locke an advocate of, 7
Egypt, on its own as Asia, 11–12
Eisenach, Eldon, 113, 125
Queen Elizabeth I, 31, 32
Elmina Castle, in Cape Coast, Ghana, 29
emancipated slaves, removing beyond the reach of mixture, 157n10
emancipation, 176–85
    baptism viewed as a form of, 100
Emancipation Proclamation, 49, 177, 180
emotional conviction, as a basis of truth, 121
empires, legacies of human trade in Africans, 178

empirical theories, explaining racial differences, 196n8
empiricism, 120–31, 120n1
empiricist, Locke as, 79
England. *See also* Britain
    sending on an average to Africa 163 ships annually in 1760, 36n40
    tyranny toward the American Colonies, 170
English, freedom of for Locke as nonnegotiable, 88
Enlightenment pioneers, 6–23
Enlightenment values, Locke on, 90
enslaved Africans, as an economic resource, 16
enslaved person, defining, 10
enslaved women, progeny of, 143
enslavement, 88, 93
equalitarian justice, denied to Africans, 84
equalitarianism, 108, 200
"errors," of the church historic for Locke, 148–49
Essay Concerning Human Understanding (Locke), 99, 123, 125
Essays of the Law of Nature (Locke), 87
ethical principles, subjecting to rational proofs, 126
ethics, derived from experience, 125
Europe, former slave-trading nations of, 180
Europeans, 5, 21, 36, 192
evil, idealization of, 190
existence of God, 122
experience, 121, 124, 125
expertise, of Locke regarding the slave trade, 71

Faiella, Graham, 124, 139
Falkland, Viscount, 109
Farr, James, on Locke, 74, 76, 89, 93, 105, 196, 197, 200, 201
Federal law, abolishing the African Slave Trade, 47
Federalists, 158, 165
female slaves, 10, 164–65, 167, 168
Filmer, Richard, 85, 86, 88, 96, 200

INDEX

Finkelman, Paul
  on American slavery as race control, 142
  on enslavement confined to a single race or ethnic group, 7
  on the evolution of the Three-Fifths Clause, 145n38
  on the freeing of Harriet Hemings, 169n59
  on Jefferson, 136, 141, 155, 156, 156n6, 157n10, 158, 158n15, 160, 169
  on proslavery thought, 147
  on the Royal African Company (RAC), 33, 74
  on Sally's children as Jefferson's, 166
  on slave masters as owners of their own children, 166
  on "slavery" appearing only once in the Constitution, 141
  on slavery in the British Empire, 63
  on *State v. Hale*, 69
  on the Three-Fifths Clause, 144, 144n35
  on Virginia stopping the baptism of slaves, 101
fishers of men, claimed to be always African, 19
"foreign slave-trade," 161
Fosset, Joe (son of Sally's sister Mary), 156n6, 169n55
foundation of knowledge, 123
Founding Fathers
  on England as an oppressive colonial power, 170
  held Blacks as slaves and property, 179
  Locke's concepts influential to, 137, 139, 203
  principles of justice, equity, and fairness, 171
  as White supremacists, 180
Fourth of July, 170, 173
Fout, John, on Godwyn, 103, 105
France, Locke's journeys to, 199n17
Franklin, Benjamin, 139, 149
"Freedom," as a central pillar of the Revolutionary War, 39

freedom of nature, 86
freedom of will and conscience, 87
freeman of Carolina, 198
freemen of Carolina, 66
Frobisher, Martin, 32
From Africa to Europe: the Middle Passage, author nugget, 77
From Europe to Africa: Their Military Subjugation, author nugget, 50
Fugitive Slave Law, making mercy a crime, 174
full-blown colonialism, slavery mutated into, 177
"function," "personification" defined by Locke, 128
Fundamental Constitutions of Carolina
  approved to govern the colony, 62n4
  dated July 21, 1669, 62
  Locke as the architect of, 64, 196
  nobility system established by, 65–66
  revisions to in 1682, 91n51
  stipulated the perpetual enslavement of Africans, 198
  versions of, 64n12
funeral speech, by Locke, 54–55

generations, perpetuating sin, 191
geometrical truth, 125n23
Gerbner, Katherine, 104
Glausser, Wayne, 15, 70, 71, 74–75, 90
God
  as all-powerful, 83
  considered as substance by Locke, 122, 122n5
  eternally separated Whites and Blacks, 146
  granted the right to all to own property, 95
  as one person, 110
  against "owning" human beings, 83
Godwyn, Morgan, 103, 104, 105, 106
grandson of Lord Ashley, 59
"great moral teacher," Jesus as, 152
Pope Gregory XVI, stigmatized the slave-trade, 45
griefs, of Blacks as transient, 156
"Grievances of Virginia," publication of, 106

INDEX

Grotius, Hugo, 82
Grzelinski, Adam, 127

Hales, John, 109
Hamilton, Walton H., 198
Haslam, David, 20–21
Hawkins, John, 31–32
Hefelbower, S. G., 152n62
Hegel, Georg Wilhelm Friedrich, 11, 12, 43, 202
Hell's Kitchen, 187
Hemings, Beverly, 169n59
Hemings, Elizabeth (Betty), 165
Hemings, Eston, 169n55
Hemings, Harriet, 167n50, 168
Hemings, James Madison, 167n50
Hemings, John (Sally's brother), 169n55
Hemings, Madison, 169n55
Hemings, Sally
    children born to, 167, 167n50
    half sister of Martha Wayles Skelton, 154
    as the half-sister of Jefferson's wife and the daughter of Jefferson's father-in-law, 166
    mother of Harriet, 168
    slave daughter of Martha Wayles Skelton's father, 165
Hemings, Thomas Eston, 167n50
Hemings, William Beverly, 167n50
Hemings family members, Jefferson's manumission of five, 169n55
Prince Henry the Navigator, slaves as gift to, 22
Herbert of Cherbury, 109n50
hereditary bondage, institution of, 93
The Heterosexual Slave Master, author nugget, 153
Hinshelwood, Brad, 55, 89, 91, 93
Hobbes, Thomas, 80n7, 112n68
Holmes, David L., on Jefferson, 149
Holy Spirit, as the power of God, 110
The Homosexual Slave Master, author nugget, 175
Hooker, Richard, Locke quoted, 197n13
Hoover, John, tortured his female slave Mira, 68
Hopkins, Samuel, 38–39

House of Burgesses, 9n7, 10
human capability, Locke's definition of, 138n8
human dignity, interpretations of by deists, 152
human equality, radical Christian message of, 108
human error, sources of, 121
human rights, 6, 90, 200
human solidarity, distortion of the concept of, 191
human trade. *See also* slave trade
    death from, 21–22
    Locke participated in, 116
    superpowers of, 184
    wealth from, 16–21
humans, Locke's forms of, 128
Hume, David, 13, 55n18, 123n14, 124n14, 199, 202
Hutcheson, Harold, 109n50
hypocrisy, of Locke, 87–88

idealization, of evil, 190
ideas
    abstract, 123n14
    complex, 124n17
    kinds of, 124n17
    Locke's categorization of, 121–22
    Locke's doctrine of, 124n14
    modes as, 122n5
    moral, 126
    simple or elementary, 121n5, 124n17
ideological platforms, of Locke, 7–8
immunity, under the American flag, 44–48
Indian slave trade, in Carolina, 62n6
individual rights, Locke an advocate of, 7
individualism, in the justification of chattel slavery, 84
Industrial Revolution, transatlantic slave trade and, 2
industrial slave trade, 43, 202
informal slave trade, 5
ingenuity, Negroe slaves in Europe and, 13
Inikori, Joseph, 18, 19–20
injustice, 189

233

INDEX

innate ideas, 121
innate "moral sense," 139
innateness, 99, 120, 126, 130, 151
intellectual capacity of all, Locke and, 95
"intensive commercial farming," slave breeding as, 163
intergenerational evil, as self-perpetuating, 190
internal slave trade, 36, 161
international slave trade, 5, 40–44
interracial marriage, Jefferson against, 157

jails and prisons, in Mississippi, 182
Jefferson, Peter (Thomas' father), 154
Jefferson, Thomas
    died on July 4, 1826, 169
    inherited substantial wealth from his father Peter Jefferson, 154
    lived far beyond his means, 160
    a man defining his time, 141
    two sides to, 160
Jefferson, Thomas (ideas of)
    emphasized reason over revelation, 151
    materialist idea of death, 151
    separation of church and state in the US, 114
    theories and practices as national standards, 194
    on unlimited religious freedom as not practical, 138n10
Jefferson, Thomas (Locke's impact on)
    adopting Locke's concept of personhood, 128
    appropriated Lockeanism, 8, 137, 201
    commentary on the power of truth, 138n11
    copied Locke on private property, 140
    indebtedness to Locke for his ideas on religious toleration, 138n6
    intellectual influences of Locke, 199
    Lockean deism and, 148–52
    Locke's influence on, 8
    as the most prominent Lockean disciple in American politics, 136, 203
    paraphrasing of Locke's *A Letter Concerning Toleration*, 138, 138n6
Jefferson, Thomas (on Blacks)
    avowed white supremacist, 155–60
    beliefs about race, 194
    believed that Blacks lacked the ability to love the way white people did, 156n6
    concluded that slaves were property and not human beings or persons, 143
    defender of White-supremacist ideas and practices, 9
    refused to appropriate any legal benefit of the law to people of African descent, 201–2
    White supremacist claims of, 14
Jefferson, Thomas (slavery and)
    approach to land ownership and those who cultivate the land, 140
    came into the presidency of the US with over 150 slaves, 136, 165
    "congo harem," 164–70
    could not live without slaves, 160
    did little to end slavery, 159
    dismissed the letter of a slave to him, 165
    enablement of the industrial slave trade and the institution of chattel slavery, 14, 135, 202
    enacted the transition from Lockean to Jeffersonian slavery, 140
    ensured the survival of chattel slavery in the US, 157
    freed eight slaves during his entire lifetime and in his will, 169
    freed Harriet while she was on the run but not Beverly, 168
    freed Joseph Fosset but not Fosset's wife and eight children, 156n6
    inherited slaves from his father and his father-in-law, 155
    intellectual architect of the slave trade, 2–3

no problem with slave breeding, 162
owned more than 150 slaves when he wrote the Declaration of Independence, 9
owned over 500 slaves at the end of his life, 167
provided a policy argument for the racialization of slavery in the US, 141
provided for the freedom of Madison and Eston Hemings but not their mother, Sally, 169
slave master and slave trader, 8, 139, 154–74, 201
sustained the institution of chattel slavery, 8, 137, 154–55
treated his slaves with dissonance, 168
Jeffersonian rights, to own property, 147
Jeffersonian slavery, 3, 135–52
Jeffersonians, 143, 157, 158, 158n15, 194
Jesus, 110, 150
Jesus Christ, 108, 187
"Jesus of Nazareth," Jefferson referring to, 150
Jim Crow laws, deaths through, 21
judges, as racist and deliberately partial, 174
"just war"
justifying slavery, 90
Locke's concept of, 15, 89
over slavery in Carolina, 62n6
slaves as captives through, 38, 90, 183
justice, 79, 174, 200
justice system, facilitating overt racial injustice, 43

Kansas-Nebraska Act of 1844, 179
Kant, Immanuel, 199, 202
Katz, Stanley N., 147, 147n46
Kaye, Mike, 63, 202
Kenney, Lucy, 145–46, 147
King of England, securing Locke's residency at Oxford, 56–57
King William's New Board of Trade, Locke as commissioner of, 71

"The Kingdom of God" address, by Rauschenbusch, 187
kings, of Spain and England profited from the slave trade, 34
knowledge, 99, 122n5, 124

labor, value of, 96
labor power, slaves having no claim to, 93–94
Lamb, Jonathan, 128
Lamprecht, Sterling P., 120–21
land, Locke wanted to justify owning, 90
Landis, Benson, 188
landowners and gentry, Locke justifying the ownership of property by, 95
Latitudinarians, 109, 111
law of nature, 80n7, 81
law officials, leasing Blacks as "convicts," 43
laws of humanity, 42–44, 131
legacy
of Jefferson, 170
of Locke, 203
legal importation, of slaves, 35
legal justification, for slavery in Britain, 63
legislative assault, on people of color, 181
A Letter Concerning Toleration (Locke), 78, 114
liberal politics, Locke laid the foundation for, 6
liberalism, of Locke as racial, 200
Licensed by the Enlightenment Thoughts, author nugget, 23
light of nature, referring to reason, 81
Ligon, Richard, 103
Lincoln, Abraham, 49, 176–77, 180
Lisbon (Portugal), 28
Liverpool, slave trade and, 16–17, 18, 21
Locke, John (biography and career of)
appointed secretary to the Lords Proprietors of Carolina, 61
collaboration with James Blair on the Board of Trade Bishop of London's Commissary in Virginia, 106

INDEX

Locke, John (biography and career of) (continued)
  continued his involvement with Carolina, 199
  "died" as Senior Censor, 54–55
  died in 1704, 203
  elected to the prestigious position of a King's Scholar in 1650, 53
  flight to Holland shrouded in secrecy, 59
  formulating and executing policies related to human trade, 73
  in "full agreement with Godwyn's position," 105
  granted the rank of landgrave in the aristocracy of Carolina, 62
  infected with Ashley's zeal for commercial imperialism, 59
  joined Ashley's new company of merchant adventurers, 74
  as a "layman" in the Church of England, 55
  as Lecturer in Greek, 53–54
  lengthy responses to Stillingfleet, 111–12
  lost the position of Secretary of Presentation to Shaftesbury in Parliament, 69
  made many influential friends at Oxford, 53
  making of, 51–60
  medical doctor, tried to achieve the degree of, 58
  meeting Lord Ashley, 55–57
  moved to the home of Lord Ashley to become his "personal physician," 58
  "personally contributed" to the global reach of Protestantism, 82
  pioneer of the Enlightenment project of reason, 6–9
  present at all expected gatherings of the Lords Proprietors of Carolina up to June of 1675, 65
  rejection of pastoral appointment, 54–55, 58
  remained in Shaftesbury's colonial affairs until late 1682, 76
  remaining at Christ Church without becoming a clergyman, 57
  a secretary for the British colony of Carolina in London from 1663 to 1696, 78
Locke, John (philosophy and religion of)
  appropriated biblical and religious ideas to establish the discovery of the law of nature, 87
  arguments for a system of inherent social inequality, 108
  choice of examples making modern readers uneasy, 195
  critique of the church and orthodox Christian theology spread to the US, 149
  deism and, 109–14
  distinction between types of knowledge, 123n14
  on freedom of men under government, 86
  influenced by the Socinians, 110
  on the law of nature seeking the welfare of all men, 81
  on the monarch as a "servant," 87–88
  not commenting on the intersection between right, property, and ownership, 83
  "owned" a copy of Godwyn's *A Supplement*," 105
  privatization of the natural rights and, 79–84
  quoting St. Paul from 1 Corinthians 7:20–24, 107–8
  radicalizing the concept of rights, 83
  on religion and civil government, 114–18
  on the separation of the soul and the body, 129
  theories and practices as national standards, 194
  theory of private property, 140
  on unlimited religious freedom as not practical, 138n10
Locke, John (slavery and)
  arguing that slaves are property and made rightless through conquest, 92

INDEX

on Black bodies are economic units, 182
defender of White-supremacist ideas and practices, 9
as fully aware of the implications of his political arguments and slave-trading practices, 197
on the industrialization of the slave trade, 73
intellectual architect of the slave trade, 2
investor in the slave trade, 70–76
legitimate caste of black slaves and, 90–91
not caring whether negroes were baptized or not, 106
only associated with slaves or Africans as property, 198
participating in and defended the industrial slave trade and the institution of chattel slavery, 202
participation in the slave trade for economic gain, 76
as a partner with Ashley in the Bahamas venture, 75
provided defenses for existence of the institution of slavery, 14
as a racist, 194–203
refused to appropriate any legal benefit of the law to people of African descent, 201–2
refusing to categorically condemn slavery, 196
rejected Filmer's argument, 86
rejected "mandatory church attendance" for slaves, 107
rejected the practice of baptizing slaves, 106–7
as a slave master and slave trader, 199, 200
as slave trader, 7, 61–76
writer of the fundamental constitutions of Carolina, 61–70
Locke, Nicholas (father of John), 51, 52
Locke, Sir William (John Locke's great-grandfather), 51
Locke, Thomas (brother of John), 55

Locke and Blair, focused on Negroes as slaves, 106
Lockean concept of right, 92
Lockean deism, Thomas Jefferson and, 148–52
Lockean empiricism, as the basis for personalism, 126
Lockean ethics, based on reason, 125–26
Lockean ideology, Jefferson as an immediate facilitator of, 136
Lockean natural rights, slavery and, 84–85
Lockean person, 127–31
Lockean philosophy, 120–31, 201
Lockean politics, 78–96, 201
Lockean presidency, in the United States, 136–41
Lockean religion, 98–119, 201
Lockean slavery
  as chattel slavery, 93–96
  defined, 183
  defining the British role in the transatlantic slave trade, 14
  exploring, 3
  formal origin in the British Parliament, 73
  to Jeffersonian slavery, 135–52, 181
  master owning production of the slave labor, 96
  as racial slavery, 7
  as rightless, 91–92
Lockean soul, having nothing to do with the body, 130
Lockean tabula rasa, 121–25
Lockeanism, provided justifications for enslavement of Black Africans, 201
London, slave trade and, 17
Lords Proprietors, of the colony of Carolina, 61, 62, 63, 90, 91
Lucas, Paul, 148

President Madison, 43, 131
"magisterial care," 116
magistrate. *See* civil magistrates
male slaves, cohabitating with female slaves, 162
malicious actions, forms of, 187

INDEX

Mann, Anika Maaza, 15, 75–76, 106
"mansteaProposalsg," 37–38, 42
Manual of Parliamentary Practice (Jefferson), 136
Mapletoft, John, 53, 70
marginalization, critique of historical forms of, 187, 190
marriages, of slaves, 146n44
Mason, George, avid slave trader, 159
mass incarceration, deaths through, 22
Massachusetts, "Mansteadeling Mandate," 37
Master of Arts degree, Locke earned, 53
Mayo, Joseph, freed close to 170 slaves, 169
medicine, Locke and, 54, 57–59
merchant adventurer, Locke as, 70
Merritt, Susan, 182
Michell, S. L., 41
Middle Passage, 22, 27, 33
Mira (slave), fatal blow to her head, 68
Mississippi, 43, 181
Miura, Nagamitsu, 80
mixed-race relationships, Jefferson's opposition to, 157
mob actions, against Black people, 21, 181
modes, as ideas constructed within the mind, 122n5
Lord Monmouth, Locke's letter of assurance from, 72
moral human, exhibiting rationality, 128–29
moral ideas, 126
moral laws, Locke attempting to ground in reason, 122
The Moral Life and Morals of Jesus of Nazareth (Jefferson), 149–50
moral truths, 125n23, 126
Morrice, William, "best friend" of Ashley, 57
mothers, enslaved, sold when babies were grown, 167

National Archives of England, on the slave trade, 20
National Trust for Scotland, on slave ships, 30–31, 34

natural human, as uncultivated, 128
natural law, identified with divine law, 122
natural reason, 79
natural revelation, 121
natural rights
 Locke and the privatization of, 79–84
 slavery and, 84–85
natural state, of man for Locke as one of liberty, 86
naturalist rejection, of Locke on innateness, 99
natural-rights philosophy, of Locke, 137
Navigation Ordinance of 1651, 32
negro, as an animal man according to Hegel, 12
Negro men, as not real men, 195
Negro slaves, as property, 142–43
negroes, as naturally inferior to whites according to Hume, 13
The Negro's and Indian's Advocate, Suing for Their Admission into the Church (Godwyn), 103
New England, slave trade flourished in, 37
New Orleans, slave ships bound for Africa came directly from, 48
New Testament, on treatment of the "least" members of society, 108
New York, as a prominent harbor for slave ships, 48
Newport, Rhode Island, flourished at the expense of Africans, 38–39
North Africa, as European, 11
North Carolina Supreme Court, on the right of masters over slaves, 69
Northwest Ordinance, 8, 174
Notes on the State of Virginia (Jefferson), 155

objective rights, 91, 92
objective sense, of *ius*, 91
ontological foundation of justice, 79
opposition, to the slave trade and chattel slavery, 145
oppression, 170, 190

INDEX

original sin, 189, 190n19
Oshinsky, David, 180
Osofsky, Gilbert, 105
other persons, referring to the slaves as, 144n35
"ownership" rights, 84
Oxford undergraduate education, as still medieval in Locke's days, 53

Paraphrase and Notes on the Epistles of St Paul (Locke), 102–3
pastor, at Hell's Kitchen church, 187, 188
pastoral appointment, declined by Locke, 54–55, 58
Paterson, William, 11, 142–43, 144n35
Patriarcha (Filmer), 85
Patriarcha Non Monarcha (Tyrrell), 85
Paz slave ship, 44–45
Peardon, Thomas, 95, 197
Pemberton, Thomas, 37
penal codes of Virginia, Jefferson designed, 8
penal slavery, developed after emancipation, 183
penal system, 180, 181
Perkinson, Robert, 182
person
    different from "man/human being," 130
    Locke used in a specialized sense, 130n42
    as simply a natural and material being, 126
    two kinds of for Locke, 128
"personalism," of Locke, 125
"pests," free blacks as, 156
philosophical and political treatises, of Locke, 79
philosophical and sociopolitical justifications, for the industrial slave trade and chattel slavery, 14
"Philosophy of Jesus," Jefferson's book as, 150–51
Pinckney, Charles Cotesworth, 145
plantations, of the New World housed and husbanded by African labor, 76

Plato's philosophy, Jefferson not believing in, 150
political absolutism, Locke on, 86
political and philosophical theories, Locke's publication of, 78, 78n2
political appointments, Locke's, 61
political argument of Locke, 79
political authority, Locke on the function of, 197
political clout, of slaves, 144–45
political society, 80, 87
politician, Jefferson as, 135–36, 138–39
Pope-Hennessy, James, 21
Popham, Alexander, 52, 52n8
Popple, William, 72–73
Portugal, 28, 29
positive laws, 81
primitive church, concept of, 113
"Principles of reason," 99n4
prison-based gerrymandering, 145
"private jurisdiction," 83
private property, 84, 115, 116, 148
"private" side (slave trader and slaveholder), of Jefferson, 160
privatization of rights, protecting owning Africans as chattel property, 84
profitability, from the slave trade, 18–21
profitableness, of evil, 190
progressive thinkers, justifying religion, 109n51
property
    egalitarian notion of, 95
    Locke not defining, 81
    Locke's concept of, 83, 94
    man controlling his own person by owning, 95
    owners of, 84
    providing the inherent foundation of a person, 127
proslavery activists, public political platform for, 194
proslavery advocates, using Locke's arguments, 131
proslavery implications, of the Three-Fifths Clause, 142n26
pseudoscientific proclamations, proslavery science and, 194

INDEX

public rights, 92
"public" side (the political hero), of Jefferson, 160
punishment, Locke's notion of as retributive, 130
"pursuit of happiness," as a reference to the Lockean notion of property, 140

Quaker Negro Act, 104
Quakers of Barbados, 104, 105
Quincy, Josiah, 165

race, defined the status of blacks, 7n4
"race riots," as pogroms, 181
race-based consciousness, of the American criminal laws, 191
race-based hypocrisy, of Jefferson, 145
"race-based slavery," Locke as the mastermind, 201
racial cognitive dissonance, of Jefferson, 169
racial distinction, reflection of Locke's notion of, 195
racial statements, of Locke as consistent, 195
racism
    in accordance with empiricist teaching, 120n1
    Locke and, 194–203
Randall, Willard Sterne, on Jefferson, 136, 139–40
Randive, Mayur, on "Elmina Castle," 29
Randolph, John, 169
the "rational," right to own property given to only, 95
rational individuals, not resigning themselves to the irrationality of religion and the church, 117
rational people, not breaking the laws, 130
rationalism, replaced in British philosophy by empiricism, 121
rationality, Locke on, 95, 131
Rauschenbusch, Walter, on sin, 186–92
REAL CHRISTIAN, a disciple of the doctrines of Jesus, 151
real men, as White men, 195

reason
    centrality of, 82
    emphasis on for Locke, 121
    established by the quest for truth, liberty, and happiness, 124
    as the law of nature, 81, 87, 122
    natural, 79
    providing the platform for the evaluation of ideas, 126
    serving as the light of nature and natural revelation, 121
    worldviews established by, 99
Reasonableness of Christianity (Locke), 111, 112, 113, 123n12
Rebecca slave ship, 44–45
redemption, 190, 192
Reedy, Gerard, 110
relations, between substances and modes, 122n5
religion, 82, 114–15, 116, 117
religious and moral convictions, not the basis for stopping breeding of Black human beings, 164
"religious dogmatism," contrasted to deism, 112
religious freedom, Locke distinguished from civil freedom, 102
religious individualism, Locke's defense of from a deistic perspective, 117
Religious Justification, author nugget, 119
religious societies (Churches), magistrate ought to tolerate, 116n84
religious tolerance, 102, 137
representation, in the new Congress based on population, 144
resolutions, of the Southern Commercial Convention, 47
revelation
    rejection of, 99, 149, 151
    voice of, 81
Revolutionary War. *See* American Revolutionary War
Rhode Island, as the biggest slave-trading location, 38
Rich, Robert, 100
Richards, Judith, 94

INDEX

"Right of man," as a central pillar of the Revolutionary War, 39
rightless, slave as perpetually, 91–92
rights. *See also* human rights; also Jeffersonian rights; natural rights; "ownership rights"; self-ownership right; subjective rights
    associated with property ownership as radically subjective, 83
    Locke's concept of, 79, 84n23, 200
    "objective and "subjective," 82n19
Roman law, 91, 201, 202
Roman slavery, compared to Lockean, 7
Romans, enslaved anyone and everyone, 7
Rosa slave ship, 44–45, 74
Rousseau, 199
Royal African Company (RAC), 30, 32–33, 34, 74–75, 200
Ruffin, Thomas, 69

Sahakian, William S., and Mabel Lewis Sahakian, 112, 113–14, 124
Sakala, Leah, 144, 145
Salley, Columbus, 22
salvation, 191
Sandy (runaway slave), 159
Saucy Jack slave ship, 44–45
scholarship, to Christ Church, Oxford, for Locke, 53
Scotland, participation in the industrial slave trade and chattel slavery, 14
scriptures, Lucy Kenney's use of, 145–46
"Sea Dogs," of Queen Elizabeth I, 32
Second Treatise of Government (Locke), on slavery, 85
secular affairs, church should not interfere in, 115
self-ownership right, 84
self-preservation, 80, 82
senses, as the basis of knowledge, 99
sensual perception, as a way to obtain knowledge, 121
Secretary Seward, suppressing the slave-trade, 49
Shaftesbury, 70, 199, 199n17

shipping companies, controlled by the Lords Proprietors, 62
Shyllon, Folarin, 100
Sidney, Algernon, 59
simple or elementary ideas, derived from experiences, 121n5, 124n17
sin
    as an act of weakness followed by shame, 190
    forms of, 191
    lacking the consciousness of, 192
    as selfishness, 189
    as social, 186, 187, 192
    as sociopolitical, economic, and racial exploitation, 186–92
sinful mind, 189, 191–92
Skelton, Martha Wayles, wife of Thomas Jefferson, 154, 167, 169
slave(s)
    appealing to the conscience of Jefferson, 164
    to blame for their own enslavement, 88
    counted as "three-fifths of all other persons," 143–44
    establishing a perpetual and legitimate class of, 90
    fear of insurrections from, 39
    narratives from William Thompson, W. L. Bost, and Chris Franklin, 166–67
    no evidence that Locke freed his, 198
    numbers of in various countries by 1775, 41
    permitting "to be admitted to that sacrament," 101
    price of rose astronomically in 1850, 46
    as property, 9, 66, 79, 90, 92, 94, 115, 161
    without justice and legal defense, 69
slave baptism. *See* baptism
slave breeding
    Jefferson engaged in it, 168
    in the slave trade and chattel slavery, 160–64

INDEX

slave codes, enacted to keep Africans from resisting or fleeing, 35–36
"slave holders' republic," United States began as, 141
slave labor, legally available and cheap, 164
slave laws, of Virginia, 9–11
"slave markets," American overstocked from 1774–75, 39
slave master(s)
    acted with absolute impunity, 66
    affairs with many enslaved women to increase the slave population, 10
    breeding of Black people, 162, 163, 167
    could not face punishment for the death of a slave, 67
    establishing a precedent by allowing a slave to be baptized, 103–4
    few freed their slaves and made provisions for them upon their death bed, 169
    free to have sex with their female slaves, 10, 146n44, 161, 166
    Jefferson as, 160
    as the lawful conqueror, 88–89
    Locke granting absolute powers and immunity to, 198, 199
    owning the labor-power and production of the slave, 96
    power over slaves, 64, 69
    refused to baptize their slaves, 102
    rights of as central to the Fundamental Constitutions, 66
    Thomas Jefferson as, 154–74
    wives consented to the slave masters' sexual seduction of female slaves, 162–63
slave owners. *See* slave master(s)
slave plantations across the United States, 46
slave ship-building state, Rhode Island as, 38
slave ships, 4, 30, 31, 44, 46, 93
slave trade. *See also* human trade
    British and, 31–36
    continued to flourish despite laws against, 41
    as distinct from chattel slavery, 49
    domestic, 5
    the Dutch and, 30–31
    end of in Britain and the United States not ending in practice, 162
    essential for the colonies' political and economic survival, 33
    Frederick Douglass on American, 161
    industrial and profit-oriented nature of, 39
    Locke's involvement in, 70–76, 200
    mutated into the institution of chattel slavery, 5
    profitability of, 15, 18, 20
    provided thousands with employment, 75
    revitalization of in the South, 47
    as sinful, 186
    superpowers of, 1
    United States and, 36
    W. E. B. Du Bois's analysis of, 2
Slave Trade Act 1807, in England, 42
slave trader
    Locke as, 7, 116
    as a powerful economic magnet, 48
slave women. *See* female slaves
slavery
    brought Locke financial and social elevation, 76
    Christian baptism as not freedom from, 100–108
    complicated legal structure for in the colonies, 63
    courts and legal system positioned themselves to protect, 69
    Declaration of Independence and, 141–42
    empiricist model making racism easy to justify, 120n1
    Locke and Filmer debate on, 85–88
    Locke defining, 88, 89
    Lockean natural rights and, 84–85
    Locke's intellectual ability and socio-political impact, 71

INDEX

mutated into penal slavery, 177
reasons for the importance of, 75
as the relationship between negroes and the Europeans, 12
as rightlessness, 91
as a social and economic enterprise, 101
as the state of war between a lawful conqueror and a captive, 88
Slavery Abolition Act, of the British Parliament, 178
slavery and slave trade, American, 173
"slave-trade clause," in the original United States Constitution, 42
slave-trading superpowers of the West, 3
Smith, Adam, Locke's impact on, 55n18
Social Gospel movement, 188
"social idealizations of evil," perpetuating, 189
social tradition, perpetuation of evils through, 189
Socinians, latitudinarians as, 110
soul, 129–30
Southern Commercial Convention, 47
Southerners
    presumed every negro to be a slave, 7n4
    used slaves to inflate their political clout, 144
Spanish, as a superpower of slave traders, 30
the state, cannot force religion on anyone, 82
state of nature, 86n32
State v. Hoover case, 68
State v. Mann case, 69
Stillingfleet, Edward, attack on Locke, 111
Stringer, Thomas, 70
Suarez, Francisco, 82
subhuman beings, Locke saw Africans as, 198
subjective rights, 91, 92
subjective sense, of *ius*, 91–92
submission, of rights to the political authority, 87
subordination, 87
substance, supporting the earth, 123

superpowers, of the slave trade, 3
The Suppression of the African Slave Trade to the United States of America 1638–1870 (W. E. B. Du Bois), 27
supremacy of the king, Locke rejected, 87
Syse, Henrik
    on Locke, 6, 82, 83, 112n68, 116, 122
    on Socinians, 110
systemic truths, examples of, 125n23

Take Your Issues to the Lord in Prayer, author nugget, 193
Taney, Roger, on inferiority Black people, 179–80
Tannenbaum, Frank, 22
theological individualism, 191
theological views, of Locke, 98
They Have Sinned Against God and the Africans, author nugget, 204
thinking, as a sense of "awareness," 127
"thinking being," "person" implying, 130
Thomas, David, 58
Thomas, Robert P., 18
Thomas and Bean's approach, 19
Thomas Jefferson Memorial Foundation, on the children of Sally, 166n44
Three-Fifths Clause, 142–48, 144n35
tolerance, Locke's concept of, 108
"toleration," Locke's notion of, 114
total servitude, for an unjust aggressor of just war, 90
tradition, adhesion to, 121
transatlantic slave trade
    among Lord Ashley's trading interests, 56
    Atlantic slave trade gave birth to, 29
    beginning in the 1400s, 3
    compared to chattel slavery, 5
    deaths through, 21
    distinctiveness of, 28
    intersected with capitalism and the industrial revolution, 16
    Locke not a bystander or accidental participant in, 73

INDEX

transatlantic slave trade (continued)
   Locke providing philosophical and political justification of, 7, 73
   Locke's political career existed in tandem with, 61–76
   mutated into full-blown chattel slavery and colonialism, 29
   mutations of, 20
   religious and philosophical validations for, 15
transgressor, becoming dangerous to Mankind, 130
treaty, granting limited Right of Search in 1862, 49
Treaty of Ghent, ending the slave trade, 43
Triangular Trade System, 77
True & Exact History of the Island of Barbados (Ligon), 103
truths, 124, 125n23
Turner, Jack, 82, 106
Two Tracts of Government (Locke), 68n26
Two Treatises on Government (Locke), 78, 86
Tyrrell, James, 85

United Kingdom. *See also* Britain
   empire-building, imperialism, and colonialism, 178
   ended the human trade in 1833, 177
   justification of slavery, 135
   politicians involved in the slave trade, 63
   redirecting all captured Africans into the West Indies, 46
United States
   as sinners, 192
   slave trade and, 36
   slavery defined by race, 7n4
"universal truth," Locke rejecting the notion of, 121
"universalism," of Jefferson, 147
"unjust aggressors and just conquerors," Locke seeing no incompatibility between, 90, 93
"unlawful bondage," former slaves kept in, 182
US Constitution. *See* Constitution of the United States

Viney, Donald Wayne, on Jefferson, 149, 151
violation, of the laws of humanity, 42–44
violence, culture of erupted, 181
virgin birth of Jesus Christ, Jefferson rejected, 151
Virginia
   Black people legally defined as slaves, property, and real estate, 67–68
   first British mainland colony establishing slavery, 8n6
   largest slave population on the North American continent, 8n6
   laws regarding slavery, 9–11, 65, 67–68, 101, 107
   master killing a slave by punishment not considered a crime, 66
"virtue" as "utility," 139
"vision of equality," Jefferson excluding Blacks from, 158
voice of revelation, referring to the Bible, 81
Voltaire, 6, 202
"voluntary" society, church as, 117–18

Washington, George, 159n20
Wayles, John
   father of Martha Wayles Skelton, 154
   father of Sally Hemings, 165
wealth, from the human trade, 16–21
Welchman, Jennifer, 102
West, Cornel, 76, 96
Westminster School in London, 52, 53
Whichcote, Benjamin, 109
White beauty, as different from Black beauty, 155
White church, divide with the Black church, 191
White man, punished for harming the slave of another White man, 69

INDEX

White supremacists
    advocated a legitimate caste system, 152
    Locke as, 196
    resorted to pseudo-interpretations of the Bible, 147
    Thomas Jefferson as, 155–60
White supremacy, 2, 8, 177
White women, proslavery campaigns of, 145
Whites
    breeding Blacks folks for sale, 163
    engaged in acts of incest, 167
    treating their own children as property, 166
"wild beasts," slaves as, 183
will, as the power to act or refrain from acting, 125–26
will (legal document), of Jefferson emancipated only five bondsmen, 159–60
Willis, Clive, 29
Wilson, Henry, 31

Witte, John, Jr., 79–80, 91, 92, 108
Woldfolk, Austin, 173
women. *See also* female slaves
    black, bred from "Oranootan," 155
    Black men preferring White, 155–56
    enslaved not controling their bodies or their children, 10
    progeny of enslaved, 143
    White, not reticent or shy about proslavery campaigns, 145
Woolhouse, Roger
    on allowing taking of slaves as "captives...in a just war," 93
    on black slaves, 84
    description of Ashley, 56
    disagreeing with Cranston's position on Locke, 65
    on Filmer, 86
    on Locke, 51, 62, 71, 199, 200

Yolton, John W., 127–28, 129, 130

www.ingramcontent.com/pod-product-compliance
Lightning Source LLC
Chambersburg PA
CBHW031727230426
43669CB00007B/271